TAKING GOD SERI‹

Is debate on issues related to faith and reason still possible when dialogue between believers and nonbelievers has collapsed? *Taking God Seriously* not only proves that it is possible, but also demonstrates that such dialogue produces fruitful results. Here, Brian Davies, a Dominican priest and leading scholar of Thomas Aquinas, and Michael Ruse, a philosopher of science and well-known non-believer, offer an extended discussion on the nature and plausibility of belief in God and Christianity. They explore key topics in the study of religion, notably the nature of faith, the place of reason in discussions about religion, proofs for the existence of God, the problem of evil, and the problem of multiple competing religious systems, as well as the core concepts of Christian belief including the Trinity and the justification of morality. Written in a jargon-free manner, avoiding the extremes of evangelical literalism and New Atheism prejudice, *Taking God Seriously* does not compromise integrity or shy away from discussing important or difficult issues.

BRIAN DAVIES is Distinguished Professor of Philosophy at Fordham University. He specializes in philosophy of religion and medieval philosophy and theology. His published books include, *The Reality of God and the Problem of Evil*, *Thomas Aquinas's "Summa theologiae": A Guide and Commentary*, *Thomas Aquinas's "Summa contra Gentiles": A Guide and Commentary*, and *An Introduction to the Philosophy of Religion*.

MICHAEL RUSE is Emeritus Professor of Philosophy at the University of Guelph in Ontario, Canada, and was the Lucyle T. Werkmeister Professor of Philosophy at Florida State University. He is a historian and philosopher of science specializing in Charles Darwin and the revolution associated with his name. Ruse has been a Guggenheim Fellow and a Gifford Lecturer. He has been awarded four honorary degrees, and has won several honours including a PROSE award for *The Cambridge Encyclopedia of Darwin and Evolutionary Thought*. He is the author or editor of more than sixty books and was the founding editor of *Biology and Philosophy*.

Taking God Seriously

Two Different Voices

BRIAN DAVIES
Fordham University

MICHAEL RUSE
University of Guelph

CAMBRIDGE
UNIVERSITY PRESS

CAMBRIDGE
UNIVERSITY PRESS

University Printing House, Cambridge CB2 8BS, United Kingdom

One Liberty Plaza, 20th Floor, New York, NY 10006, USA

477 Williamstown Road, Port Melbourne, VIC 3207, Australia

314–321, 3rd Floor, Plot 3, Splendor Forum, Jasola District Centre, New Delhi – 110025, India

79 Anson Road, #06–04/06, Singapore 079906

Cambridge University Press is part of the University of Cambridge.

It furthers the University's mission by disseminating knowledge in the pursuit of education, learning, and research at the highest international levels of excellence.

www.cambridge.org
Information on this title: www.cambridge.org/9781108491075
DOI: 10.1017/9781108867375

© Cambridge University Press 2021

First published 2021

A catalogue record for this publication is available from the British Library.

ISBN 978-1-108-49107-5 Hardback
ISBN 978-1-108-79219-6 Paperback

Contents

Preface

Michael Ruse and Brian Davies are both English-born and were educated at the University of Bristol, in the southwest of that country. They are now professors of philosophy in the United States: Ruse at Florida State University in Tallahassee (now retired), and Davies at Fordham University, the Jesuit university in New York City. There the similarities end.

Ruse was raised a Quaker, but around the age of twenty his faith started to fade and since then he has been a nonbeliever, more agnostic than atheist. A philosopher of science, he is nevertheless much appreciative of his Christian childhood. Intellectually, he has been led to work on the science–religion relationship, and so, somewhat naturally, he has spent much time and effort trying to understand the work and influence of the nineteenth-century naturalist Charles Darwin, author of the 1859 evolutionary work *On the Origin of Species*.

Davies was raised Roman Catholic and, around the age of twenty-six, decided to train for the priesthood and joined the Dominican Order. Intellectually interested in philosophical questions on and around religion, equally naturally he has spent much time and effort trying to understand the work and influence of the thirteenth-century theologian and philosopher St. Thomas Aquinas, author of the *Summa theologiae* and of many other writings.

Ruse and Davies are friends of increasingly long-standing, and while they have very different world pictures (Ruse much influenced by Darwinism and Davies by Aquinas), they have nonetheless found their interactions highly stimulating and fruitful. These interactions have led to the present book, which lays out our differences. We have deliberately restricted our discussion, most pertinently to Christianity rather than to religion in general. This is partly a function of personal interests and partly a function of competence. We have still found much to discuss.

As we began work on this project, we agreed that there were a number of topics that had to be discussed, and we have structured the book accordingly. There are seven chapters. Each has one half written by Ruse and one half written by Davies. The contributions in each chapter match, but for the first six chapters we wrote independently. Realizing that this is an ongoing dialogue, in the final chapter we respond to each other directly. No significance should be read into the fact that Ruse's contribution leads each chapter. We decided the order simply on the principle of "age before beauty." The reader should feel free to read the contributions in the sequence that they prefer.

We are philosophers. We know that there is never a last word on any subject. The journey is as important as the destination. There are always old problems to be rethought and new problems to be tackled. We have found this interaction enjoyable, stimulating, and enlightening. We very much hope that you will too.

Acknowledgments

We both very much want to thank our editor, Beatrice Rehl. She has been the Platonic Form of editor. She has been welcoming, encouraging, supportive, and ever ready to give a word of advice and to suggest that revision may be needed. We are very fortunate. Individually, Brian Davies would like to thank Christopher Arroyo, Noah Hahn, and Paul Kucharski, fellow members of the Fordham University Philosophy Department, all three of whom gave him comments on his text. Michael Ruse likewise would like to thank Antonios Kaldas (of Sydney, Australia) for comments on his text. More generally, Ruse would like to thank five scholars with whom he has, over the years, discussed pertinent issues of religion and science: John Kelsay (Florida State University), Edward J. Larson (Pepperdine University), Ronald L. Numbers (University of Wisconsin), Michael L. Peterson (Asbury Seminary), and Robert J. Richards (University of Chicago). Above all, he thanks the members (mainly liberal Christians) of the Institute for Religion in an Age of Science, with whom he shares an annual conference week on Star Island, off the coast of New Hampshire. As modest in person as the society is pretentious in name, no group (since the Quakers of his childhood) has influenced him more on our shared journey to the Celestial City (the nature of which, he suspects, they find more problematic and hidden than he).

Faith

Michael Ruse

FAITH AND ITS DISCONTENTS

"I BELIEVE IN GOD, THE FATHER ALMIGHTY, CREATOR OF HEAVEN and earth." This is the beginning of the Apostle's Creed, shared by both Catholics and Protestants. I take it to be at the center – the very heart – of the Christian religion. If you believe this, then you are on the way to being a Christian. If you do not believe this, then you are not a Christian. I say "believe," but in this context I am not inclined to make much of the difference between knowledge and belief. "For I know that my Redeemer lives, and that at the last he will stand upon the earth."[1] You might say that there is a difference and that is that knowledge is justified true belief, or some such thing. Fair enough, but for now I am going to ride roughshod over such issues, for all that they have given fellow philosophers many happy hours of thinking up counter-examples. Obviously, many people believe in the existence of God. No one knows that God exists – because, he doesn't! For the moment, though, I shall take it that when someone recites the Apostle's Creed, they think that God really does exist. They know that God exists.

Why do they believe or know that God exists? Because they have faith. "Now faith is the assurance of things hoped for, the conviction of things not seen."[2] It is here that the New Atheists – biologist and popular science writer Richard Dawkins, philosopher Daniel Dennett, sometime graduate student and neurobiologist Sam Harris, and the journalist the late Christopher Hitchens – become eloquent. In *The God Delusion* (2006), Richard Dawkins says, "Faith is an evil precisely because it requires no justification

[1] Job 19:25.   [2] Hebrews 11:1.

and brooks no argument."[3] The title of Sam Harris's book, *The End of Faith*, tells the tale. He states flatly that "the truth is that religious faith is simply unjustified belief in matters of ultimate concern – specifically in propositions that promise some mechanism by which human life can be spared the ravages of time and death. Faith is what credulity becomes when it finally achieves escape velocity from the constraints of terrestrial discourse – constraints like reasonableness, internal coherence, civility, and candor."[4]

Others hold forth in the same way. A more recent member of the group, Chicago biologist Jerry Coyne, laments that the problem is not with religion as such but with "its reliance on and glorification of faith – belief, or if you will, 'trust' or 'confidence' – without supporting evidence." Faith is dangerous both to science and to society. "The danger to science is how faith warps the public understanding of science: by arguing, for instance, that science is based just as strongly on faith as is religion; by claiming that revelation or the guidance of ancient books is just as reliable a guide to the truth about our universe, as are the tools of science; by thinking that an adequate explanation can be based on what is personally appealing rather than what stands the test of empirical study."[5]

DOES FAITH MATTER?

Let us focus in a little more on this dreadful phenomenon. You might be inclined to say that we could escape altogether having to discuss this obviously dated issue. Coyne brings up the matter of science, and if anything is true it is that we today – as compared with even the most recent past – are living in an age of science and technology. That spells reason and evidence. Why don't we just jump therefore to possible alternatives for getting at the Almighty and pick up the God discussion there? What reason and evidence are there to believe in the Christian God? We shall turn to this issue in later chapters, but I am afraid that right now there is no getting away from the faith question. That faith is all-important is right at the heart of the Christian religion. Whatever the powers of reason and evidence, they are trumped by faith.

---

[3] R. Dawkins, *The God Delusion* (New York: Houghton, Mifflin, Harcourt, 2006), 308.
[4] S. Harris, *The End of Faith: Religion, Terror, and the Future of Reason* (New York: Free Press, 2004), 65.
[5] J. A. Coyne, *Faith vs. Fact: Why Science and Religion Are Incompatible* (New York: Viking, 2015), 225–26.

Jesus set the scene. The disciple Thomas, on meeting the risen Lord, expressed some doubt. astonishment.

> Then he said to Thomas, "Put your finger here and see my hands. Reach out your hand and put it in my side. Do not doubt but believe."
> Thomas answered him, "My Lord and my God!"
> Jesus said to him, "Have you believed because you have seen me? Blessed are those who have not seen and yet have come to believe."[6]

This is and always has been the essential Christian tradition. Faith is where it is at. Saint John Paul II, in his encyclical *Fides et Ratio* (1998), affirmed this position strongly. "The results of reasoning may in fact be true, but these results acquire their true meaning only if they are set within the larger horizon of faith: 'All man's steps are ordered by the Lord: how then can man understand his own ways?'"[7]

WHAT IS FAITH?

So, we're stuck with faith. First, let us ask a bit more about it and how it functions. Without in any sense intending irreverence, it is a bit like a direct Skyping line with God. Calvin – and his later followers like Alvin Plantinga – spoke of a *sensus divinitatis*.

> That there exists in the human minds and indeed by natural instinct, some sense of Deity, we hold to be beyond dispute, since God himself, to prevent any man from pretending ignorance, has endued all men with some idea of his Godhead, the memory of which he constantly renews and occasionally enlarges, that all to a man being aware that there is a God, and that he is their Maker, may be condemned by their own conscience when they neither worship him nor consecrate their lives to his service.[8]

The *sensus* is not faith itself but leads to faith. This, in the Christian context, is perfectly reasonable. We humans are made in the image of God. We are not the only care of God – "Are not two sparrows sold for a penny? Yet not one of them will fall to the ground apart from your Father"[9] – but we are the uniquely loved and favored. Jesus did not die on the cross for

---

[6] John 20:27–29.
[7] John Paul II, *Fides et Ratio: Encyclical Letter of John Paul II to the Catholic Bishops of the World* (Vatican City: L'Osservatore Romano, 1998), 16. Quoting Proverbs 20–24.
[8] J. Calvin, *Institutes of the Christian Religion* (Grand Rapids: Eerdmans, [1536] 1962), chapter 3, section 1.
[9] Matthew 10:29.

kangaroos, even though one supposes that in some sense they are tainted by sin because they die. One would expect humans to be directly aware of God. Can we dig a little further? Let us turn to a couple of faith experiences. First, most famously, that of Saul of Tarsus. He has set out for Damascus to find and persecute Christians. Then it happened.

> Now as he was going along and approaching Damascus, suddenly a light from heaven flashed around him.
> He fell to the ground and heard a voice saying to him, "Saul, Saul, why do you persecute me?"
> He asked, "Who are you, Lord?" The reply came, "I am Jesus, whom you are persecuting."[10]

Famously, Saul has been struck blind. He is taken to Damascus, where Ananias comes to him.

> So Ananias went and entered the house. He laid his hands on Saul and said, "Brother Saul, the Lord Jesus, who appeared to you on your way here, has sent me so that you may regain your sight and be filled with the Holy Spirit."
> And immediately something like scales fell from his eyes, and his sight was restored. Then he got up and was baptized.[11]

Paul, it will be remembered, was the chap who took faith very seriously, valuing it over good works.

> Therefore, since we are justified by faith, we have peace with God through our Lord Jesus Christ, through whom we have obtained access to this grace in which we stand; and we boast in our hope of sharing the glory of God.[12]

So much for the Sermon on the Mount. A sympathetic explanation is that Paul is reflecting on his own experience of being saved without having any merits to his name. The point is that, through his love, his grace, God gives us understanding without our having earned it.

There is more to faith than just a spartan knowledge component: $2 + 2 = 4$ sort of thing. There is an overwhelming feeling of love, irresistible. The eminent (English) philosopher of religion John Hick wrote of his conversion to Christianity as a late teenager. He was resisting the call. Then it happened. "An experience of this kind which I cannot forget, even though it happened forty-two years ago [1942], occurred – of all places – on the top deck of a bus in the middle of the city of Hull.... As everyone will be very conscious who

---

[10] Acts 9:3–5.   [11] Acts 9:17–18.   [12] Romans 5:1–2.

can themselves remember such a moment, all descriptions are inadequate. But it was as though the skies opened up and light poured down and filled me with a sense of overflowing joy, in response to an immense transcendent goodness and love."[13]

Of course, Paul did not think that faith meant there was no more to be done. Like the shipwrecked sailor in the A. A. Milne poem, there was so much to be done

– And he wanted a hat,
and he wanted some breeks;
And he wanted some nets, or a line and some hooks –

In the end, the sailor sat on his bottom.

But he never could think which he ought to do first.
And so in the end he did nothing at all,
But basked on the shingle wrapped up in a shawl.
And I think it was dreadful the way he behaved –
He did nothing but basking until he was saved![14]

This was very much not St. Paul. His bottom went unused. No sooner was he converted than he set about preaching and writing, without pause, until his life was ended by an executioner's sword in Rome. Hick had a less grisly end, but he was through his life a great force for religious and racial harmony, working in the British Midlands industrial city of Birmingham on and within interfaith groups and the like, nonstop.

Faith is this sense of being embraced by love, an experience over which one has no control. It does not necessarily come in a flash, but it comes and it cannot be resisted. C. S. Lewis, conservative Anglican and now the idol of the evangelicals:

You must picture me alone in that room in Magdalen, night after night, feeling, whenever my mind lifted even for a second from my work, the steady, unrelenting approach of Him whom I so earnestly desired not to meet. That which I greatly feared had at last come upon me. In the Trinity Term of 1929 I gave in, and admitted that God was God, and knelt and prayed: perhaps, that night, the most dejected and reluctant convert in all England.[15]

[13] J. Hick, *An Autobiography* (London: Oneworld Publications, 2005), 205.
[14] A. A. Milne, "The Old Sailor," in *Now We Are Six* (London: Penguin, [1927] 1988), 36–41.
[15] C. S. Lewis, *Surprised by Joy: The Shape of My Early Life.* (London: Geoffrey Bles, 1955), 115.

Dejected and reluctant, perhaps. Compulsively sharing his experience, certainly.[16]

AND THE WORLD SAID

Now what are we to say about all of this? Or rather, what is a nonbeliever to say about all of this? I am a case in point. I was born in England in 1940, early in the years of the Second World War. My father was a conscientious objector, I think mainly for political (he was very far left) than for religious reasons. Unsurprisingly, he came into contact with members of the (pacifist) Religious Society of Friends, Quakers. After the war, he and my mother joined that group, and I was raised very intensely within it. In my teens, I went to a Quaker boarding school. Yet around the age of twenty, my faith started to fade and has never returned. It was quite independent of my becoming a philosopher. If anything, I think it was connected to my intense dislike of my headmaster, an emotion reciprocated. My identification of God was with the worse kind of Old Testament bully – the God of the New Atheists – and it was as much with relief as regret that my identification as a Christian faded away. I don't hate religion. If you are raised a Quaker, you don't hate religion. It is just not for me.

So, what does a nonbeliever have to say on the faith issue? On the one side, the Christians; on the other side, the New Atheists. You cannot just dismiss those who have faith as stupid or weak or ignorant. Like a lot of us, I often have my doubts about St. Paul, but anyone who can write I Corinthians 13 – the King James Version! – has my money over Richard Dawkins. Apparently, *The God Delusion* has sold a mere 3 million copies. I hope, in Paradise, St. Paul will not be too condescending when they compare sales figures. Although I am closer to Dan Dennett than (let us say) to St. Augustine on the God question, the saint has my vote in the *Philosophical Gourmet*'s competition for the "Ten Greatest Philosophers of All Time." And John Hick? Intellectually and morally, he has it over the rest of the motley crew. But because you respect the people of faith – not just men but women of faith, like Sophie Scholl of the White Rose Group, who died on the guillotine for her opposition to the Nazis – if you do not have

---

[16] I do not intend to imply that every person of faith had a road-to-Damascus experience. Some have faith naturally, as it were, all their lives. Others, notably Mother Teresa, have ongoing doubts (*Mother Teresa: Come Be My Light*, New York: Image, 2009). What I claim is that there is a shared experience of knowledge and love of God that is simply part of one's being, without need of argument. It is given, not earned.

faith yourself, you should not be pushed or bullied into pretending faith for yourself. Or into going all subjectivist and saying truth for me is not necessarily truth for them, and their position is just as good as mine. It seems to me that John Hick is a bit prone to this last fault, something that I shall pick up on later.

I doubt the New Atheists and fellow travelers will be much impressed by the point I have just made – they tend not to be impressed by any points but those they themselves make – so let us keep pressing the case. There is in the writings of Dawkins and company a contempt – not just implicit – for anyone who has faith-like experiences and who takes them seriously. Real white men – as critics have pointed out, the New Atheists tend to be at least as sexist and Eurocentric as any fervent Evangelical[17] – don't have such experiences or, if they do, they brush them to one side. Science, mathematics, logic, evidence, observation, experiments make faith simply untenable in any direction. Someone like St. Paul may not seem weak, but obviously he was given to delusion. Most probably, the fear of death drove him to his conversion experience and future activities. However, let us leave on one side the cowardly nature of St. Paul, who knowingly preached up to his expected execution, and dig a little further. I do this even though, as a nonbeliever, I do – must – conclude that there is something inauthentic about faith. Only by making the strongest positive case can we then turn to criticism.

THE FAITH EXPERIENCE

What about the faith experience itself? An overwhelming sensation, experience, that is out of your hands and that leads to new insights. Is this, in itself, a sign of weakness? It is certainly a sign of being human, but weakness is another matter. Take falling in love, a very human experience, for all the obvious biological and social reasons. David Copperfield, in Charles Dickens's novel of that name, still a (late) teenager, is articled to become a proctor. This was a kind of lawyer who dealt with the oddest mélange of issues – wills and misbehaving clergymen and (very strange to say) nautical matters. After a few months, David is invited down for the weekend to the home of the (widowed) senior partner, where he meets the daughter.

---

[17] T. Crane, *The Meaning of Belief: Religion from an Atheist's Point of View* (Cambridge, MA: Harvard University Press, 2017).

We went into the house, which was cheerfully lighted up, and into a hall where there were all sorts of hats, caps, great-coats, plaids, gloves, whips, and walking-sticks. "Where is Miss Dora?" said Mr. Spenlow to the servant. "Dora!" I thought. "What a beautiful name!"

We turned into a room near at hand ..., and I heard a voice say, "Mr. Copperfield, my daughter Dora, and my daughter Dora's confidential friend!" It was, no doubt, Mr. Spenlow's voice, but I didn't know it, and I didn't care whose it was. All was over in a moment. I had fulfilled my destiny. I was a captive and a slave. I loved Dora Spenlow to distraction!

She was more than human to me. She was a Fairy, a Sylph, I don't know what she was - anything that no one ever saw, and everything that everybody ever wanted. I was swallowed up in an abyss of love in an instant. There was no pausing on the brink; no looking down, or looking back; I was gone, headlong, before I had sense to say a word to her.[18]

Not much reason or evidence here. Yet - as always with Dickens - so human, so very human. And if this doesn't at once click with John Hick on the top of the omnibus, I can only conclude that you are not human, so very human. The experiences are nigh identical. We have seen how people of faith stress that although it has a propositional content - God exists - there is so much more. Faith "seeks acceptance as an expression of love." The sense of being swept up by a force stronger than oneself - a force that is entirely good and beautiful.

So, let us have no more nonsense about faith being untrustworthy simply because of its nature. If this is simple weakness, then thank God for weakness. We know weakness. Lydgate in *Middlemarch*, who, when faced with difficult decisions, doesn't have the guts to choose the right option. The young soldier in the Great War who cowered in the trenches as his comrades went over the top. Paul, Hick, and David are not weak in this way. Does this mean that their experiences are beyond criticism? No indeed! People who fall in love often make disastrous decisions - both Dorothea and Lydgate in *Middlemarch*. (Fortunately, Dorothea gets a second chance.) So, for the moment, keep this in mind about religious experiences. More importantly, for all their similarities, there is surely a major difference between David Copperfield and John Hick. David, and the rest of us, would understand (and probably approve of) his emotions, but we would see them in some sense relative. David thinks - believes, knows - that Dora is the most beautiful person in the world, an object of irresistible attraction. We think - believe, know - that David thinks - believes, knows - that Dora is the most

[18] C. Dickens, *David Copperfield* (Oxford: Oxford University Press, [1850] 1948).

beautiful person in the world, an object of irresistible attraction. However, we don't think – believe, know – that Dora is the most beautiful person in the world, an object of irresistible attraction.

We surely know why David feels as he does, and we probably have a pretty good idea of why we don't share that emotion. We may already ourselves be in love with another. We may find Dora not quite to our taste. As serious thinkers we would prefer a bluestocking over the rather shallow little person Dora proves to be. Not that we are not glad for David, for apart from anything else he is no longer a competitor for the person I want as my beloved. The point is that it is all relative. Objectively, Dora is not the most beautiful person in the world, an object of irresistible attraction. Whereas the believer wants to claim that objectively God exists, Jesus is his son, and these truths are given to us by an irresistible overwhelming force. And those of us who do not have faith are left outside wondering why we should accept this as an objective truth. In the end, given the similarities and differences between love and faith claims, it seems that one cannot – should not – condemn a faith experience because of what it is, namely, not reason and evidence, but that does not in itself confer self-validating status on such an experience.

SCIENCE VERSUS FAITH

The New Atheist will keep hammering. Let's take up the all-important question of science and what it tells us about faith. The answer is simple. Science tells us that faith is quite unreliable; it is just a crutch for the inadequate. Dawkins takes without argument that the God question is a scientific question. "Either he exists or he doesn't. It is a scientific question; one day we may know the answer, and meanwhile we can say something pretty strong about the probability."[19] Significantly less than 1 percent! Jerry Coyne is eloquent on the subject. In *Faith vs. Fact* (2015) – a title that tells of where he goes and how – he speaks of Charles Darwin's *Origin of Species* as the "greatest scripture-killer ever penned." He argues that "science and religion are engaged in a kind of war: a war for understanding, a war about whether we should have good reasons for what we accept as true."[20] To use a wicked metaphor, Coyne has a statement of faith.

My claim is this: science and religion are incompatible because they have different methods for getting knowledge about reality, have different ways

[19] Dawkins, *God Delusion*, 48.   [20] Coyne, *Faith vs. Fact*, xii.

of assessing the reliability of that knowledge, and, in the end, arrive at conflicting conclusions about the universe. "Knowledge" acquired by religion is at odds not only with scientific knowledge, but also with knowledge professed by other religions. In the end, religion's methods, unlike those of science, are useless for understanding reality.[21]

Why, then, are people deceived? Someone like John Hick may be as deluded as the alcoholic who sees pink rats running up the wall, but he is not an alcoholic. He is a solid citizen. Here we get into (scientific) explanations of religion and its hold on people. Opinion is divided. Some think it an evil phenomenon that has a life and history of its own, a life and history that involves humans but not their welfare. This is Dennett's position. He regards religion as a parasite, just as much as the liver fluke is a parasite on sheep. "You watch an ant in a meadow, laboriously climbing up a blade of grass, higher and higher until it falls, then climbs again, and again, like Sisyphus rolling his rock, always striving to reach the top." Why does this happen? The ant gets nothing out of all this activity. "Its brain has been commandeered by a tiny parasite, a lancet fluke (*Dicrocelium dendriticum*), that needs to get itself into the stomach of a sheep or cattle in order to complete its reproductive cycle. This little brain worm is driving the ant into position to benefit *its* progeny, not the ant's."[22] Just as the liver fluke is up to no good for sheep, so religion is up to no good for humans.

Some think religion is just a by-product of more useful adaptations. This is Richard Dawkins's position. It could be that the clear biological utility of learning from your seniors, your parents, and others – stay away from the cliff; red berries give you stomachache; crocodiles are not friendly – backfires and leads to religious conviction. "To say the least, there will be a selective advantage to child brains that possess the rule of thumb: believe, without question, whatever your grown-ups tell you. Obey your parents, obey the tribal elders, especially when they adopt a solemn, minatory tone. Trust your elders without question."[23] Regrettably, this is just what happens with religion, and, like a Dennettian parasite, one has it because it is good at propagating itself for itself.

A third suggestion makes religion of great adaptive importance. This is the position of Edward O. Wilson, today's most distinguished Darwinian evolutionist. "The highest forms of religious practice, when examined more

---

[21] Coyne, *Faith vs. Fact*, 64.
[22] D. Dennett, *Breaking the Spell: Religion as a Natural Phenomenon* (New York: Viking, 2006), 3–4.
[23] Dawkins, *God Delusion*, 174.

closely, can be seen to confer biological advantage. Above all they congeal identity. In the midst of the chaotic and potentially disorienting experiences each person undergoes daily, religion classifies him, provides him with unquestioned membership in a group claiming great powers, and by this means gives him a driving purpose in life compatible with his self-interest. His strength is the strength of the group, his guide the sacred covenant."[24] Religion makes for a sense of self-worth set within a functioning society.

To be honest, I am not quite sure what to make of these explanations. Parasites are not always that harmful, and learning from your elders does not, as such, make religion a bad thing. Group identity and these sorts of things have certainly been of fundamental importance in some societies. One thinks of people in the Middle Ages and how the elaborate Catholic Church – with beliefs and rituals and the like – gave a meaning to a life that otherwise would, in the words of Thomas Hobbes, have been "solitary, poor, nasty, brutish, and short." The same seems to have been true of American settlers in the early years of the Republic. Their Protestant, Bible-based evangelical religion gave them a stability and meaning that was quite lacking in the deism of the founders of the nation.[25]

What we can certainly give to the critics of faith is that there must surely have been naturalistic reasons for the attractions of faith. These are not necessarily signs of weakness, or – the implication – that this makes faith untrustworthy. Needing a Gospel when facing native people and drought and illness and loneliness and more is an understandable human need, not necessarily a flawed human need. If you say that a receptivity to faith beliefs does not demand a naturalistic explanation, then I guess the discussion ends there. For myself, I would be prepared to say that faith beliefs themselves can have naturalistic explanations. This does not, in itself, make them false or unreliable. I don't see any reason to deny the authenticity of Hick's conversion simply because it is explicable in terms of adolescent psychology. Is the sky not blue simply because the sensation is explicable in terms of optics and physiology?

What about the central claim that science and faith are, as it were, naked mud wrestling and that science wins, always? That is another matter. Obviously, science does win over religion, whether this involves faith-based claims or not. Someone who claims to have faith that the Bible is universally, literally true is going to say that Adam and Eve and Noah and his Ark and

[24] E. O. Wilson, *On Human Nature* (Cambridge, MA: Harvard University Press, 1978), 188.
[25] A. Porterfield, *Conceived in Doubt: Religion and Politics in the New American Nation* (Chicago: University of Chicago Press, 2012).

the sun stopping for Joshua are given to us on faith. They are true because faith tells us that they are true. But they aren't – true, that is. There was no historical Adam and Eve. The human species may have gone through bottlenecks, but the population was never fewer than 10,000 or so. Likewise, Noah and his ark never existed – certainly not one holding all the animals – and there was no worldwide flood. Geology tells us that this is not true and geology is right on this. And as for Joshua and the sun? Give us a break!

Even the Christian should admit that if we are made in the image of God, then we are not going to be deceived by science all the time. God gave us the talents to explore this world. He is not about to mess up things every time we do use these talents. This thinking, incidentally, is very much part of the Christian tradition. St. Augustine was adamant that the Bible is not a work of science – the ancient Jews were not educated people like we Romans – and so we should not look to the Bible for scientific guidance. Supposedly, the sun was created on the fourth day (in Genesis 1:16), whereas light has already been around since the first day (in Genesis 1:3). Both claims cannot be true. Hence, "we should not think either of those days being the ones governed by the sun nor of that working resembling the way that God now works in time."[26]

FAITH CONCLUDED

Where do we end our discussion? I have done my best for faith; but, in the end, was my best is good enough? I don't have faith. Should I simply walk away and say the conflict ended with no winner? I respect people of faith, but now a judgment must be made. Let's assume that everything is now on the table, for all that, as the discussion proceeds, we shall see is much to be queried. Cutting to the quick, I fear that, as things stand at the moment, for all the concessions, faith is going out with the tide. Putting empathy on one side, let us stop pussyfooting around. If – because I have love and respect for people of faith – I am not prepared to say this myself, let someone say it on my behalf. You have given a sympathetic hearing to the faith defenders. You have come up empty-handed. Little wonder that you yourself have admitted that you don't have faith. Clearly, you think that the defenders of faith are wrong, that in some sense it is a delusion, and that ultimately it all comes down to fear of the unknown, of extinction. William James knew the

[26] St. Augustine, *The Literal Meaning of Genesis*, trans. J. H. Taylor (New York: Newman 1982).

problem and the solution. On the one hand, the "sanest and best of us are of one clay with lunatics and prison inmates, and death finally runs the robustest of us down." On the other hand, thanks to religion, thanks to faith, "what we most dreaded has become the habitation of our safety, and the hour of our moral death has turned into our spiritual birthday. The time for tension in our soul is over, and that of happy relaxation, of calm deep breathing, of an eternal present, with no discordant future to be anxious about, has arrived."[27]

This is not enough. Belief in God may make me feel happy. That's not the point. Is there reason for me to believe in God? Good question. I have not yet seen a lot of reason to believe in God. Trying not to be insulting, I think believers are kidding themselves, probably because they are scared of the unknown and frightened of nonbeing. But that is not a good enough answer. Faith? No thanks.

Brian Davies

INTRODUCTION

When people think about faith, they often suppose that it is second-rate compared with knowledge. Why? Because they suppose that faith is belief that lacks *grounds* or *reasons* or *evidence*. The big idea here seems to be this: (1) knowledge is always *good* since it rests on reason, and (2) faith is always *bad* since it does not. It is also sometimes said that faith is bad since it frequently amounts to belief held *despite* reason, belief that resolutely ignores the presentation of good reasons for supposing that what is believed "on faith" is false.

One thing to be said in favor of these conclusions is the fact that knowledge seems to guarantee truth, while belief does not. I might believe that everyone is out to get me, but they might not be. Yet I cannot be wrong if I *know* that such and such is the case. From "John *believes* that Paris is the capital of France" it does not *follow* that Paris *is* the capital of France (even though it is). But if we accept that John *knows* that Paris is the capital of France, we are committed to agreeing that Paris *is* the French capital.

Yet is it easy to distinguish between faith and knowledge in a clear way? Do those with faith automatically fail to have knowledge? Should we think that those with knowledge do not rely on faith? My view is that it is not easy

---

[27] W. James, *Varieties of Religious Experience: A Study in Human Nature* (New York: Longman, 1902), 47.

to distinguish sharply between faith and knowledge. I also think that those with faith do not automatically fail to have knowledge and that those with knowledge always somehow rely on faith.

KNOWLEDGE AND FAITH

In adopting this view, I confess to being influenced by what Ludwig Wittgenstein (1889–1951) argues in reflections written shortly before he died, which were published under the title *On Certainty*.[28] He begins by drawing attention to a lecture delivered by G. E. Moore (1873–1958) titled "Proof of an External World."[29] Philosophers have often been skeptical when it comes to the claim that material things exist. You might suppose that "No material things exist" is a stupid claim, but some philosophers have accepted it, and in "Proof of an External World,"[30] Moore aims to rebut them. He tries to do so by holding up his hand and declaring that both he and his audience find it unquestionable that he has a hand. Moore's "proof" seems to amount to the following argument: (1) I know that *p* if the falsity of *p* is inconceivable. (2) It is inconceivable that I do not have a hand. (3) So, I *know* that I have a hand and therefore know that there is "an external world." In another work, *A Defence of Common Sense*, Moore claimed that propositions such as his "I have a hand" are "truisms," examples of what we all *know*.[31] This knowledge, says Moore, is what refutes skepticism concerning the existence of material things.

Wittgenstein thinks that Moore is onto something important here. But he also thinks that Moore is wrong to suppose that he can *prove* the truth of his "common sense propositions" just by saying that he *knows* them to be true. Wittgenstein takes Moore's "I know" to be intellectually redundant since, rather than showing why Moore is right to say, "I have a hand," it merely serves as a way of *emphasizing* that assertion. Wittgenstein agrees that it makes sense to speak of us proving what might be doubtful and going on to say that we therefore *know* what we are talking about. But he sees no sense in the notion of proving the truth of propositions *whose falsity is inconceivable* by simply claiming to know that they are true. Such propositions, he

---

[28] Ludwig Wittgenstein, *On Certainty*, ed. G. E. M. Anscombe and G. H. von Wright, trans. Denis Paul and G. E. M. Anscombe (Oxford: Basil Blackwell, 1974). I take Wittgenstein to be one of the greatest of Western philosophers.

[29] G. E. Moore, "Proof of an External World," *Proceedings of the British Academy* 25 (1939).

[30] Here, of course, we might ask "external" to "what"?

[31] G. E. Moore, "A Defence of Common Sense," in J. H. Muirhead, ed., *Contemporary British Philosophy*, 2nd series (London: Allen and Unwin, 1925).

suggests, are not *suppositions* or *hypotheses* for which there could be *grounds* or *evidence*. Rather, they are propositions that we (or at least most of us) draw on when deciding what *counts* as grounds or evidence. They are not propositions *to which* we reason but are *what we rely on* when determining what it is reasonable to believe. And here I agree with Wittgenstein.

Whenever we attack an opponent intellectually, or whenever we defend ourselves intellectually, or whenever we claim knowledge or express doubt, we are trusting in certain truths. Aristotle (384–322 BC) expressed this point by noting that, on pain of an infinite regress, all arguments have to proceed from what is not proved or known to be true on the basis of some previous reasoning or evidence.[32] Having cast doubt on Moore's claim to *know* that he has a hand, and without doubting that Moore has a hand, Wittgenstein moves to a conclusion similar to that of Aristotle, though he does not make reference to the notion of infinite regress, as does Aristotle. Instead, he draws attention to the extent to which what we take to be knowledge rests on a huge amount of assumptions that we take for granted, not because we are paying *insufficient attention to evidence*, but because these assumptions are things in the light of which we determine what *counts* as evidence. Moore thinks that "I just know" can be a good answer to "How do you know?" By contrast, Wittgenstein asks us to note that "I just know" normally invites the question "How do you know?" while implying that this is a question we inevitably answer while *ultimately* relying on what we take *for granted*.

Wittgenstein is not saying that claims to know something should not be backed up by reasons. He is noting that what we take to be reasons always rests on beliefs to which we have not reasoned, beliefs that he calls the "scaffolding of our thoughts," which are groundless and amount to "judgements used as principles of judgement."[33] Hence we find Wittgenstein saying, "I did not get my picture of the world by satisfying myself of its correctness; nor do I have it because I am satisfied of its correctness. No: it is the inherited background against which I distinguish between true and false."[34] At another place he observes, "If you tried to doubt everything you would not get as far as doubting anything. The game of doubting itself presupposes certainty."[35] Again, he writes: "In general I take as true what is found in textbooks, of geography for example. Why? I say: all these facts have been confirmed a hundred times over. But how do I know that? What is my evidence for it? ... I believe what people transmit to me in a certain

---

[32] I take an infinite regress in a series of propositions to be something that arises if proposition 1 depends on proposition 2, and 2 on 3, and 3 on 4 ... and so on without end.
[33] See *On Certainty*, §§211 and 214.   [34] *On Certainty*, §94.   [35] *On Certainty*, §115.

manner. In this way I believe geographical, chemical, historical facts, etc. That is how I *learn* the sciences. Of course, learning is based on believing.... Knowledge is in the end based on acceptance.... The child learns by believing the adult. Doubt comes *after* belief."[36]

This line of thinking is also defended by Elizabeth Anscombe (1919–2001), especially in her essay "What Is It to Believe Someone?"[37] Her focus here is on what she calls "believing the person." By this phrase she means "believing *x* that *p*," which she takes to be *relying on x for it that p*, not just agreeing with *x* for reasons that one may already have. And, as Anscombe notes, such believing the person is of enormous importance in our lives. Or, as she puts it:

> The greater part of our knowledge of reality rests upon the belief that we repose in things we have been taught and told.... Nor is what testimony gives us entirely a detachable part, like the thick fringe of fat on a chunk of steak. It is more like the flecks and streaks of fat that are distributed through good meat; though there are lumps of pure fat as well. Examples could be multiplied indefinitely. You have received letters; how did you ever learn what a letter was and how it came to you? You will take up a book and look in a certain place and see "New York, Dodd Mead and Company, 1910". So, do you know from personal observation that that book was published by that company, and then, and in New York? Well, hardly. But you do know it *purports* to have been so. How? Well, you know that is where the publisher's name is always put, and the name of the place where his office belongs. How do you know that? You were taught it. What you were taught was your tool in acquiring the new knowledge. "There was an American edition" you will say, "I've seen it". Think how much reliance on believing what you have been told lies behind being able to say that. It is irrelevant at this level to raise a question about possible forgery; without what we know by testimony, there is no such thing as what a forgery is *pretending* to be. You may think you know that New York is in North America. What is New York, what is North America? You may say you have been in these places. But how much does that fact contribute to your knowledge? Nothing, in comparison with testimony. How did you know you were there? Even if you inhabit New York and you have simply learned its name as the name of the place you inhabit, there is the question: How

---

[36] *On Certainty*, §§162, 170, 378, and 160.
[37] This essay has been reprinted a number of times, most recently in *Faith in a Hard Ground: Essays on Religion, Philosophy and Ethics by G. E. M. Anscombe*, ed. Mary Geach and Luke Gormally (Exeter: Imprint Academic, 2008), from which I quote in what follows. For a comparable essay by Anscombe, see "Faith," in G. E. M. Anscombe, *Collected Philosophical Papers*, vol. 3 (Oxford: Basil Blackwell, 1981).

extensive a region is this place you are calling 'New York'? And what has New York got to do with this bit of a map? Here is a complicated network of received information.[38]

Indeed, there is such a complicated network, and this should leave us uneasy with the claim that reason dictates that there always must be something wrong with belief that does not rest on an evaluation of reasons. What we think of as reasons depends to a huge extent on what we believe without them. In this sense, what we take to be knowledge and rational thinking most definitely rests on what can be thought of as faith. Even René Descartes (1596–1650), often taken to be the "father of modern philosophy," shows us that this is so in his attempt to undermine total skepticism (though not in the reasoning he uses to ground the attempt).

In his *Meditations on First Philosophy* (1641), worried about skepticism concerning all that he takes to be true, Descartes relentlessly strives to hit on what he can *know* to be true without question. To begin with, in his second meditation he famously arrives at the thought "I certainly know that if I am thinking, then I must exist since, even if I am wrong in thinking as I do, I have to exist in order to be thinking wrongly."

But in *Meditation* III it strikes him that even what he takes to be most clearly true might be doubted and that the doubt cannot be finally done away with unless it can be proved that God exists and is not a deceiver.

Descartes then offers a proof that God exists, and that God is no deceiver. In doing so, however, he relies on exactly the kind of reasoning that led him to assert his own existence – reasoning that rests on what he takes to be "clearly and distinctly perceived" by him to be true. In *Meditation* III Descartes agrees that he cannot know that any of his "clear and distinct perceptions" are true without first proving that God exists, and that God is no deceiver. But he cannot undertake to present such a proof without taking some of his clear and distinct perceptions to be true. At this stage in his *Meditations*, therefore, he is trying to get himself in the air by pulling himself upward on the shoes in which he is standing. Descartes's claim to know that *such and such* is the case rests on beliefs that he does not attempt to prove. One of the most important of these is "I understand the words I am using and know that words do not change their meaning from moment to moment." Of course, Descartes might have raised doubts concerning this

[38] Geach and Gormally, eds., *Faith in a Hard Ground*, 30–31. Cf. G. E. M. Anscombe, "Grounds of Belief," in Mary Geach and Luke Gormally, eds., *Logic, Truth and Meaning: Writings by G. E. M. Anscombe* (Exeter: Imprint Academic, 2015).

proposition, but it is hard to see how he could have *argued* against it since his arguments would have had to presuppose what he would then be denying.

One thing I take all of what I have just been saying to imply is that it would be wrong to suppose that someone who believes that God exists but cannot argue the matter is *automatically* being irrational. We often believe that such and such is true while citing reasons, sometimes challenged, for doing so. Yet we often believe an uncountable number of things by "believing the person" directly, as Anscombe has it. So, there is no reason in principle why someone should be thought to be irrational just because they believe x that p even if p is "God exists" (unless it can be proved that God does not or cannot exist). My belief that there are black holes derives entirely from people who tell me that they exist while themselves taking many things on trust. But I do not see that my belief in black holes as derived from the current scientific community is unreasonable. Unlike Michael Ruse, I am not an expert on evolutionary biology. If asked whether I believe that millions of things on earth have evolved over very many centuries, I will say "Yes." But only by appealing to people such as Michael and what they have to say. And if you think that I am not flying in the face of reason when doing so, you should, in principle, also concede that the same could be true of someone who believes that God exists on the say-so of someone else, not on the basis of their own research. You should concede this even if you happen to think that good reasons can be given for asserting that God exists.

If you agree with me on this matter, however, are you not committed to supposing that people can be reasonable when believing anything at all, even what might be deemed to be incredible? Suppose that you tell me that witches and wizards exist because of what we read in the Harry Potter novels. Would I be right or reasonable simply to believe you on your say-so? Again, would I be right or reasonable to continue in my belief that Santa Claus exists just because I believed my parents when they told me about him when I was a child? The right answer to both questions is "Obviously not." But nothing that I have said above while drawing on Wittgenstein and Anscombe should be taken as suggesting otherwise. These philosophers are not saying that someone should believe *anything* that *anyone* tells them. Rather, they are drawing attention to the error that would be presented in a slogan such as "Knowledge, always *good*; belief, always *bad*." The error consists in supposing that knowledge is gained without dependence on what is believed without reasons or justifications or evidence.

In paragraph 167 of *On Certainty* Wittgenstein observes:

It is clear that our empirical propositions do not all have the same status, since one can lay down such a proposition and turn it from an empirical proposition into a norm of description. Think of chemical investigations. Lavoisier makes experiments with substances in his laboratory and now he concludes that this and that takes place when there is burning. He does not say that it might happen otherwise another time. He has got hold of a definite world-picture – not of course one that he invented: he learned it as a child. I say world-picture and not hypothesis, because it is the matter-of-course foundation for his research and as such also goes unmentioned.

Wittgenstein is not here telling us not to worry about reasons for believing. He is saying that the boundary between what we might call "faith" and "reason" is not a sharp one. He is noting that there is no such sharp boundary since, in Anscombe's words, "the greater part of our knowledge of reality rests upon the belief that we repose in things we have been taught and told."

BELIEF AND EVIDENCE

It has often been claimed that a rational person will believe only what is self-evident, evident to the senses, or derivable from this. Yet it is not self-evident, or evident to the senses, or derivable from what is self-evident or evident to the senses, that this claim is true. I take "All triangles have three sides" to be self-evident. And I take it that my cat now being on my lap is evident to me at a sensory level. But where is the comparable evidence for it being true that a rational person will believe only what is self-evident, evident to the senses, or derivable from this? There is none. None that I know of, anyway. We may commit ourselves to this thesis because of faith. But it would be faith and not reason on which we would be drawing when doing so.

In response to this point someone might insist that if faith is a matter of belief as opposed to knowledge, and if belief is always fallible, then faith is always fallible; so, best to stick with knowledge and steer clear of faith entirely. And with this thought in mind, some have said that in order to be rational we must always proceed on the basis of *evidence*, or *sufficient* evidence. A famous exponent of this conclusion is W. K. Clifford (1845–1879). He was an English mathematician and is especially remembered philosophically for an essay called "The Ethics of Belief," published in 1877.[39] In this work he roundly declares: "It is wrong always, everywhere, and for anyone, to believe anything on insufficient evidence." Clifford does not assert that knowledge is what we end up with *only* if we have "sufficient" evidence. But he does seem to be saying that we are morally at fault if we believe *without* such evidence. Yet is that so?

We might doubt that it is, because we might wonder when evidence is "sufficient" and when it is not. Yet Clifford moves to his conclusion by considering cases that seem to support it very well when reflecting on what we might think of as "real life" scenarios. For example, he asks us to consider a shipowner wanting to put one of his vessels to sea with a host of immigrants on board. This ship had done good service, and, though sometimes needing repairs, it had always performed well. When some (unspecified) people with knowledge of ships suggested that the ship might not be seaworthy, its owner worried for a time but eventually decided to let the ship sail while relying on the fact that it had never sunk yet. Yet the ship sank and all aboard were drowned. Clifford argues that the shipowner here was negligent, and it seems hard to disagree with this conclusion. To take a parallel case, would we not be rightly outraged to learn that pilots of a plane took off without having very good reason to believe that the plane was up and ready for takeoff, apart from the fact that it had never crashed before? Surely, we would. So, there are instances when beliefs (such as "This ship is seaworthy" or "This plane is safe for takeoff") can be faulted with respect to a lack of attention to evidence in defense of them or against them. Indeed, that we should form our beliefs with an eye to evidence for and against them might seem like a rational truism.

But is believing without evidence always irrational? The famous philosopher David Hume (1711–1775) once declared: "A wise man proportions his belief to the evidence."[40] In its context, this remark seems to mean that one should believe only what accords with previous sensory experience, for Hume goes on to say that, since reports of miracles contradict what sensory experience confirms abundantly, the evidence against the truth of such reports is as strong as could be. The "wise man," claims Hume, should never believe that any miracles have occurred, even though people have reported them as having occurred.[41]

---

[39] See W. K. Clifford, *Lectures and Essays*, 2nd ed., ed. Leslie Stephen and Frederick Pollock (London: Macmillan, 1886).
[40] David Hume, *An Inquiry Concerning Human Understanding*, ed. Tom. L. Beauchamp (Oxford: Clarendon Press, 2000), 84.
[41] Hume, *Inquiry*, 84–88.

"Evidence," however, is a slippery notion. What is evidence for one conclusion might be entirely irrelevant to another. Nor, so to speak, does evidence grow on trees. I mean that while you will know exactly what I am telling you to do if I ask you to count the number of apples on a certain tree, you will not know what I am telling you to do when asking you to count the number of pieces of evidence on the tree – or anywhere else. "Evidence" is not a noun signifying anything belonging to a natural kind. Cats and dogs belong to natural kinds. Pieces of evidence do not. So how do we identify them for what they are?

We frequently declare that we have evidence for this or that being the case. People get legally indicted because of what is taken to be evidence, and juries often acquit for what they regard as a lack of evidence. But how do we end up being able to cite what we think of as evidence? It can hardly be because all our evidence rests on previous evidence, for that would lead us into an infinite regression. If I need evidence for asserting that my first piece of evidence is truly evidence, then I presumably need evidence for asserting that this second bit of evidence is also truly evidence. And so on, without end. If all evidence needs to be backed up by further evidence, then nobody is going to be able to offer any evidence, just as nobody can obey the command "Never ask for permission without first asking for permission." Yet we do take ourselves sometimes rightly to try to bring discussions to a reasonable close by appealing to "the evidence" or to what we might refer to as "good reason." Notice, though, that in order to get to this stage we need what I can only think of as an "education."

In this connection, consider what we often find in the stories about Sherlock Holmes in the writings of Sir Arthur Conan Doyle (1859–1930). In these, the following scenario is reported again and again. (1) Someone of whom Holmes previously knew nothing visits him at home in Baker Street so as to consult him in his role as a private detective. (2) On such occasions, Holmes is in the company of his friend, Dr. Watson. (3) Within a few seconds, Holmes makes a whole lot of true statements about the person who is visiting him. (4) Along with Holmes's visitor, Watson is amazed and asks Holmes, "How on earth do you know all that?" (5) Holmes says that it is all perfectly obvious, and then proceeds to note facts about the visitor that support what he has said. In these scenarios Holmes and Watson are looking at one and the same person. But Holmes can interpret what he sees in a way that Watson cannot. Why so? Because he is a much better detective than Watson and can identify as clues to certain truths things that Watson cannot recognize for what they are until his attention is drawn to them. But how did Holmes, or anyone comparable to him, get to be that way? Was it *always* by attending to evidence in something like Hume's sense of "evidence"?

Obviously, it was not. Holmes, like all of us, learned how to identify such and such as evidence for this or that. He did not come into the world as an expert detective. He started as a child being taught by teachers whom he believed as they tried to teach him. While believing his teachers, he acquired what he took to be knowledge, and he drew on this in his subsequent cases while becoming the expert he turned out to be when identifying X or Y as evidence for Z. I stress the role of teaching here since, as I have argued, so much that we take ourselves to know derives not from inspection and evaluation of evidence but from beliefs we have somehow acquired independently of anything that might be thought to be evidence. As I have said, what we typically think of as knowledge derives from beliefs that we do not question but take on what I would call "faith."[42] Hence, for example, geologists who end up formulating geological laws presume that there is a material world to investigate and that things in the material world behave in a regular way (hence the metaphorical notion of "*laws* of nature" regularly "*obeyed*" by material things). But from where did the geologists derive such presumptions? Was it from an inspection of evidence? Hardly. They *presumed* them, or as I would say, took them on faith. And so we might therefore conclude, there is nothing necessarily wrong with believing on faith if that is taken to mean "believing something without recourse to evidence that is supposed to confirm the thing that we believe."

HOW A DEMAND FOR EVIDENCE OR REASONS MIGHT BE LEGITIMATE

Yet it certainly does not follow from anything I have been saying above that requests for evidence or philosophical arguments are always out of place when it comes to certain beliefs. Clifford was arguably right to have chided the shipowner of which he speaks. On the other hand, however, my belief that there is such a place as London (in which I was born) was most certainly not something that I arrived at because of evidence or argument. It is a belief that I take to be basic in the sense that, if people came to dispute it, I would take them or myself to be deranged. I would say that if I came to believe that London is not a place, then I would not know what to think about anything. That London is a place is, for me, something not to be questioned. Should I come seriously to question it, I would be at a loss when it comes to

---

[42] I am not here concerned with what is sometimes called knowledge of necessary truths such as "All triangles have three sides," though I suspect that such knowledge in some ways falls under what I am now talking about.

reasoning as I do. If I am wrong about London being a place, then I am wrong when it comes to most of what I think since so much of what I think is, in a hugely complicated way, bound up with the idea that London is the city in which I was born. It does not follow from this fact that reasons cannot be given for supposing that London is a place. Indeed, I can give you all sorts of reasons for believing in the existence of London. What I cannot do, however, is give you reasons that proceed to infinity, one reason always depending on another one. There must be a stop when it comes to the giving of reasons. The giving of reasons or the appeal to evidence depends on believing without reasons or evidence; it depends on taking certain things for granted, things that are not themselves conclusions inferred on the basis of what we might grandly refer to as "reason."

Still, good reasons can be given for various conclusions. Scientists are in the business of trying to provide good reasons for various conclusions that they draw. And why should they not try to do this? Again, what I have been saying does not mean that good reasons cannot be given for the claim that God exists. In the religious tradition to which I belong there have been many who have sought to explain why we have reason to assert that God exists – people like St. Anselm of Canterbury (1033–1109) and St. Thomas Aquinas (1226–1274). But neither of these authors disparaged people who believe that God exists without philosophical argument for "God exists." It is also highly unlikely that either of them came to believe that God exists because of a philosophical investigation. But when trying to explore what they took "God exists" to mean, they ended up arguing that there are good reasons for concluding that God exists, a conclusion formally ratified by the first Vatican Council (1879–1870) in its declaration that "Holy Mother Church holds and teaches that God, the beginning and end of all things, may be certainly known by the natural light of human reason, by means of created things."[43] Vatican I did not explain *how* human reason can come to a knowledge of God's existence. But that is unsurprising since the decrees of Vatican I are not intended to be read as a series of philosophical essays. In what it says about reason and the knowledge of God, Vatican I was just taking its stand on what St. Paul says in Romans 1, where he teaches that "ever since the creation of the world" God's "eternal power and divine nature, invisible though they are, have been understood and seen through the things he has made" (Romans 1:20). But I see nothing wrong in asking whether the claim that

---

[43] Vatican I, *Dogmatic Constitution on the Catholic Faith (Dei Filius)*, chapter 1.

God's existence can be known from what God has created can be sustained by reasonable argument. If it can, then I take it that we would have good reason for claiming that God exists.

With that said, however, I now need to note two things that I take to be of historical importance. The first is that people like Anselm and Aquinas do not deny that knowledge claims rest on what is taken for granted. The second is that they, and the whole Catholic tradition, make a distinction between reason and faith while holding that there are true teachings to which our reason cannot be thought to lead, teachings that are revealed by God. Belief in such teachings is what Catholics, and many other Christians, typically refer to when they speak about the religious virtue of faith.

People often say that those with faith are people who believe that God exists or people who are in some vague way religious. But authors such as Anselm and Aquinas do not think in this simplistic way. They take it as obvious that belief that one true God exists is common to the three monotheistic religions of Judaism, Islam, and Christianity, some members of which have argued philosophically that God exists. But they also recognize that these religions also teach significantly different things. So, they distinguish between belief that God exists and what they call the "articles of faith" – these being uniquely Christian beliefs such as the doctrine of the Trinity and the doctrine of the Incarnation, to which Jews and Muslims do not subscribe. The justification for this distinction between belief that God exists and the articles of faith is simply that, given Judaism and Islam, it is clear that one can believe, or maybe even know, that God exists without believing that God is somehow triune or that God, in the words of John 1:14, "became flesh and lived among us."

The big idea here is that we should distinguish between what we can figure out by reason (drawing on faith as it might) and what must be *revealed* to us by God. According to Aquinas, the religious virtue of faith (which he refers to as a *theological* one) amounts to firmly believing something without being compelled by what we might think of as proof or decisive evidence. So, he takes faith to be halfway between opinion and knowledge, meaning that someone with faith is firmly committed to a certain teaching without thinking that there is no rational option but to accept that teaching. And he takes the theological virtue of faith to be had by one who believes what God teaches, not just what can be worked out philosophically. So, he says that the object of faith is God since "faith assents to anything only because it is revealed by God."[44]

This distinction between reason and revelation is a traditional one made by many theologians both earlier and later than Aquinas, and it is central to Roman Catholic teaching. It is also not an odd one to make if we reflect on the notion of teaching. Teachers spend a lot of their time imparting what they take to be truths that their students need to learn without being able to arrive at them on their own, truths on the basis of which they might go on to engage in what we call "research." Teachers, we might say, are in the business of sharing their knowledge with us. When it comes to the traditional approach to faith, however, faith is not merely believing what a human being tells one; it is believing *God* when it comes to what cannot be proved or shown probable by human reasoning. As St. Paul says in Galatians 3:6, "Abraham believed God and it was reckoned to him as righteousness." Here we clearly have Anscombe's notion of believing x that p. Obviously, believing x that p might sometimes leave one in a state of error. Yet what if it is *God* whom one is believing? Aquinas, and the Catholic tradition in general, assumes that to have Christian faith is to believe what God is teaching and to believe on God's say-so alone. And what could be wrong with that conclusion if, indeed, one is believing what God is declaring?

This question, however, obviously leads to another question: What would we be doing if we take God to be declaring or teaching? I suppose that the best answer to this question is that we would be taking ourselves to believe the teaching that is offered to us as coming from God, teaching that amounts to divine revelation and which might be compared to the revelation that teachers often present to their students. But why this appeal to uniquely Christian faith in the first place? Instead of resorting to articles of faith supposedly derived from faith in divine revelation, why not try to figure everything out reasonably? The traditional answer to this question, which I accept, is that the articles of faith are not teachings that can be proved to be true or shown to be probably true. When it comes to the articles of faith, we are talking of such things as the doctrine of the Trinity and the Incarnation as laid down by ecumenical church councils such as those of Chalcedon (451) and the first council of Nicaea (325). And when looking at what these doctrines proclaim, one can see why one might

---

[44] *Summa Theologiae*, 2a2ae, 1, 1 and 2.

conclude that they are neither provable nor probable when held before the bar of human reason.

Take, for example, the doctrine of the Trinity. This asserts that there is but one God who is Father, Son, and Holy Spirit (the "persons" of the Trinity) and that each of these persons is wholly divine while being one God and not three gods. What kind of argument could show that this must be so or that it is probably so? I know of none. Indeed, I suggest that the orthodox doctrine of the Trinity is a teaching that we can *prove* to be one that *cannot* be proved – as Aquinas argues. In *Summa theologiae* 1a, 1, 32, 1, he observes:

> Through natural reason man can know God only from creatures; and they lead to the knowledge of him as effects do to their cause. Therefore, by natural reason we can know of God what characterizes him necessarily as the source of all beings.... Now the creative power of God is shared by the whole Trinity; hence it goes with the unity of nature, not with the distinction of persons. Therefore, through natural reason we can know what has to do with the unity of nature, but not with the distinction of persons. He who tries to prove the trinity of persons by natural powers of reason detracts from faith in two ways. First on the point of its dignity, for the object of faith is those invisible realities which are beyond the reach of human reason. St. Paul says that *faith is of things that appear not* (Hebrews 11:1). Second, on the point of advantage in bringing others to faith. For when one someone wants to support faith by unconvincing arguments, he becomes a laughingstock for the unbelievers, who think that we rely on such arguments and believe because of them.

What Aquinas says here depends on it being true that reason can lead us to God only by inference from creatures to God as their cause – a line of thought to which I shall later return, one that denies that we are all born with an innate knowledge that God exists or an inbuilt understanding that God cannot be thought not to exist. Granted that Aquinas is right on this point, however, his argument seems to me to work. He has explained how it is demonstrable that the truth of the doctrine of the Trinity cannot be demonstrated, that it is demonstrably undecidable. He has shown why reason cannot establish the doctrine of the Trinity and allows one to make sense of the claim that the articles of faith, if true, must be revealed by God. I might add that the notion of demonstrable undecidability is not one to which only a theologian like Aquinas might have recourse. It is a commonplace among mathematicians, especially because of the incompleteness theorems of Kurt Gödel (1906–1978).[45]

[45] For Gödel, see the *Stanford Encyclopedia of Philosophy*, https://plato.stanford.edu/entries/goe del/#FirIncThe.

So, I end this section of the present book while commending to you the following theses. (1) Much that we take ourselves to know rests on what we believe without reliance on reason or evidence. (2) All arguments have to rely on what is taken for granted at some stage. (3) What we take to be reasons or evidence inevitably draw on what we do not conclude on the basis of reasons or evidence. (4) It does not follow from (1)–(3) that it is foolish to consider reasons for the truth of the claim that God exists. (5) While allowing for there being reasons to claim that God exists, traditional Christians (in the Catholic tradition at any rate) think of the religious virtue of faith as a matter of believing God that certain propositions are true. (6) This view of faith coheres with the fact that it can be reasonable to believe what has been declared to one even though one cannot prove the truth of what has been declared to one. (7) This view of faith rightly holds that specifically Christian articles of faith, such as the doctrines of the Trinity and the Incarnation, are demonstrably undecidable.

But can we reasonably claim to have knowledge of God based on what those who believe that God exists take to be things that God has made to exist? Can we claim to have knowledge of God on other grounds? These questions are what motivate philosophers writing about what is commonly referred to as "natural theology" as opposed to "revealed theology."[46] By "natural theology" I understand any attempt to argue philosophically that God exists without relying on anything taken to be faith in divine revelation. On this understanding, especially famous exponents of natural theology include Aristotle, St. Augustine of Hippo (354–430), Anselm and Aquinas, John Duns Scotus (d. 1308), Descartes, Gottfried Wilhelm Leibniz (1646–1716), William Paley (1743–1805), and Frederick Tennant (1866–1957). Exponents of natural theology often differ when it comes to their understanding of what God is, but they are united in thinking that philosophical reflection gives us grounds to think that God exists. As one might expect, their arguments have been subjected to criticism by those who think that, ultimately, we have no reason to say that God exists – criticisms of many different kinds, some of them favored by Michael Ruse. And Michael and I shall be reflecting on some of them in later sections of this book. Before we do that, however, we need to consider the view that natural theology should be cast into outer darkness since God is somehow beyond reason, and that there is something intrinsically wrong with any attempt to argue

---

[46] For an overview of the history of natural theology, together with many essays dealing with a variety of perspectives in natural theology, see Russell Re Manning, ed., *The Oxford Handbook of Natural Theology* (Oxford: Oxford University Press, 2013).

philosophically for God's existence. It has been said that arguments for the existence of God must be misguided since "God exists" cannot be thought to be even a *possibly* true proposition. It has also been said that sound theological thinking ought to convince us that the notion of arguing for God's existence conflicts with what proper belief in God amounts to. In my section of Chapter 2, I shall be considering versions of each of these conclusions and the reasons given for them.

Reason

Michael Ruse

ATHENS AND JERUSALEM

*W*AS THE CONCLUSION IN CHAPTER 1 – THAT, IN THE END, faith is inadequate – the end of the discussion? Clearly not. Let me use an analogy to show you my thinking at this point. I don't have faith and I am inclined to think that those who do are deceiving themselves. What will the believers, the people of faith, say in response? Most certainly, that in some sense the nonbeliever is lacking a sense. Often the analogy is with sight:

I once was lost
But now I'm found
Was blind, but now I see.

Can the nonbeliever speak to this? Very much so. If not having faith is like being blind, then why would a blind person be willing to allow that they are deficient and that others do have the sense of sight? Through reason and evidence! I (blind) and a friend (sighted) walk into a room and the friend says that on a table in the room is a book in braille. We walk over there. I feel the table, then the book, and finally I open it and am able to read it by touch. It is – perhaps this is the very reason my friend took me into the room – *The Wit and Wisdom of Thomas Aquinas* by Brian Davies. So now the question is whether I have reason and evidence to think I am blind and my friend is sighted, and obviously the answer is that I do. Even though I am blind, reason and evidence persuade me that I am missing something. There is, I suppose, the follow-up question of why he is sighted and I am blind. We cannot just put it down to chance, some problem of embryonic develop- ment, say, caused by the ingestion of some drug while my mother was pregnant. If the Christian is right, we are both made by a good God and – all other things being equal – we should both be sighted.

If you feel uncomfortable about sight – since, after all, I am not really blind – then try a sixth sense. Is the person who claims to have such a sense truly that much more able or capable than I or any other person with the standard five senses? Basically, it is the same situation as before. Reason and evidence! If your sixth sense tells you things we don't know previously (and could not be expected to know previously) – What will my teenager do next? – then it is reasonable to claim that you do have such a sense. Not otherwise. So, although you have faith, it is legitimate for me – more than that, binding – to use my reason. And if you cannot tell me, through reason and evidence, why faith is legitimate – as the sighted person shows the blind person – I have nothing forcing me to accept faith. And there may be reasons why I should reject faith and think you are simply deluding yourself. And when you tell me that I lost my sight because of my own carelessness or whatever, that is not necessarily true. I might have been born blind. That is answer enough for those who say that my absence of faith in some wise reflects my sinfulness or whatever. At the age of twenty I didn't kill someone and then lose my faith. I just lost it.

Which now swings me back to the main thread of my argument. What if you say that the analogy with sight is only an analogy? You don't trust reason enough to let it have the role I want it to play? Now it is up to me to show that this move is blocked, that you have already shown your faith (!) in reason. I may not be able to change your mind, because you think faith trumps reason. But you must allow that it is legitimate for me to use reason and, if I can show that there is no reason for me to take faith-claims seriously, to conclude that you are living in cloud-cuckoo land. You may think I am wrong, but you are not allowed to think I am insincere or being false to my own premises.

Start with a bit of history. Christianity is an amalgam. On the one hand, Christianity is a growth out of Judaism, the religion of the Old Testament, or, as it is sometimes called, the Hebrew Bible. This is absolutely and completely a religion of faith. Abraham, Moses, David, they are not in the business of proving God's existence. "Trust in the Lord with all your heart, and do not rely on your own insight. In all your ways acknowledge him, and he will make straight your paths."[1] Jesus and his followers were no exceptions. "For we walk by faith, not by sight."[2] Then, on the other hand, we have the philosophy of the Greeks, several centuries before Jesus arrived on Earth. This is absolutely and completely a philosophy of reason. Technically, I suppose, both Plato and Aristotle were pagans, although I don't think either of them was given to stripping stark naked, dancing around the fire,

---

[1] Proverbs 3:5–6.   [2] 2 Corinthians 5:7.

and having sex under the sacred oak while calling down the moon. I wouldn't put it past Socrates if he could upset the staid and self-important. If there were good-looking young men, also stark naked, dancing around the fire, that would be appreciated. The point is that both Plato and Aristotle believed in an eternal universe, with a deity whose creative powers were certainly not those that we identify happily with the Christian God of the Bible.[3] Plato believed in the rational Form of the Good, akin to the sun in our physical universe, which gives sustenance and being to all the world. The Good did not create the world; but, in the *Timaeus*, Plato suggests that in some sense it is the Designer. Opinion is mixed, but it is generally thought that this Design was not a phenomenon of one fixed point in time, but more a principle of design, pervading the universe, that has been there infinitely. Certainly, the Designer was working on the given. Aristotle had his Unmoved Mover, toward the perfection of which all strive. His system then is totally teleological. However, the Mover is unaware of the existence of anything but itself. It does the only thing a perfect thing can do, namely, contemplate its own perfection. I have young relatives who practice this with considerable skill.

The great philosopher-theologians Augustine, Anselm, and Aquinas picked up on all this, and – despite the differences – incorporated it into their Christian theology. Augustine never read Plato – he may have known a fragment or two – but through the Neo-Platonist Plotinus, he got the system. Particularly, that the deity had to be eternal, outside space and time. The *Confessions* is the key work.

> Thy years neither go nor come; but ours both go and come in order that all separate moments may come to pass. All thy years stand together as one, since they are abiding. Nor do thy years past exclude the years to come because thy years do not pass away. All these years of ours shall be with thee, when all of them shall have ceased to be. Thy years are but a day, and thy day is not recurrent, but always today. Thy "today" yields not to tomorrow and does not follow yesterday. Thy "today" is eternity.[4]

Same for space.

Anselm is famous for his ontological argument that God is a necessary being – "that than which none greater can be thought."[5] Thinking in an Augustinian manner, Aquinas, much influenced by Aristotle, was into end-directed proofs of God's existence. More on these later, but the key point is

---

[3] M. Ruse, *On Purpose* (Princeton: Princeton University Press, 2017).

[4] Augustine, *Confessions*, trans. H. Chadwick (Oxford: Oxford University Press, [396] 1998), 396.

[5] St. Anselm, *Anselm: Proslogium, Monologium, an Appendix on Behalf of the Fool by Gaunilon; and Cur Deus Homo*, trans. S. N. Deane (Chicago: Open Court, 1903).

that God had in some sense to be necessary, cause of himself. Else we are caught in infinite regresses. "Therefore it is necessary to admit a first efficient cause, to which everyone gives the name of God."[6] What, then, does this all add up to? The Christianity of the last two millennia has two sides. Revealed religion or theology – the religion of faith, especially as given to us through the Bible (for Catholics, through the Church also) – and natural religion or theology – the religion of reason and evidence, especially as given to us through some standard and well-polished arguments.

WHY NOT REASON?

The primary question now is whether natural theology is an essential part of Christianity. If it is, then, even if faith fails us – in the sense that I don't have it, even if you do – we have reason as an alternative. We both accept that. I cannot get to God through faith – if you can, you are not getting to God in such a way that convinces a nonbeliever like me that this is a route I should take – but perhaps you can get to God through reason and that is enough, or more than enough. You might at this point ask, "Enough, or more than enough" for whom? My answer is: the Christian. I am committed to working through reason. If it can be shown that the Christian is likewise committed to working through reason, then the avenue to fruitful dialogue is made open. We are not arguing at cross purposes. And this means that, if I am honest, it is "more than enough" for me too. I must be open to a change of mind on the God question. Faith may not do the trick, but reason might.

So, what about natural theology, meaning getting at the God question through reason? The great Catholic theologians accepted it and developed it. However, staying with Western Christianity, the leaders of the Protestant Reformation urged a return to a more primitive, Bible-based Christianity – *sola scriptura* – and so expectedly we find in Protestantism a strong strain of wariness if not outright hostility to natural theology. Not always. The Elizabethan Compromise in Britain – walking a careful line between the Catholic religion of the past (and all of those annoying Jesuit missionaries intent on martyrdom) and the newly returned, joy-killing Calvinists who had hidden out in Geneva during the reign of Bloody Mary (1553–1558) – made much of natural theology, something that fit well with the British bent to science and technology.[7] Generally, however, many

---

[6] St. Thomas Aquinas, *Summa theologiae*, I (London: Burns, Oates and Washbourne, 1952), 1a, 2, 3.

[7] M. Ruse, *Darwin and Design: Does Evolution Have a Purpose?* (Cambridge, MA: Harvard University Press, 2003).

had sympathy with Martin Luther: "Reason is a whore, the greatest enemy that faith has; it never comes to the aid of spiritual things, but more frequently than not struggles against the divine Word, treating with contempt all that emanates from God."[8]

The most famous to turn from reason was the nineteenth-century theologian Søren Kierkegaard. He spoke of a leap of faith, meaning that religious commitment had to go beyond reason and evidence into the unjustified, the absurd. If it didn't, then in some sense faith is downgraded. You don't really need faith if reason is there, backing you up.

> If naked dialectical deliberation shows that there is no approximation, that wanting to *quantify* oneself into faith along this path is a misunderstanding, a delusion, that wanting to concern oneself with such deliberations is a temptation for the *believer*, a temptation that he, keeping himself in the passion of faith, must resist with all his strength, lest it end with his succeeding in changing faith into something else, into another kind of certainty, in substituting probabilities and guarantees, which were rejected when he, himself beginning, made the *qualitative* transition of the leap from unbeliever to believer . . .

Continuing:

> When someone is to leap he must certainly do it alone and also be alone in properly understanding that it is an impossibility. . . . the leap is the *decision*. . . . But if a resolution is required, presuppositionlessness is abandoned. The beginning can occur only when reflection is stopped, and reflection can be stopped only by something else, and this something else is something altogether different from the *logical*, since it is a resolution.[9]

And:

> Faith is the objective uncertainty with the repulsion of the absurd, held fast in the passion of inwardness, which is the relation of inwardness intensified

---

[8] Like many oft-used quotations, it is difficult to pin down exactly where and when Luther said this. It does seem to be extracted from Luther's last sermon in Wittenberg (January 17, 1546). So, it is a genuine sentiment, in Luther's words, but the context makes very clear that Luther's intent is to privilege faith, rather than diss reason. In the same sermon he says: "Everything should be subject to faith, or rather, the fine gift of conceit should not be wiser than faith. See to it that it is in accord with it." And: "Reason must be subject and obedient to this faith." For (much) more detail, consult https://beggarsallreformation.blogspot.com/2018/01/luther-reason-is-devils-whore-throw.html.

[9] S. Kierkegaard, *Concluding Unscientific Postscript to Philosophical Fragments, vol. 1 (Kierkegaard's Writings, Vol. 12.1)*, trans. H. V. Hong, and E. H. Hong (Princeton: Princeton University Press, 1992), 11–12, 102, 113.

to its highest. This formula fits only the one who has faith, no one else, not even a lover, or an enthusiast, or a thinker, but solely and only the one who has faith, who relates himself to the absolute paradox.[10]

Karl Barth in the twentieth century followed in this tradition, as have many others.

In many respects, this approach resonates with someone like me, raised as I was in the Religious Society of Friends. For me, despite my jokes about God as a headmaster, he was never really something that could or should be captured by reason. He was indeed something – or Something – that reason would in some sense undermine. In the words of the philosopher John Hick, toward the end of his life a Quaker and, incidentally, a pupil at the same Quaker school as I – separated by the Second World War and a change in headmasters:

> Let us begin with the recognition, which is made in all the main religious traditions, that the ultimate divine reality is infinite and as such transcends the grasp of the human mind. God, to use our Christian term, is infinite. He is not a thing, a part of the universe, existing alongside other things; nor is he a being falling under a certain kind. And therefore, he cannot be defined or encompassed by human thought. We cannot draw boundaries around his nature and say he is this and no more. If we could fully define God, describing his inner being and his outer limits, this would not be God. The God whom our minds can penetrate and whom our thoughts can circumnavigate is merely a finite and partial image of God.[11]

The core of Quaker theology is that God is an unknown, one we can approach only through a nigh-mystical experience.[12] So for Friends, as for many other Protestants, it is faith or nothing. At the risk of sounding a complete hypocrite – "The test of a first-rate intelligence is the ability to hold two opposed ideas in mind at the same time and still retain the ability to function"[13] – this is very much my own position. If faith is to mean anything, it must be a leap of trust, into or toward the Unknowable. As Kierkegaard saw, reason giving you a comfortable backup spoils the whole thing.

---

[10] Kierkegaard, *Concluding Unscientific Postscript*, 610–11.
[11] J. Hick, *God and the Universe of Faiths: Essays in the Philosophy of Religion* (New York: St. Martin's Press, 1973), 139.
[12] In the language of the theologians, Quakers reject "theistic personalism," where God is a kind of super-human, the kind of guy who buys the first round of drinks. More later on this view.
[13] F. Scott Fitzgerald, *The Crack-Up* (New York: New Directions, 1945).

FAITH AND REASON

Yet before you think that I have gone over completely to the dark side, let me raise one or two uncomfortable points against the Kierkegaardian position. Most directly, there is the fact that while the Bible generally stresses faith, this is not always true. There is the Psalm: "The heavens are telling the glory of God; and the firmament proclaims his handiwork."[14] St Paul chips in too: "Ever since the creation of the world his eternal power and divine nature, invisible though they are, have been understood and seen through the things he has made."[15] This doesn't sound like a religion that has given up on reason!

For the second, more philosophical point, we must dig a little more deeply and turn to history. We have just heard the Protestants on the topic. What did the great Catholic theologians have to say on the subject? Start with the fact that, as with the Protestants, faith is all-important. This is and always has been the essential Christian tradition. Generations of philosophy students, whose only acquaintance with St. Thomas Aquinas is in books of readings that have extracted his five proofs, think that by the Middle Ages all that faith nonsense had been dropped. Not so! All the major theologians have endorsed the importance of faith at one level or another. Aquinas thought that, often, reason can get there in the end: "For certain things that are true about God wholly surpass the capability of human reason, for instance that God is three and one: while there are certain things to which even natural reason can attain, for instance that God is, that God is one, and others like these."[16] Note, however, that reason – where we could be wrong – is limited, and in the end, faith – where we cannot be wrong – is top dog. "The truth of the intelligible things of God is twofold, one to which the inquiry of reason can attain, the other which surpasses the whole range of human reason."[17]

Ultimately, without faith you get only part of the story, and Aquinas makes clear that faith trumps all – how else could the ignorant or stupid or lazy get knowledge of God? What then of reason, what of natural theology and the like? The right position is that of John Henry Newman: "I believe in design because I believe in God; not in a God because I see design."[18] As a

---

[14] Psalms 19:1.   [15] Romans 1:20.

[16] St. Thomas Aquinas, *Summa contra Gentiles*, trans. V. J. Bourke (Notre Dame: University of Notre Dame Press, [1259–65] 1975), 5.

[17] Aquinas, *Summa contra Gentiles*, 7.

[18] J. H. Newman, *The Letters and Diaries of John Henry Newman, vol. 25*, ed. C. S. Dessain and T. Gornall (Oxford: Clarendon Press, 1973), 97.

Christian, one believes on faith all about the Christian God, and then one fleshes this out by looking at the world and using reason. After all, that is what being made in the image of God is all about. Qualified but categorical. First, we saw biblical reasons for taking reason seriously. Now, for all that is said about the dominance of faith, we have theological reasons for taking reason seriously. We are made in the image of God. God is the apotheosis of reason. Hence, we too can and must use reason. It is not, compared with faith, a second-rate source of information. On its own, it is as good as faith. That it is not on its own enough is our fault, not God's. Had we not sinned, reason could be all-powerful. But we did sin and so reason cannot be all-powerful. We need faith. Faith embracing reason, not rejecting it.

I would nevertheless add a kind of codicil to this discussion, drawing attention to a problem that hovers over the whole concept of faith, certainly faith as set in the Kierkegaardian tradition, which I have admitted is the one to which I am most strongly attracted. The problem is that, with this juggling of faith and reason, Christians are in danger of trying to run with the hare and hunt with the hounds. On the one hand, faith, God is unknowable, beyond our understanding – "the ultimate divine reality is infinite and as such transcends the grasp of the human mind." One the other hand, there must be something more – given in reason? – or what is God to us? You must know something of God, or you are de facto an agnostic, even verging toward the atheistic. You are worshipping a black hole. Of course, the Christian position is that we can know about God – through analogy. We know that he is Creator, he is loving, he has a special place in his heart for us. Agree, these cannot be the characteristics of a human person, but they have meaning for us, nevertheless.

Yet, with respect, what meaning can we give to God's characteristics? What sense can we give to "God is loving"? The person of faith has a response. Even if we cannot know the sense, we know there is an answer. And there's the rub! That is just not enough for the nonbeliever. They are out in the cold; but better, perhaps, than the false warmth within. Declaring my own hand, I am all the way with the population geneticist J. B. S. Haldane: "Now my own suspicion is that the Universe is not only queerer than we suppose, but queerer than we can suppose."[19] Is there something more? I don't know. Backing this is the wise reflection of Richard Dawkins – I bet neither you nor he ever thought I would say that – that there is no reason why we should be able to peer into ultimate mysteries. We were not

---

[19] J. B. S. Haldane, *Possible Worlds and Other Essays* (London: Chatto and Windus, 1927), 49.

designed that way. "Modern physics teaches us that there is more to truth than meets the eye; or than meets the all too limited human mind, evolved as it was to cope with medium-sized objects moving at medium speeds through medium distances in Africa."[20] That is why my leaping takes me to agnosticism, not Christianity.

ROOT METAPHORS

Back to where we came in. For all the issues, the Christian can have a dialogue with the likes of me. Even more, I can have a dialogue with the likes of a Christian. If the Christian refuses to do so, on the grounds that faith trumps reason, it is still open for me as a nonbeliever to discuss the claims of the Christian. All very civilized and a reason why, at this point, the New Atheist will explode in frustration. We are ignoring the elephant in the room. We saw in Chapter 1 that science trumps religion, right down the line. Remember the wise words of St. Jerry of Chicago: "'Knowledge' acquired by religion is at odds not only with scientific knowledge, but also with knowledge professed by other religions. In the end, religion's methods, unlike those of science, are useless for understanding reality."[21] Whatever the basis on which religion makes its claims – faith or religion – they are worthless. Science shows them wrong.

But is this necessarily so? I think not. Start with the fact that science is not out of *Dragnet* – "just the facts, ma'am, just the facts." It is always a kind of Kantian activity of observation and interpretation. Objects in the world do things. We understand this activity through laws. The laws do not exist "out there." They are "in here," and are applied to the out there. Most important for science is metaphor – understanding one thing in terms of another, better-known thing.

> Let me not to the marriage of true minds
> Admit impediments. Love is not love
> Which alters when it alteration finds,
> Or bends with the remover to remove:
> O no; it is an ever-fixed mark,
> That looks on tempests, and is never shaken;
> It is the star to every wandering bark,

---

[20] R. Dawkins, *A Devil's Chaplain: Reflections on Hope, Lies, Science and Love* (Boston: Houghton Mifflin, 2003), 19.

[21] J. A. Coyne, *Faith vs. Fact: Why Science and Religion Are Incompatible* (New York: Viking, 2015), 64.

Whose worth's unknown, although his height be taken.
Love's not Time's fool, though rosy lips and cheeks
Within his bending sickle's compass come;
Love alters not with his brief hours and weeks,
But bears it out even to the edge of doom.
If this be error and upon me proved,
I never writ, nor no man ever loved.[22]

Love is not marriage. Humans marry, not emotions. Love doesn't look at anything, let alone tempests. Humans do that through their eyes. Love is not male. Females love too and are hardly male when they do so. Love could not be subject to a sickle, bending or otherwise. And yet, how brilliantly Shakespeare captures love! Can anyone who loves or is loved deny the power of this poem? How truly it captures the emotion. A hundred volumes of Alfred Kinsey and his crew would be farcical beside these fourteen lines.

Scientists are like Shakespeare. They use and rely on metaphors through and through. Force, work, attraction, orbits, charm, strings, tree of life, natural selection, arms races, gay genes, Oedipus complex, and the list grows and grows. Linguists point to the fact that metaphors are not isolated. They can fit together and be subsumed under broader metaphors, ultimately under what are called "root" metaphors.[23] If you think of an argument as being a battle, then you bring in subsidiary metaphors – attacked, countered, diverted, reinforced, gave way, triumphed, accepted defeat. "Until next time!" Same in science. Before the Scientific Revolution of the sixteenth and seventeenth centuries, the world was seen as an organism. Kepler of all people tells us that "as the body displays tears, mucus, and earwax, and also in places lymph from pustules on the face, so the Earth displays amber and bitumen; as the bladder pours out urine, so the mountains pour out rivers; as the body produces excrement of sulphurous odor and farts which can even be set on fire, so the Earth produces sulphur, subterranean fires, thunder, and lightning; and as blood is generated in the veins of an animate being, and with it sweat, which is thrust outside the body, so in the veins of the Earth are generated metals and fossils, and rainy vapor."[24]

Then came the change. From organism to machine, the root metaphor of modern science. We see the world in a mechanical fashion. Robert Boyle, the

---

[22] W. Shakespeare, *The Oxford Shakespeare: The Complete Sonnets and Poems* (Oxford: Oxford University Press, 2008), Sonnet 116.

[23] G. Lakoff and M. Johnson, *Metaphors We Live By* (Chicago: University of Chicago Press, 1980).

[24] J. Kepler, *The Harmony of the World*, trans. E. J. Aiton, A. M. Duncan, and J. V. Field (Philadelphia: American Philosophical Society, [1619] 1977), 363–64.

seventeenth-century philosopher-chemist, argued that the world is "like a rare clock, such as may be that at Strasbourg, where all things are so skillfully contrived that the engine being once set a-moving, all things proceed according to the artificer's first design, and the motions of the little statues that at such hours perform these or those motions do not require (like those of puppets) the peculiar interposing of the artificer or any intelligent agent employed by him, but perform their functions on particular occasions by virtue of the general and primitive contrivance of the whole engine."[25] (In fairness to Kepler, he used this metaphor also. Old ways die hard. Newton was into alchemy.)

From an organism to a machine. Thomas Kuhn, in his later writing, stressed that his controversial concept of a paradigm was, in many respects, speaking of metaphor.[26] Now you see the world one way. Now you see the world another way. Important is that, as Kuhn stressed, part of the power of a metaphor/paradigm is that it rules out many questions.[27] It puts blinkers on the scientist so that he or she does not waste time asking questions that cannot be answered within the metaphor/paradigm. Are Shakespeare's lovers any good at mathematics or are they Protestant or Catholic? We don't know and we don't care. We do know that love lasts despite troubles and changes, and doesn't give up when things go wrong. Same in science. The machine metaphor simply doesn't answer some questions. They may well be genuine questions, but they are not within its domain.

FOUR QUESTIONS

There are a range of questions not answered by science under the machine metaphor. Let me pick out four of pertinence to us.[28] Why is there something rather than nothing? This what Heidegger called "the fundamental question of metaphysics."[29] Wittgenstein said it was a pseudo-question, but it doesn't look that way to most of us. The point is that science doesn't even

---

[25] R. Boyle, *A Disquisition about the Final Causes of Natural Things: Wherein It Is Inquir'd Whether, and (if at all) with What Cautions, a Naturalist Should Admit Them?* (London: John Taylor, 1688), 12–13.

[26] T. Kuhn, "Metaphor in Science," in *Metaphor and Thought*, 2nd ed., ed. Andrew Ortony, 533–42 (Cambridge: Cambridge University Press, 1993).

[27] T. Kuhn, *The Structure of Scientific Revolutions* (Chicago: University of Chicago Press, 1962).

[28] M. Ruse, *Science and Spirituality: Making Room for Faith in the Age of Science* (Cambridge: Cambridge University Press, 2010).

[29] M. Heidegger, *An Introduction to Metaphysics* (New Haven: Yale University Press, 1959), 1.

set out to answer it. Like the cookbook, first take your hare. Suppose I am explaining a pendulum. Where did the brass come from? We can trace it back. Ultimately, we must take things as given and get on with the job of measuring times and so forth. To say that Big Bangs explain ultimate origins is to miss the point. Big Bangs don't just happen. Why do they happen? And if you can answer that, then push the question back a step. The question is simply not one of mechanical science.

What ought we to do? Ethics. David Hume made it clear that science doesn't get into this game. There is a difference between "is" and "ought." The former involves factual claims and the latter moral claims. And "as this ought, or ought not, expresses some new relation or affirmation, 'tis necessary that it should be observed and explained; and at the same time that a reason should be given, for what seems altogether inconceivable, how this new relation can be a deduction from others, which are entirely different from it."[30] Of course, science might get into explaining why we are moral and why perhaps we think that ethics does have a foundation. This is another matter and will be tackled in a later chapter. No need to do so now.

Third, what is mind? Again, modern science has no answer to this – and can have no answer. Machines don't think. Leibniz is good on this.

> It has to be acknowledged that perception can't be explained by mechanical principles, that is, by shapes and motions, and thus that nothing that depends on perception can be explained in that way either. Suppose this were wrong. Imagine there was a machine whose structure produced thought, feeling, and perception; we can conceive of its being enlarged while maintaining the same relative proportions among its parts, so that we could walk into it as we can walk into a mill. Suppose we do walk into it; all we would find there are cogs and levers and so on pushing one another, and never anything to account for a perception. So perception must be sought in simple substances, not in composite things like machines.[31]

Fourth, what is the point of it all? Of course, machines do have purposes. Lawn mowers are for cutting grass and computers are for writing books on religion. But the way the machine metaphor is used in science drops such purpose talk, and all the focus is on unbroken laws working ceaselessly. You can talk about function within the system, as in the purpose of the flower is to attract insect pollinators, but not outside the system. Flowers in themselves, cosmically, have no purpose. The Nobel Laureate Steven Weinberg

[30] D. Hume, *A Treatise of Human Nature* (Oxford: Oxford University Press, [1739-40] 1978), III, I, 1.
[31] G. F. W. Leibniz, *Monadology and Other Philosophical Essays* (New York: Bobbs-Merrill, 1714).

wrote: "The more the universe seems comprehensible, the more it also seems pointless."[32] Why am I not surprised? Simply because the machine metaphor does not ask questions of meaning.

I am sure you can see the direction in which my argument is going. I argue that these are all genuine questions that science under the machine metaphor does not answer and does not even set out to answer. They are, however, questions that religion can and does answer. Why is there something rather than nothing? Because a good God created the world out of nothing. "In the beginning when God created the heavens and the earth."[33] Repeatedly, elsewhere. Hebrews again: "By faith we understand that the worlds were prepared by the word of God, so that what is seen was made from things that are not visible."[34] What is the basis for morality? The will of God. "Who can confront it and be safe? – under the whole heaven, who?"[35] We should do what God wants us to do.

> Now the works of the flesh are obvious: fornication, impurity, licentiousness, idolatry, sorcery, enmities, strife, jealousy, anger, quarrels, dissensions, factions, envy, drunkenness, carousing, and things like these. I am warning you, as I warned you before: those who do such things will not inherit the kingdom of God. By contrast, the fruit of the Spirit is love, joy, peace, patience, kindness, generosity, faithfulness, gentleness, and self-control. There is no law against such things.[36]

What is mind? The image of God. That is what makes us human and not as other animals. "So God created humankind in his image, in the image of God he created them; male and female he created them."[37] What is the point of it all? Eternal bliss with our Creator, made possible by the sacrifice of his son on the Cross. "Not everyone who says to Me, 'Lord, Lord,' shall enter the kingdom of heaven, but he who does the will of My Father in heaven."[38] Or: "In my Father's house there are many dwelling places. If it were not so, would I have told you that I go to prepare a place for you?"[39]

ON TO THE ARGUMENTS

The conclusion here is that, with respect to questions like these, there is no conflict between science and religion here because science simply doesn't have a dog in the fight. Jerry Coyne and his chums miss the point. Do note,

---

[32] S. Weinberg, *The First Three Minutes: A Modern View of the Origin of the Universe* (New York: Basic Books, 1977), 154.
[33] Genesis 1:1.   [34] Hebrews 11:3.   [35] Job 41:11.   [36] Galatians 5:19–23.   [37] Genesis 1:27.
[38] Matthew 7:21.   [39] John 14:2.

however, what this means. It does not mean that we must accept religion's answers. It means that, for those of us who cannot or will not turn to faith, it is still open to see where reason will lead us. And this will be the task of the next two chapters. First, we will look at the positive arguments. We want to know if reason can speak to the questions posed above. What about the Creator God business, and the long-term implications for us? (Morality will be left to a later chapter.) Then we want to see if reason can give us arguments to doubt or deny the whole God business. If reason points us that way, those of us who reject faith can feel comfortable in our denial. I would add that it is because of this point, you should not think that, in this chapter, I have given away the whole game to the Christian. I have agreed that science cannot do it, so I have opened the way for religion to do it. True, but I have also opened the way to showing that religion cannot do it, and that – thanks to reason – it should be rejected. I am a nice guy but that doesn't mean that I am a softy.

Brian Davies

INTRODUCTION

Exponents of natural theology argue that God exists without relying on anything that might be called faith in "divine revelation." They offer *philosophical* arguments. Classical exponents of natural theology include Anselm, Aquinas, Duns Scotus (1266–1308), Descartes, and Leibniz. More recently, philosophical arguments for "God exists" have been presented by philosophers such as David Braine (1940–2017), William Lane Craig (b. 1949), Edward Feser (b. 1968), Germain Grisez (1929–2018), Barry Miller (1923–2006), Alvin Plantinga (b. 1932), and Richard Swinburne (b. 1934).[40]

Yet it has often been suggested that we should not even bother to allow the arguments of natural theologians to be given a serious hearing. The idea here is that there are grounds for dismissing *all* natural theology *on principle*, and I now aim to explain why some people have defended this claim and why I think that what they say may be challenged.

---

[40] Cf. David Braine, *The Reality of Time and the Existence of God* (Oxford: Clarendon Press, 1988); William Lane Craig, *The Kalām Cosmological Argument* (London: Macmillan Press, 1979); Edward Feser, *Five Proofs of the Existence of God* (San Francisco: Ignatius Press, 2017); Germain Grisez, *Beyond the New Theism* (Notre Dame: University of Notre Dame Press, 1975); Barry Miller, *From Existence to God: A Contemporary Philosophical Argument* (London: Routledge, 1992); Alvin Plantinga, *The Nature of Necessity* (Oxford: Clarendon Press, 1974); Richard Swinburne, *The Existence of God*, 2nd ed. (Oxford: Clarendon Press, 2004).

PHILOSOPHICAL ARGUMENTS FOR OBJECTING TO NATURAL THEOLOGY ON PRINCIPLE

If one of my students says that she wants to write an essay explaining why Descartes disagreed with Aristotle, I would look forward to reading the essay. But how should I respond to a student proposing to work on an essay explaining why square circles exist? I should say that she is wasting her time since square circles cannot possibly exist. And something like this line of thinking is one that a number of philosophers have offered when dismissing the notion of natural theology – the main argument being that God is not something that could exist and that it is therefore pointless to consider arguments for God actually existing.

A famous philosophical proponent of this conclusion is David Hume. At one point in his *Inquiry Concerning Human Understanding* he writes: "If we take in our hand any volume; of divinity or school metaphysics, for instance; let us ask, *Does it contain any abstract reasoning concerning quantity or number?* No. *Does it contain any experimental reasoning concerning matter of fact and existence?* No. Commit it then to the flames: For it can contain nothing but sophistry and illusion."[41] Hume is not bluntly declaring that "God exists" is on the same level as "Square triangles exist." But he is claiming that, given that the reality of God is not something supposed to be established empirically (by checking with our senses), then it should not be taken seriously.

In the twentieth century this idea became the foundation stone of a philosophical movement now commonly referred to as "Logical Positivism."[42] Supporters of this movement held that properly factual statements are ones the truth of which can be verified by sensory experience. And some of these supporters appealed to this principle while ruling out talk about God as meaningless. Hence, for example, A. J. Ayer (1910–1989) maintained: "The term 'God' is a metaphysical term. And if 'god' is a metaphysical term, then it cannot even be probable that a god exists. For to say that 'God exists' is to make a metaphysical utterance which cannot be either true or false. And by the same criterion, no sentence which purports to describe the nature of a transcendent god can possess any literal significance."[43]

---

[41] Hume, *Inquiry*, 123.

[42] For an introduction to this, see Oswald Hanfling, *Logical Positivism* (Oxford: Blackwell, 1981), and Oswald Hanfling, ed., *Essential Readings in Logical Positivism* (Oxford: Blackwell, 1981).

[43] A. J. Ayer, *Language, Truth and Logic*, 2nd ed. (New York: Dover, 1952), 115.

The truth in this line of thinking is that when we make what might be called "ordinary factual assertions" we are taking them to be assertions that can be empirically verified in some way. If a doctor tells a patient that they have cancer, the doctor will be expected to back up the diagnosis by drawing attention to the results of various medical tests. Yet God is not supposed to be something open to sensory investigation. So, assertions about God are, indeed, unusual if understood to be factual ones, and it is not surprising that they baffle people like Ayer. A theist might suggest that such people display a woeful lack of imagination. But to *imagine* something is to form a *picture* of it, and God is not supposed to be picturable. Nobody takes Michelangelo's ceiling portrait of God creating Adam to be anything comparable to a photograph. And the gospel of John declares, "No one has ever seen God."[44]

Yet nothing I have just noted shows that talk about God is meaningless and that natural theology has therefore to be a fruitless undertaking. Statements about God can be dismissed in advance if the only way of arriving at knowledge of what exists is to verify empirical hypotheses. But theists have never taken "God exists" to be an empirical hypothesis, and it seems as odd to attack them for not doing so as it is to complain that wrestlers do not score goals or that basketball players do not manage to achieve a "hole in one" (as in golf). If theists do not think of "God exists" as an empirical hypothesis, then what is the point of attacking them for not doing so? You might say that if "God exists" is meant to tell us something true, and if it is not confirmable as empirical hypotheses are, then it possesses no "literal significance" (Ayer's phrase). It is meaningless. But why tie meaningfulness to empirical verifiability?

Some logical positivists did so because they accepted a strong version of what came to be known as the "verification principle." According to this, a purportedly factual statement that cannot be *conclusively* verified empirically is devoid of any meaning. But there are serious objections to this thesis. For one thing, it is hard to see how its truth could be conclusively verified empirically; so it does not live up to its own standards when it comes to meaningfulness. Again, there are examples of purportedly factual statements that are meaningful even though they cannot be conclusively verified empirically. Consider "All people spend part of their time asleep." That statement is intelligible. Yet it is not *conclusively* verifiable by sensory investigation. However many people we inspect, it is always *possible* that we might eventually find one who never sleeps at all.

Conscious of worries such as this, logical positivists such as Ayer defended a weaker version of the verification principle. According to this, a

---

[44] John 1:18.

purportedly factual statement is meaningful only if sense experience can confirm it in *some* way. But even this weaker version leaves us with the question "How can sense experience confirm in *any* way that a statement is meaningful only if sense experience can confirm it in some way?" And why should we think that a statement is meaningless just because it cannot be empirically verified? Consider the statement "Some of the toys that to all appearances stay in the toy cupboard while people are asleep and no one is watching, actually get up and dance in the middle of the night and then go back to the cupboard, leaving no traces of their activity."[45] Few of us would find this assertion to be credible, and it is not verifiable empirically. But the assertion is hardly *meaningless*, and film producers in Hollywood have made money while trying to depict exactly the scenario that the statement now in question proposes. Hence the popular movie *Toy Story* (1995) and its sequels.

With all of that said, however, perhaps the strongest objection to any verification theory that takes "God" to be a word without meaning lies in the history of natural theology. For natural theologians have offered several arguments for it being true to think that God exists. If you are as rigorously empiricist in your thinking as are people such as Hume and Ayer, then you might be disinclined in advance to pay attention to any of these arguments. But what if the arguments have value? If any of them do, then it is silly to rule out natural theology on principle and with reference to either the strong or weak verification principle. Surely, the thing to do would be to examine the arguments rather than declaring in advance that there could not be any that present good philosophical reasoning for the assertion "God exists."[46]

THEOLOGICAL ARGUMENTS FOR OBJECTING TO NATURAL THEOLOGY ON PRINCIPLE

Many theologians have favored the enterprise of natural theology. But some theologians have positively *reviled* natural theology. Here I think of authors such as Karl Barth (1886–1968), and Colin Gunton (1941–2003). They were both ordained Christian ministers, but they were opposed to natural theology. According to Barth, "Natural theology does not exist as an entity

---

[45] I owe this example to Richard Swinburne. See Richard Swinburne, *The Coherence of Theism*, revised ed. (Oxford: Clarendon Press, 1993), 28.

[46] Ayer came to admit this himself. In response to an argument presented by Alonzo Church (1903–1995), he ended up agreeing that the verification principle cannot be formulated in any satisfactory way. For Church's argument, see his review of the second edition of *Language, Truth and Logic* in *Journal of Symbolic Logic* 14 (1949): 52ff. For Ayer's admission, see his *The Central Questions of Philosophy* (London: Pelican Books, 1976), 27.

capable of becoming a separate subject within what I consider to be real theology – not even for the sake of being rejected. If one occupies oneself with real theology one can pass by so-called natural theology only as one would pass by an abyss into which it is inadvisable to step if one does not want to fall. All one can do is turn one's back upon it as upon the great temptation and source of error, by having nothing to do with it."[47] Arguing in a vein similar to Barth, Gunton claims that natural theology represents a "metaphysic of being in which God is named by what is essentially a method of philosophical abstraction."[48] For both Barth and Gunton, natural theology amounts to a wrongheaded attempt on the part of reason to pass judgment on God (and on divine revelation) using human, philosophical categories. Since it does this, they suggest, natural theology fails because (1) it does not allow for the profound difference between God and creatures; (2) it refuses to give supremacy to faith; and (3) it conflicts with the approach to God presented in the Bible. Yet are Barth and Gunton right here?

I agree with Barth and Gunton that if God exists, then God is profoundly different from any of God's creatures. Theists hold that since God is the Creator of all things "visible and invisible," God makes everything nondivine to exist for as long as it exists, that the existence of everything other than God derives directly and at all times from God, who is not something the existence of which is derived from anything. That, at any rate, is what Jews, Muslims, and Christians have traditionally believed. If they are right to do so, however, then we should hardly take the word "God" to be the name of anything whose nature we can fully comprehend. One might suppose this to be obvious simply on biblical grounds, for the Bible often insists on the mystery of God. Hence, for example, St. Paul says in 1 Corinthians 2:11: "No one comprehends what is truly God's except the Spirit of God." For now, though, let me just make the point by saying that God cannot be an *individual*.

By "individual" I mean "a member of a natural kind of which there could be more than one member of that kind." We may ask how many individuals are in the room and expect an answer that tells us how many *people* are in the room, or how many *cats* or *dogs* are there. So, if God accounts for the existence of everything other than God, then God cannot be an individual in *this* sense. Such individuals are inhabitants of the world and therefore cannot be thought of as its Creator. Something can be intelligibly thought of as an individual *such and such* (an individual belonging to a natural kind) only

---

[47] "No!," in Emil Brunner and Karl Barth, *Natural Theology* (Eugene: Wipf and Stock, 2002), 75. Barth's essay was originally published in 1934.
[48] Colin Gunton, *Act and Being* (Grand Rapids: William B. Eerdmans, 2002), 12.

because it can be picked out as something that exists and because it can then be compared and contrasted with a range of things that are individuals belonging to natural kinds. I do not, however, see how God the Creator could be picked out and compared with other things in this way. If he could, he would be part of his creation, a point that Anselm and Aquinas make by insisting that God is *simple*.

On their account, which echoes what was said by earlier theologians, God is not material and is therefore no object of scientific inquiry and classification. As we scientifically classify things, we assign individuals to kinds and ascribe properties to them. Yet such classification implies a genuine distinction between individuality and nature. To say, for example, that Rover is a dog is to imply that there are other dogs and that Rover (*this* dog) is not what we mean when we refer to what it is to be a dog, since he is but an example of canine nature. But, say Anselm and Aquinas, *what* God is (God's nature) is not similarly distinguishable from *God*; or, if you like, there is no serious distinction to be made between *who* God is and *what* God is. When it comes to God, says Anselm, nothing "that is predicated truly" of his essence "is to be taken as a predicate of quality, or quantity, but of what it is."[49] God, says Aquinas, "is the same as his essence or nature."[50] And I agree with that line of thinking. It raises all sorts of philosophical questions. But it seems to me that it, or something very like it, is what needs to be embraced by those who hold that everything in the universe owes its being to God.

So, I think that Barth and Gunton are right to insist on what we might call the "radical otherness" of God or the "mystery" of God. Yet classical natural theologians also emphasize these things. Barth appeals to what he calls the "infinite qualitative distinction" between God and creatures. But such a distinction (or something very like it) can be found governing all that Anselm and Aquinas have to say. Many people assume that when reflecting on God, we should be hugely constrained by what we can know to be true about ourselves, the idea being that certain true thoughts about ourselves can be somehow turned into a true understanding of God (the assumption being that God and human beings belong to a kind of some sort). But Anselm and Aquinas do not assume this. Yet both (and, so far as I can see, the Catholic theological tradition in general) do not, therefore, want to conclude that God

---

[49] *Monologion*, chapter 17. Cf. *Proslogion*, chapter 18. For English translations of these texts, see Brian Davies and G. R. Evans, eds., *Anselm of Canterbury: The Major Works* (Oxford: Oxford University Press, 1998).

[50] *Summa theologiae*, 1a, 3, 3. I quote from Brian Davies and Brian Leftow, eds., *Aquinas: Summa theologiae, Questions on God* (Cambridge: Cambridge University Press, 2006).

is utterly beyond reason. For they also want to say that, even abstracting from matters of revelation, there are things we can know to be true when it comes to God.

Not being a veterinarian, I am quite unable to give a lecture on the anatomy of cats. But I own a cat, and I know quite a lot about it. I also think that it is obvious that one can have knowledge of something without knowing *all* that is true of it. So, might we not suggest that there are things to be known about God even apart from revelation? An obvious way to settle the matter would be to look at the history of natural theology and to consider whether any good reasons have ever been given for supposing that there is anything corresponding to what God has traditionally been taken to be. Without depending on explicitly Christian premises, Anselm, for example, offers arguments for there being a creative source of the universe, one that is omnipotent, omniscient, eternal, and good. Again, without depending on explicitly Christian premises, Aquinas argues that there must be an unchanged source of all change, one that makes things to be from nothing, one that is active in everything, one that is the beginning and end of all things. Are the arguments of Anselm and Aquinas good ones? Are comparable arguments coming from other natural theologians good ones? If any of them are, then God is not entirely beyond reason. If natural theologians have good arguments, then that ought to be enough to show that there is *some* knowledge of God to be had apart from revelation. And it ought to be enough to show that reason and faith should not be starkly opposed to each other.

Yet that is not how Barth and Gunton see things, for they object to the idea that one can properly and truly talk of God while not talking about God incarnate or God as Trinity. For them, all talk of God should be about what God has revealed himself to be in Christ. Everything else is irrelevant and probably impious. And, so Barth insists, this is emphatically the view of the Bible. But why should we believe any of this? I suggest that we have positive reasons for *disbelieving* it.

At one level, of course, it is natural for a Christian to reply to the question "What is God?" with an answer such as "The Father of Jesus Christ," or "Three persons in one substance" or "The One who has saved us and addresses us in the Bible." For this indeed *is* what God is for orthodox Christians. But it does not therefore follow that to talk about God without homing in on key Christian teachings ("articles of faith," as Aquinas calls them) is not to talk about God. If it were, then, for example, the prophet Isaiah was not talking about God, which would surely be a strange theological conclusion for a Christian to embrace. As far as Fred is concerned, the most important facts about Mary might be that she is his wife and the mother of his children. But someone can know a lot about Mary without knowing these truths about her. By the same token, I see no reason to suppose that someone who has never even heard of specifically Christian teaching must, simply by virtue of that fact, be ignorant of God. You might say that such a person has been denied access to some exciting and liberating truths. But not to know *all* that is true of something is not necessarily to know *nothing* about it.

Another tactic that theological critics of natural theology use is to claim that our reason is infected by sin and that we therefore know nothing of God by virtue of reason and must rely only on revelation. But that is a claim that needs to be tested by looking at natural theology rather than dismissing it in advance. If Michael Ruse tells me that he has decided to walk the Appalachian Trail, I might mock him and say, "You don't have it in you. You are just not fit enough." And I may be right to think that. But it would be perfectly in order for Michael to reply: "Well let's see if I *can* make it." Suppose that he then sets off on the trail and walks it from end to end. *Now* my view of Michael has been refuted by his *success*. And, as far as I can see, so it might be with the claim that sin confines our knowledge of God to what revelation teaches. If natural theologians can be shown to have good arguments for what they say about God in abstraction from revelation, then the harm that sin does just *cannot* extend to making us totally ignorant of God at the level of reason. We often think about what we *choose* to think about, and our reasoning can accordingly be adversely affected since our choosing may be affected by our vices. Yet these observations do not entail that we cannot sometimes think rightly and to the point, and they do nothing to settle the question "Is there anything of value in the arguments of natural theologians?"

Anyway, why should one suppose that reason is not a *God-given* way of coming to know something about God, even if not too much? Why should we not take reason to be a way in which God does something to *reveal* himself to us? Barth and Gunton belong to a venerable Protestant tradition drawing on theologians such as John Calvin (1509–1564), who said that reason without revelation leaves us like someone without spectacles who can know they are holding a book in his hand, and can know quite a bit about it, but cannot actually read it.[51] But nothing I am now suggesting is intended as a critique of Calvin's view here. The image that he conjures up would, I suspect, have been amenable to people such as Anselm and Aquinas (stressing, as they do, *both* God's incomprehensibility *and* the possibility of some limited knowledge of God apart from revelation). To the suggestion

---

[51] John Calvin, *Institutes*, I, vi, 1.

that reason might be thought of as a way in which God reveals himself, you might object that reason and revelation are completely distinct things, and here you might appeal to the fact that many theologians have for centuries made a sharp distinction between them. But some of these theologians have also claimed that, without being able to demonstrate what Aquinas would have called the "articles of faith," those who believe them have knowledge of God in that they *somehow* share in God's knowledge of himself by virtue of revelation. For a comparison here, think of me (someone who *truly* knows next to *nothing* about neuroscience) saying that I know that I have terminal brain cancer because the doctors in one of the best cancer hospitals in the world tell me that I have brain cancer. Again, and reverting to speaking of "knowledge" as opposed to "faith in revelation," what might be revelation to some people need not be so for all. I may just have to believe or have faith in my doctor when I am told that I am suffering from malaria. But my doctor does not have to think of the diagnosis as an act of faith on their part, or as depending on a revelation of any kind (let alone one that is needed because the doctor's reason is "infected by sin"). By the same token, so it has been suggested, while certain truths about God may have to be accepted by some people on faith, it does not follow that there are none for whom these truths are a matter of knowledge arising from the gift of reason. Aquinas is someone who famously takes this line. He defends the claim that we can demonstrate the truth of "God exists" (*Deus est*) in response to the view that "it is an article of faith" that God exists. In doing so, he speaks of what can be known of God by reason as that which the articles of faith *presuppose*, adding that "there is nothing to stop people from accepting on faith some demonstrable truth that they cannot personally demonstrate." Aquinas is not here denying that there are truths that need to be accepted by *all* people on faith. He is defending the project of natural theology as something that might explain what we can know of God by reason and independently of divine revelation.

Barth's reply to this line of thinking is to say that *revelation* condemns natural theology because the *Bible* does so. Yet this suggestion has been thoroughly undermined by James Barr (1924–2006) in *Biblical Faith and Natural Theology*. Barr rightly acknowledges that the Bible never presents anything that reads like sustained philosophical essays in natural theology. But why should we expect it to do so? The Bible is no more a collection of philosophical texts (in the contemporary sense) than it is a collection of scientific or historically accurate texts (in the contemporary sense). Yet, so Barr makes clear, it leaves plenty of room for there being a knowledge of God *apart* from Christian revelation.

Take, for example, Acts 17. Here we are told that St. Paul once preached in Athens. He praises the Athenians for being "extremely religious" while noting their altar inscribed "To an unknown God." He goes on to say: "What therefore you worship as unknown, this I proclaim to you." The Barthian reading of Acts 17 holds that Paul is denying to the Athenians any genuine knowledge of God. But the text of Acts 17 does not license this interpretation at all. Without any reference to the Old Testament, Acts 17 clearly has Paul, in a thoroughly Gentile context, appealing to a knowledge of God, not, to begin with, as one who raised Jesus from the dead, but as one "who made the world and everything in it." All human beings, says Paul, come from God, *as even Athenian poets have said.*[52] The most natural reading of Acts 17 is to see it as attempting to place specifically Christian belief in the context of a more universal knowledge of God, one independent of Christian (or Jewish) revelation. As Barr observes: "Acts 17 cannot be fully expounded without opening the gate to some sort of natural theology."[53]

Again, consider the first chapter of Paul's letter to the Romans. Friends of the notion that knowledge of God does not depend only on revelation, or that it must be a matter of "blind faith" for everyone, have long appealed to this text in defense of their position. Aquinas does this. So does the First Vatican Council, which teaches that "God, the beginning and end of all things, can be known, from created things, by the light of natural human reason," while immediately citing Romans 1:20: "Ever since the creation of the world his [God's] eternal power and divine nature, invisible though they are, have been understood and seen through the things he has made." The Barthian reading of Romans 1 has Paul saying that "the light of natural human reason" of which Vatican I speaks is really a darkness in which God is unknown, a darkness in which people stand condemned by God as "without excuse," a darkness for which God gave them up to "impurity" and "degrading passions."

As an exegesis of Romans 1, however, this is absurd. Paul's argument in Romans 1 (and it clearly is an *argument*) can be straightforwardly represented thus:

1. God's wrath is revealed against all who are ungodly and wicked (v. 18).
2. These people know something about God since his power and nature have been understood and seen through what he has made (vv. 19–20).
3. These people are, therefore, without excuse for engaging in idolatry and making images of God in the form of people and animals (vv. 19–23).

---

[52] Acts 17:28.
[53] James Barr, *Biblical Faith and Natural Theology* (Oxford: Clarrendon Press, 1993), 26.

4. So, as punishment, God "gave them up" to "impurity" and "degrading passions" (vv. 24–27).
5. And, for the same reason, God "gave them up" to all sorts of wrongdoing (vv. 28–32).

Far from denying a knowledge of God apart from Christian revelation, Paul is here clearly supposing such knowledge and attacking those who distort it in the direction of idolatry. As Barr observes, Romans 1 appears "to imply that there is something 'known of God,' which is revealed through his created works, which is accessible to all human beings through their being human."[54] And, as Barr goes on to note, it is not astonishing that Paul should think along these lines since he had precedent for doing so in both the Old Testament and the writings of Hellenistic Judaism. In the Old Testament, we might, for example, note Psalm 104, which points to the world as evidence and manifestation of God's generosity, and Psalm 19, with its insistence that "the heavens are telling the glory of God; and the firmament proclaims his handiwork." When it comes to Hellenistic Judaism, the book of Wisdom comes especially to mind. As Paul does in Romans 1, Wisdom declares that there is a knowledge of God on which people have culpably failed to act, a failure leading to vices of all kinds.

Once again, I am not suggesting that the Bible contains anything like a series of essays in natural theology or "philosophy of God." And Jesus of Nazareth, as portrayed in the New Testament, does not speak like a contemporary philosopher. That said, however, the Bible proclaims that God can somehow be known by human reason. So, if it is said that God is beyond reason because of what the Bible asserts, the claim should be rejected. Or, as Barr makes the point: "If you thoroughly reject natural theology, and if natural theology underlies the Bible in any significant degree, then you must judge that the Bible is inadequate as a theological guide."[55]

It might, of course, be replied that natural theology, or a "reason-based" approach to God, falls short of what Christians mean by faith in God. And I can see sense in this thought. Kierkegaard develops it at length, but let me make the point I have in mind now by saying that Christians do not normally speak of their central religious beliefs as *hypotheses*. A hypothesis is something one entertains while allowing that it might be proved false. And it is arrived at on the basis of some pretty careful sifting of (typically empirical) evidence. Yet Christians commonly take their faith as certain

---

[54] Barr, *Biblical Faith and Natural Theology*, 43f.
[55] Barr, *Biblical Faith and Natural Theology*, 104.

and not as something they might be prepared to give up. Nor do they typically embrace it in the wake of a sifting of evidence while concluding that it is probably true. If the Vatican suddenly announced that "probable" or "probably" should be inserted at various stages when the Nicene Creed is recited in church, the majority of Christians would, I suspect, be stunned. They would be even more amazed if told that "so far as we can see for the present," or a similar phrase, should be added to the creed somewhere. It is not surprising that people might not want to take Christian faith and the conclusions of rational inquiry to be one and the same thing. And such people might, I think, sensibly develop their case by noting that it is surely odd to suppose that Christian faith is a "merely intellectual" matter.

Someone might produce a series of philosophical arguments for the belief that God exists, just as another person might produce a series of philosophical arguments for the belief that time travel is impossible. But would mere subscription to philosophical argument make someone a person with belief in God? Arguably not. Surely, more is required. As Norman Malcolm once said:

> If a man did not ever pray for help or forgiveness, or have any inclination toward it; nor ever felt that it is "a good and joyful thing" to thank God for the blessings of this life; nor was ever concerned about his failure to comply with divine commandments – then, it seems clear to me, he could not be said to believe in God. Belief in God is not an all or none thing; it can be more or less; it can wax and wane. But belief in God in any degree does require, as I understand the words, some religious action, some commitment, or if not, a bad conscience.[56]

Malcolm is here saying that belief in God is not just "in the mind," so to speak. It must also show itself in behavior. And Malcolm seems right to me. "A theist is as a theist does," you might say. Yet nothing I have just said entails that there is no decent natural theology, or that people of faith should distance themselves from it on principle. Natural theologians have never suggested that those who believe that God exists should be worried about the possibility of concluding that this or that bit of natural theology might prove to be mistaken for some reason or other. Nor have they suggested that those who believe in God must all be able to offer a set of philosophical arguments in defense of "God exists," or that uniquely Christian beliefs stand or fall on the basis of a set of philosophical arguments, or that belief in God is a mere hypothesis, or that the Christian creed is "more probable than not." What

---

[56] Norman Malcolm, "The Groundlessness of Belief in God," in Stuart C. Brown, ed., *Reason and Religion* (Ithaca: Cornell University Press, 1977), 155.

they have normally said is that not all truths about God have to be thought of as accessible to people only by virtue of a special divine revelation, and that is a conclusion that can be seriously dealt with only by evaluating the arguments offered in its defense.

THE GOD OF THE PHILOSOPHERS AND THE GOD OF THE BIBLE

It is sometimes said that natural theology leaves us with a God who is totally different from God as presented in the Bible. The thought here is that God as depicted in the Bible differs remarkably from the God whose existence is defended by natural theologians such as Aquinas. But I disagree with this view, on which I offer the following thoughts.

To begin with, a lot depends on what notion of God we have in mind. Here I think that we need to distinguish between what I have elsewhere referred to as "classical theism" and "theistic personalism."[57]

By "classical theism" I mean the view of God that one can find in the teaching of the Catholic Church, in the writings of some of the Protestant reformers, and in the texts of authors such as Anselm and Aquinas. For classical theists, God is the Creator of all that is not divine by making it to exist from second to second. For classical theists, God is also immutable, omnipotent, omniscient, and highly mysterious to us. On the classical theistic understanding, God is no spatiotemporal individual and is not, unlike you and I, to be seriously thought of as belonging to a kind or class of which there are or could be more than one member.

For "theistic personalism," by contrast, God is strongly comparable to us on the understanding that we are essentially noncorporeal thinking things, or so many immaterial centers of consciousness, as, for example, Descartes famously took us to be.[58] On this account, which is sometimes defended by people who self-identify as natural theologians, God is a person to be added to the list of persons that now exist and that have existed in the past. Theistic personalists (whether speaking as defenders of natural theology or not) regularly agree that God differs from persons such as us by lacking a body and by being much more powerful and knowledgeable than we are. For theistic personalists, however, the differences between us and God seem to

---

[57] Brian Davies, *An Introduction to the Philosophy of Religion*, 3rd ed. (Oxford: Oxford University Press, 2004), chapter 1.
[58] René Descartes, *Meditations on First Philosophy*, Second Meditation. For an English edition of this, see *The Philosophical Writings of Descartes*, vol. 2, trans. John Cottingham, Robert Stoothoff, and Dugald Murdoch (Cambridge: Cambridge University Press, 1984).

be matters of *degree*: God has *more* of what we have – as Einstein might be said to have had more scientific knowledge than I do. What I am calling "theistic personalism" is something of a late development in the history of ideas. I have no doubt that it squares with what masses of "card-carrying" Christians have thought since New Testament times. But from Augustine to Descartes and beyond, philosophers (and a ton of theologians) writing about God have in mind what classical theism amounts to. Yet many philosophers today assume that "Does God exist?" is asking whether the God of theistic personalism exists. Among contemporary examples of authors working on this assumption I would (among philosophers) instance Richard Swinburne and Alvin Plantinga, and (among theologians) Jürgen Moltmann.[59] I also think that it is theistic personalism that is the target of "New Atheists" such as Richard Dawkins, Daniel Dennett, and Sam Harris.[60]

Now, given my distinction between classical theism and theistic personalism, it seems to me that there is some (albeit slight) reason to identify "the God of the Bible" with the God of theistic personalists. I mean, to put it briefly, that both "gods" are presented as being seriously comparable to human persons. They undergo thought processes, they favor some people and disfavor others, they live a life spread out in time, and they undergo reactions as they learn about (or perhaps foreknow) what goes on in the world. Theistic personalists seem to think of God as a kind of Top Person, and it is not hard to see why people often read authors of many biblical passages as agreeing with them.

Typically, however, those who worry about the God of the Bible seriously differing from the God of natural theology are not thinking of God in theistic-personalist terms. Their worry stems from what they take defenders of *classical theism* to be saying. Their main point is that, unlike the God of the Bible, the God of classical theism is impersonal and uninvolved in the world. Sometimes they suggest that the God of classical theism is an odd kind of hangover from what certain Greek philosophers, especially Plato (427–347 BC) had in mind when saying that there are "pure forms" in which worldly things somehow "participate." These forms were supposed to be abstract objects (as some have taken numbers to be). They were not *living*

---

[59] See Richard Swinburne, *The Coherence of Theism*, 2nd ed. (Oxford: Oxford University Press, 2016); Alvin Plantinga, *Does God Have a Nature?* (Milwaukee: Marquette University Press); Jürgen Moltmann, *The Crucified God* (Minneapolis: Fortress Press, 1993).

[60] See Richard Dawkins, *The God Delusion* (Boston: Houghton Mifflin, 2008); Daniel Dennett, *Breaking the Spell* (New York: Penguin Books, 2007); Sam Harris, *The End of Faith* (New York: W. W. Norton, 2004). I offer comments on "New Atheism" in general in "The New Atheism: Its Virtues and Its Vices," *New Blackfriars* 92 (2011).

beings, and they did not *act* in any way. They were *ideals*. And, so it is often said, the God of classical theism sounds just like them and is obviously nothing like the God of the Bible. But this view of classical theism rests on what I take to be a serious misunderstanding of it. When trying to defend that conclusion I obviously cannot pretend to speak on behalf of everyone writing in the tradition of classical theism. So, I shall briefly focus on Aquinas, whom I take to be the most classical of classical theists.

Perhaps the first thing to say about Aquinas as a natural theologian is that he does not think of God as a platonic form. He explicitly rejects what he takes to be Plato's views on pure forms.[61] For Aquinas, as for biblical authors, God is the knowing and willing Creator of all that is not divine. The thought of there being such a creator is not something that we find promoted by ancient Greek philosophers (among whom I include Plato and Aristotle). It is an Old Testament notion. But Aquinas (biblical theologian as he is) buys into it while going on to argue that in God there is knowledge, life, will, love, and power.[62]

Yet Aquinas is also at pains to remind us that if God is the Creator of all things, if God is the answer to the question "How come something rather than nothing?," then God cannot be a spatiotemporal individual as, for example, I am. Aquinas wrote a large number of commentaries on biblical texts, so he is well aware of how biblical authors frequently portray God as something like an invisible human being with more power and knowledge than we have.[63] But he also thinks that the Bible does not interpret itself and has to be read in the light of what we can know of God by reason.

If God is the maker of the spatiotemporal universe, can God be a spatiotemporal individual? While having no problem with biblical texts depicting God in human terms, Aquinas thinks not. To think otherwise, he argues, would be to take God to be part of the "something" we might have in mind when wondering why there is something rather than nothing. So, he spends much time noting what God *cannot* be. He argues, for example, that God cannot be bodily or perishable or dependent for existence on something other than it. He also argues that God cannot be part of the universe, that God cannot be one more individual in the world to be lined up for counting among other such things. So, he denies that God is a member of a group of which there could be more of the same kind – as each egg in a basket is one

---

[61] Cf. *Summa theologiae*, 1a, 84,4.   [62] Cf. *Summa theologiae*, 1a, 14, 18, 19, 20, and 25.

[63] Aquinas's biblical commentaries include expositions of Isaiah, Jeremiah, Job, Psalms, Matthew, John, and several of the letters attributed to St. Paul.

among many eggs. He also denies that God can literally undergo change or suffering.

Some readers of Aquinas have read him as thereby asserting that God is static or lifeless. Such readers, however, are failing to note that to say what something is *not* is not to explain what it *is*. If I tell you that I am not French, you have no business concluding that I am, therefore, Dutch or Australian. And it would be wrong to suppose that, when Aquinas says that God does not change or suffer as we do, he means that God is inert or static. What he means is that the "maker of all things, visible and invisible," cannot be thought of as being *acted on* by something external to him or as being *vulnerable* to any such thing. To think of God in those terms, Aquinas argues, would be to think of God as a creature, as something that owes its life history to things around it. It has been said that Aquinas's view of God holds that God has no compassion for people since God cannot literally suffer. But even *we* do not have to suffer in order to have compassion with those who suffer. And, far from being uninvolved with those who suffer, the God of classical theism is most intimately involved with them. The point is nicely made by Herbert McCabe. Speaking on behalf of classical theism, he observes:

> Our only way of being present to another's suffering is by being affected by it, because we are outside the other person. We speak of *sympathy* or *com*passion, just because we want to say that it is *almost* as though we were not outside the other, but living her or his life, experiencing her or his suffering. A component of pity is frustration at having, in the end, to remain outside. Now, the Creator cannot in this way ever be outside his creature; a person's act of being as well as every action done has to be an act of the Creator. If the Creator is the reason for everything that is, there can be no actual being which does not have the Creator at its centre holding it in being. In our compassion, *we* in our feeble way, are seeking to be what God is all the time: united with and within the life of our friend. We can say in the psalm "The Lord is compassion" but a sign that this is metaphorical language is that we can also say that the Lord has no need of compassion; he has something more wonderful, he has his creative act in which he is "closer to the sufferer than she is to herself."[64]

So, I end this section of the present book while commending to you the following theses. (1) The enterprise of natural theology is not to be dismissed in advance because God is not supposed to be something to be investigated by means of our senses. (2) Various theological objections to natural

---

[64] Brian Davies and Paul Kucharski, eds., *The McCabe Reader* (London: Bloomsbury T&T Clark, 2016), 74.

theology rest on highly dubious premises. (3) To engage in natural theology is not to set oneself against biblical teaching since the Bible itself sanctions what we can think of as natural theology. (4) It is false to suggest that the God of classical theism is something quite different from the God spoken of by biblical authors.[65]

Of course, nothing that I have just been saying does anything to show that there are any good philosophical reasons to believe that God exists. Whether or not there are is a question that Michael and I shall be discussing next.

---

[65] For a good development of this thesis, see Eleonore Stump, *The God of the Bible and the God of the Philosophers* (Marquette: Marquette University Press, 2016).

3

Arguing for God

Michael Ruse

THE ONTOLOGICAL ARGUMENT

*F*OR TWO OR THREE YEARS, I WAS A HEGELIAN. I REMEMBER THE exact moment when I became one. I had gone out to buy a tin of tobacco, and was going back with it along Trinity Lane, when I suddenly threw it up in the air and exclaimed: 'Great God in Boots! – the ontological argument is sound!'"[1] This was not a lasting commitment, and before long Russell became the most famous Anglophone atheist, until Richard Dawkins arrived on the scene. Pipe smokers or not, let us follow in Russell's footsteps – if not in Cambridge – and see where the arguments for the existence of God land us. With the possible exception of the teleological argument – the argument from design – I don't pretend to any special or new knowledge on these very much discussed topics. My discussion is (and is intended to be) quite standard. I will take in turn the ontological argument, the causal or cosmological argument, and, third (because this is my area of specialty), the teleological argument or the argument from design. I will leave the argument from miracles and the moral argument for God's existence until later chapters, although in a way the moral argument interests me most of all.

Mention was made in the previous chapter of the ontological argument. Now, let's dig into it, starting with the fact that it is exceptional because it is an a priori argument, making appeal only to logical or nonempirical claims, trying to show the very idea of God implies his necessity. There are two standard versions or presentations. The first that of Anselm. He defines God as that than which none greater can be conceived. Does God exist? If he does not, then there is a greater that can be conceived, namely, an existent God. Hence, God necessarily exists. "Truly there is a God, although the fool hath

---

[1] B. Russell, *My Philosophical Development* (London: Allen and Unwin, 1959), 60.

said in his heart, There is no God." Continuing: "even the fool is convinced that something exists in the understanding, at least, than which nothing greater can be conceived. For, when he hears of this, he understands it. And whatever is understood, exists in the understanding. And assuredly that than which nothing greater can be conceived cannot exist in the understanding alone. For, suppose it exists in the understanding alone: then it can be conceived to exist in reality; which is greater." From which it follows, by a reductio, that "if that than which nothing greater can be conceived exists in the understanding alone, the very being than which nothing greater can be conceived, is one, than which a greater can be conceived. But obviously this is impossible. Hence, there is no doubt that there exists a being, than which nothing greater can be conceived, and it exists both in the understanding and in reality."[2]

The second version several centuries later is from Descartes's *Meditations*. God is defined as that which has all perfections. Existence is a perfection. Hence, God exists.

> I clearly see that existence can no more be separated from the essence of God than can its having its three angles equal to two right angles be separated from the essence of a [rectilinear] triangle, or the idea of a mountain from the idea of a valley; and so there is not any less repugnance to our conceiving a God (that is, a Being supremely perfect) to whom existence is lacking (that is to say, to whom a certain perfection is lacking), than to conceive of a mountain which has no valley.[3]

Expectedly, Richard Dawkins is contemptuous of this line of thought, despite failing to explain it or refute it, dismissing it as an "infantile argument." Perhaps more perceptively than he intends, he continues: "I mean it as a compliment when I say that you could almost define a philosopher as someone who won't take common sense for an answer."[4] With friends like this, what need has one of enemies! He does put his finger on a point, though, namely that the mark of a real philosopher is to find the argument quite stunning in its presumption to get so much from so little. Something with the elegance of the Euler identity: $e^{i\pi} + 1 = 0$. Sensible people like my wife really cannot understand me at all – but then, she never worried about whether she was asleep or awake.

[2] Anselm of Canterbury, *The Major Works*, trans. B. Davies, and G. R. Evans (Oxford: Oxford University Press, 2008), 87–88.
[3] R. Descartes, Meditations, in *Philosophical Essays* (Indianapolis: Bobbs-Merrill, 1964), 59–143, 121.
[4] R. Dawkins, *The God Delusion* (New York: Houghton, Mifflin, Harcourt, 2006), 83.

Stunning or not, it cannot be valid. At once, a contemporary of Anslem, Gaunilo, wrote a response on behalf of the fool. Philosophical humor hasn't changed too much through the centuries either. Neither has the way we go after arguments we think invalid. Think of an analogous case that shows the absurdity of the argument. In Gaunilo's case, he supposed an island better than anyone could otherwise conceive.

> If a man should try to prove to me by such reasoning that this island truly exists, and that its existence should no longer be doubted, either I should believe that he was jesting, or I know not which I ought to regard as the greater fool: myself, supposing that I should allow this proof; or him, if he should suppose that he had established with any certainty the existence of this island.[5]

As far as Descartes is concerned, Kant put his finger on the issue – red, heavy, beautiful are predicates. Existence is not a predicate, more an indication of whether a certain spot or conception is filled.

> Being is evidently not a real predicate, that is, a conception of something which is added to the conception of some other thing. It is merely the positing of a thing, or of certain determinations in it. Logically, it is merely the copula of a judgement. The proposition, God is omnipotent, contains two conceptions, which have a certain object or content; the word is, is no additional predicate – it merely indicates the relation of the predicate to the subject. Now, if I take the subject (God) with all its predicates (omnipotence being one), and say: God is, or, There is a God, I add no new predicate to the conception of God, I merely posit or affirm the existence of the subject with all its predicates – I posit the object in relation to my conception.[6]

For me, this is definitive. End of argument. Admittedly, recently some have tried to resuscitate it. Alvin Plantinga argues that if we think of an entity with "maximal greatness," then it obviously exists in some possible world, which means it must exist in all possible worlds.[7] The problem here seems to be the same that Kant picked out: somehow you are slipping existence into greatness and the conclusion follows. But the question first is whether greatness exists, not that it must necessarily exist.

---

[5] Anselm, *Works*, 109.
[6] I. Kant, *Critique of Pure Reason*, trans. J. M. D. Meiklejohn (New York: Colonial Press, [1781] 1899), 348.
[7] A. Plantinga, *The Nature of Necessity* (Oxford: Oxford University Press, 1974).

However, this does point to something of real value in the ontological argument. It draws our attention to the nature of God's existence. If he exists, then he is not one of the chaps.[8] He exists necessarily. Hard as it may be for people to imagine, Brian Davies and Michael Ruse might not exist. God is different. If he does exist, then he exists necessarily. This of course is built into the neo-Platonic God of Augustine. He is like the Form of the Good, and the Forms are a level above mathematics. Mathematics is necessary (2+2 could not equal 5), and so the Forms are necessary. The question therefore becomes whether God could exist necessarily and, if so, what this can mean. Which takes us onto our next argument.

THE COSMOLOGICAL ARGUMENT

The following is the argument made famous by Aquinas.

> In the world of sense we find there is an order of efficient causes. There is no case known (neither is it, indeed, possible) in which a thing is found to be the efficient cause of itself; for so it would be prior to itself, which is impossible. Now in efficient causes it is not possible to go on to infinity, because in all efficient causes following in order, the first is the cause of the intermediate cause, and the intermediate is the cause of the ultimate cause, whether the intermediate cause be several, or only one. Now to take away the cause is to take away the effect. Therefore, if there be no first cause among efficient causes, there will be no ultimate, nor any intermediate cause. But if in efficient causes it is possible to go on to infinity, there will be no first efficient cause, neither will there be an ultimate effect, nor any intermediate efficient causes; all of which is plainly false. Therefore it is necessary to admit a first efficient cause, to which everyone gives the name of God.[9]

The obvious response – the Richard Dawkins response – is: "What caused God?" Aquinas's answer seems to be, in the spirit of Anselm, nothing caused God. He exists necessarily. David Hume worried about this.

> [T]here is an evident absurdity in pretending to demonstrate a matter of fact, or to prove it by arguments a priori. Nothing is demonstrable, unless the contrary is a contradiction. Nothing, that is directly conceivable, implies a contradiction. Whatever we conceive as existent, we can also

[8] Part of the reason to reject theistic personalism.
[9] St. Thomas Aquinas, *Summa theologiae*, I (London: Burns, Oates and Washbourne, 1952), 1a, 2, 3.

THE COSMOLOGICAL ARGUMENT   63

conceive as non-existent. There is no being, therefore, whose non-existence implies a contradiction. Consequently there is no Being whose contradiction is demonstrable.[10]

Now notice here that the kind of necessity we and Hume are thinking of is logical necessity, or perhaps mathematical necessity if the two are different. And this seems to be the necessity of Anselm's God. He couldn't not exist. Now, what you might say here is that what is going wrong is that you are committing what philosophers call a "category mistake." You are confusing two entirely different sorts of things. If I say "Tuesday is tired," you know that there must be something wrong because Tuesdays are just not the sorts of things that could be tired. Brian Davies might be tired on Tuesday – the Pope was so interested in his views on the candidacy for sainthood of Michael Ruse that Davies had to take a later flight and he didn't get to NYC until nearly midnight – but Tuesdays as such are never tired or not tired. They cannot be. So, if I say God is necessary, I am committing a similar sort of category mistake. If I say "either Michael Ruse was born in England or he was not born in England" – "p or not-p" – then it just has to be true. It is logically necessary. If I say just "Michael Ruse was born in England," it might be true or it might not be true. It is not logically necessary. I might have been born in Ruritania. It is a category mistake to think that Michael Ruse's birth, in or out of England, had to be necessary. It is the same with God. "God exists" is by its very nature not logically necessary. Hence, God cannot be a logically necessary entity.

The great philosophers, especially Aquinas, knew this. Hence, for them, there had to be something about God that did make his existence necessary. It might not be logical necessity, but it had to be necessary nonetheless. The term used is "aseity," and the claim is that God's very essence implies his existence. Just as the essence of a triangle implies that its angles add up to two right angles, so the essence of God implies his existence. The $64,000 question is just how God's essence implies his existence. You might say that it cannot be done. I guess that would be Hume's position. Having allowed the legitimacy of the question "Why is there something rather than nothing?," I am not sure I want to go in that direction. My problem, if problem it be, is that, if you insist on an answer to the fundamental question, why we cannot just take the Greek (or Buddhist for that matter) option and say that, given there was no Creator God, the very existence of things is in some sense necessary.

---

[10] D. Hume, *Dialogues Concerning Natural Religion*, in *Hume on Religion*, ed. R. Wollheim (London: Fontana, [1779] 1963), 93–204, 189.

Not individual things, but existence as a whole. It couldn't not exist. After all, given that it does exist, why does it exist? Is existence purely contingent? To be honest, I am not quite sure what that means. But either way, I am not sure that one must bring in God. Existence just is. No proofs of deities, I am afraid.

THE TELEOLOGICAL ARGUMENT

The teleological argument or the argument from design has a long history.[11] It is to be found in Plato's *Phaedo*, the dialogue about Socrates' last day on earth.

> I thought before that it was obvious to anybody that men grew through eating and drinking, for food adds flesh to flesh and bones to bones, and in the same way appropriate parts were added to all other parts of the body, so that the man grew from an earlier small bulk to a large bulk later, and so a small man became big.[12]

Plato acknowledges that this is not a bad explanation – we do get bigger, thanks to eating and drinking – but it is in some sense incomplete. Why would one bother to eat and drink? Why would one want to grow and put on weight? The answer is that we are – or rather will be – better off if we grow.

> One day I heard someone reading, as he said, from a book of Anaxagoras, and saying that it is Mind that directs and is the cause of everything. I was delighted with this cause and it seemed to me to be good, in a way, that Mind should be the cause of all. I thought that if this were so, the directing Mind would direct everything and arrange each thing in the way that was best.[13]

Note one very important thing. Plato, through the mouthpiece of Socrates, is not proving the existence of a Creator God. The great Greek philosophers did not believe in such a God. Rather, he is proving the existence of a Designer God. Plato certainly believed in this entity, in the *Timaeus* giving a detailed discussion of how the "Demiurge" works. As noted in Chapter 2, there is some debate about whether this being actually did a job of designing or is more a principle of design; but when the Christian philosophers and theologians got hold of the notion, it became a being – the Christian God. Aquinas gives the most famous version of the argument. Having given four arguments for God's existence – the cosmological argument and others – Aquinas turns to the question of design.

---

[11] M. Ruse, *Darwin and Design: Does Evolution Have a Purpose?* (Cambridge, MA: Harvard University Press, 2003); *On Purpose* (Princeton: Princeton University Press, 2017).

[12] J. M. Cooper, ed., *Plato: Complete Works* (Indianapolis: Hackett, 1977), 83–84; *Phaedo*, 96c–d.

[13] Cooper, *Plato*, *Phaedo*, 97c–d.

The fifth way is taken from the governance of the world. We see that things that lack knowledge, such as natural bodies, act for an end, and this is evident from their acting always, or nearly always, in the same way, so as to obtain the best result. Hence it is plain that they achieve their end, not fortuitously, but designedly. Now whatever lacks knowledge cannot move knowledge and intelligence, as the arrow is directed by the archer. Therefore, some intelligent being exists by whom all natural things are directed to their end; and this being we call God.[14]

Parenthetically, I must note that – as mentioned in Chapter 2 – Aquinas was much influenced by Aristotle, and this shows in his version of the design argument. Whereas for a Platonist, the teleology is external – meaning a designer who puts the design in place through an efficient cause – for an Aristotelian, the teleology is internal – meaning any inference of design comes from a final cause as things move toward desired ends. For Plato, the evidence of design comes from the hand that was made (efficient cause) for a purpose (final cause). For Aristotle, the evidence of design comes in the growth of a plant (driven by efficient causes) to the mature fruit-laden form (final cause). Aquinas in the passage just quoted is thinking in an Aristotelian mode, although overall as a Christian he was committed to a Platonic designer.

Note that either way, Platonic or Aristotelian, this being creates and designs the inorganic as well as the organic world, as one would expect of the Creator of all. But after the Scientific Revolution, the design focus was on the organic. Francis Bacon and Robert Boyle and others wanted no part of design – what they called "final causes" and what in the eighteenth century was called "teleology" – in the physical sciences. Boyle, probably the most subtle writer on the topic, argued that design has a proper place, but in theology not science.

For there are some things in nature so curiously contrived, and so exquisitely fitted for certain operations and uses, that it seems little less than blindness in him, that acknowledges, with the Cartesians, a most wise Author of things, not to conclude, that, though they may have been designed for other (and perhaps higher) uses, yet they were designed for this use.[15]

(Descartes argued that we can never know God's intentions.)

As part of their promotion of natural theology, the English always had a love for the argument from design. Most famous of all is the textbook writer Archdeacon William Paley of Carlisle. His *Natural Theology* (1802) – written

---

[14] Aquinas, *Summa theologiae*, 11, Man (1a. 2, 3).
[15] R. Boyle, "A Disquisition about the Final Causes of Natural Things," in *The Works of Robert Boyle*, ed. T. Birch (Hildesheim: Georg Olms, [1688] 1966), 5:397–98.

in a happy Platonic (externalist) mode – gave what many took to be the definitive statement.

> In crossing a heath, suppose I pitched my foot against a stone, and was asked how the stone came to be there; I might possibly answer that, for anything I knew to the contrary, it had lain there forever, nor would it perhaps be very easy to show the absurdity of this answer. But suppose I had found a watch upon the ground, and it should be inquired how the watch happened to be in that place; I should hardly think of the answer which I had before given, that, for anything I knew, the watch might have always been there.[16]

The watch shows organization, marks of design. The stone does not. Hence, there must be an organizer. Shall we simply say that the watch just happened? "Or shall it, instead of this, all at once turn us round to an opposite conclusion, viz. that no art or skill whatever has been concerned in the business, although all other evidences of art and skill remain as they were, and this last and supreme piece of art be now added to the rest? Can this be maintained without absurdity? Yet this is atheism."[17] Organisms are in the same boat. They too show marks of design. Hence, as the eye is like a telescope, so analogous to the telescope designer there must be the Great Optician in the Sky.

The paradox or irony of all of this is that Paley was writing several decades after David Hume had launched a withering attack on the argument. In his *Dialogues Concerning Natural Religion*, started in the 1750s but eventually published (anonymously) in 1779, shortly after the philosopher's death, he showed that the argument from design is riddled with problems. Who is to say that there is only one designer, and who moreover is to say that this designer got things right straight off? Our experience of complex entities is that usually this is a group effort, drawing on the experience of many attempts – sometimes failures, sometimes successes – in the past.

> But were this world ever so perfect a production, it must still remain uncertain, whether all the excellences of the work can justly be ascribed to the workman. If we survey a ship, what an exalted idea must we form of the ingenuity of the carpenter who framed so complicated, useful, and beautiful a machine? And what surprise must we feel, when we find him a stupid mechanic, who imitated others, and copied an art, which, through a long succession of ages, after multiplied trials, mistakes, corrections, deliberations, and controversies, had been gradually improving?[18]

[16] W. Paley, *Collected Works, vol. 4: Natural Theology* (London: Rivington, [1802] 1819), 1.
[17] Paley, *Natural Theology*, 13–14.   [18] Hume, *Dialogues*, 77.

Was it just one workman? "And what shadow of an argument ... can you produce, from your hypothesis, to prove the unity of the Deity? A great number of men join in building a house or ship, in rearing a city, in framing a commonwealth; why may not several deities combine in contriving and framing a world?" The trouble is, of course, that you are reading your conclusion – a unique, all-powerful deity – right into your premises and then thinking that you have discovered or proved something.

End of argument! But, given Paley and his huge success, obviously not. Hume does point to something very important, for, despite his attack, at the end of the *Dialogues* he rather concedes that there must be something – or Something.

> That the works of Nature bear a great analogy to the productions of art, is evident; and according to all the rules of good reasoning, we ought to infer, if we argue at all concerning them, that their causes have a proportional analogy. But as there are also considerable differences, we have reason to suppose a proportional difference in the causes; and in particular, ought to attribute a much higher degree of power and energy to the supreme cause, than any we have ever observed in mankind. Here then the existence of a DEITY is plainly ascertained by reason: and if we make it a question, whether, on account of these analogies, we can properly call him a mind or intelligence, notwithstanding the vast difference which may reasonably be supposed between him and human minds; what is this but a mere verbal controversy?[19]

"Plainly ascertained by reason"? What on earth is going on here? The best explanation is that it is a mistake to think of the argument from design as a simple analogical argument – the eye is like a telescope, telescopes have telescope designers, hence the eye has a designer, or Designer. It is, rather, what is known in the philosophical trade as an "abduction" (to use the term introduced by the Pragmatist Charles Sanders Peirce) or, more commonly today, "an argument to the best explanation." Sherlock Holmes knew all about these. In *The Sign of the Four*, he nailed it in his explanation to Dr. Watson. "How often have I said to you that when you have eliminated the impossible, whatever remains, however improbable, must be the truth?" The point being made is that the organized complexity that we see in organisms particularly must have some explanation. Pure chance will not do the job. Therefore, there must be a designer, and since we know that the designer was not human, there must be a God – or god(s), because we are not necessarily talking about the Christian God.

---

[19] Hume, *Dialogues*, 130.

DARWINISM

The weakness in this argument, if such it be, is that when a more successful competitor comes along, the conclusion vanishes. Enter Charles Darwin. In his *Origin of Species*, published in 1859, he offered a natural – law-bound, without reference to a deity – explanation of the design-like nature of the organic world.[20] Note, he was not denying the design-like nature of the organic world. Anything but. At the University of Cambridge, he had been brought up on a diet of Paley.[21] Rather, he explained it without the need to invoke God. First, Darwin raised the name of the late eighteenth-century cleric and political economist Thomas Robert Malthus, who argued that there would be inevitable "struggles for existence" due to population numbers outstripping supplies of space and food. Then, having convinced himself that new variations are constantly appearing in populations, Darwin argued that in the struggle those with the better variations – the fitter – would out-reproduce those with fewer adaptations – the less fit. As in the barnyard, this would lead to a constant choosing in the direction of fitness, and thus through "natural selection" new variations, design-like variations, adaptations, would appear.

> A struggle for existence inevitably follows from the high rate at which all organic beings tend to increase. Every being, which during its natural lifetime produces several eggs or seeds, must suffer destruction during some period of its life, and during some season or occasional year, otherwise, on the principle of geometrical increase, its numbers would quickly become so inordinately great that no country could support the product. Hence, as more individuals are produced than can possibly survive, there must in every case be a struggle for existence, either one individual with another of the same species, or with the individuals of distinct species, or with the physical conditions of life.[22]

Then to natural selection:

> Let it be borne in mind how infinitely complex and close-fitting are the mutual relations of all organic beings to each other and to their physical conditions of life. Can it, then, be thought improbable, seeing that variations useful to man have undoubtedly occurred, that other variations useful in some way to each being in the great and complex battle of life,

---

[20] C. Darwin, *On the Origin of Species by Means of Natural Selection, or the Preservation of Favoured Races in the Struggle for Life* (London: John Murray, 1859).

[21] J. Browne, *Charles Darwin: Voyaging, Volume 1 of a Biography* (New York: Knopf, 1995).

[22] Darwin, *Origin*, 63–64.

should sometimes occur in the course of thousands of generations? If such do occur, can we doubt (remembering that many more individuals are born than can possibly survive) that individuals having any advantage, however slight, over others, would have the best chance of surviving and of procreating their kind? On the other hand, we may feel sure that any variation in the least degree injurious would be rigidly destroyed. This preservation of favourable variations and the rejection of injurious variations, I call Natural Selection.[23]

The all-important point is that this cause – natural selection – points to adaptation, to final cause. The eye is created as it is in order to see. The flower to attract pollinators. The fangs of the snake to kill. The instincts of the nest-building bird to promote and continue life. It is not just change but change of a particular kind:

> Under nature, the slightest difference of structure or constitution may well turn the nicely-balanced scale in the struggle for life, and so be preserved. How fleeting are the wishes and efforts of man! how short his time! and consequently how poor will his products be, compared with those accumulated by nature during whole geological periods. Can we wonder, then, that nature's productions should be far "truer" in character than man's productions; that they should be infinitely better adapted to the most complex conditions of life, and should plainly bear the stamp of far higher workmanship?[24]

Note, by a rather delicious irony, Darwin is not denying the existence of God. Although later he became an agnostic, at this time he was a deist, thinking God works through unbroken law. However, like Boyle, Darwin felt that these sorts of thoughts belong to religion, not to science. Science begins and ends with unbroken law. In a way, we might say that Darwin started out in a Platonic mode – thinking of the hand and eye as if designed by a designer – but gave an Aristotelian-type solution – natural selection points organisms to the end of successful survival and reproduction. This means that although you can continue to believe in a Platonic designer or Designer God, you don't absolutely have to.

Making just this last point, Richard Dawkins has said, with respect to this argument, that Darwin makes it possible to be "a fulfilled atheist."[25] This is surely true. The argument to the best explanation has backfired. Aristotle over Plato. However, do note that it does not mean you have to be an atheist. Darwin wasn't! It is more John Henry Newman's already-quoted point:

[23] Darwin, Origin, 80–81.   [24] Darwin, Origin, 83–84.
[25] R. Dawkins, The Blind Watchmaker (New York: Norton, 1986).

"I believe in design because I believe in God. I do not believe in God because I believe in design."[26] I will be coming back to this thought in the next chapter. But, for now, I will leave it and turn to (what was certainly to me and I suspect most biologists) a rather surprising new development concerning the design argument.

THE ANTHROPIC PRINCIPLE

I have said (truly) that, up to the Scientific Revolution, it was agreed that the design argument works for the inorganic as well as the organic. However, Aristotle, who was a biologist, was even back then focusing on the organic. In talking of final causes, he wrote: "This is most obvious in the animals other than man: they make things neither nor after inquiry or deliberation.... If then it is both by nature and for an end that the swallow makes its nest and the spider its web, and plants grow leaves for the sake of the fruit and send their roots down (not up) for the sake of nourishment, it is plain that this kind of cause is operative in things which come to be and are by nature."[27] It doesn't mean that "by nature" Aristotle didn't think something more was involved – the Unmoved Mover – but the point is that it is in the organic that we really see the action.

Then, in the sixteenth and seventeenth centuries, the inorganic was taken out of the discussion. No final causes there. This doesn't mean that, at the theological level, we never had thereafter discussion of final causes in the inorganic world. William Whewell worried about planets other than ours.[28] What is their purpose? If there are intelligent beings on some or all of them, does this mean that Jesus might have to die on a cross almost every Friday? If they are barren, why make them in the first place? Whewell came up with a couple of answers, neither of which was entirely satisfactory. On the one hand, he argued for what is sometimes known as the "argument (for God's existence) from law," that you really don't need useful ends – what are sometimes called "utilitarian" ends – to show design. Any kind of law-bound pattern will do:

---

[26] J. H. Newman, *The Letters and Diaries of John Henry Newman*, vol. 25, ed. C. S. Dessain and T. Gornall (Oxford: Clarendon Press, 1973).

[27] Aristotle, *De generatione de animalium*, in *The Complete Works of Aristotle*, ed. Jonathan Barnes, 1111–218 (Princeton: Princeton University Press, 1984).

[28] W. Whewell, *Of the Plurality of Worlds. A Facsimile of the First Edition of 1853: Plus Previously Unpublished Material Excised by the Author Just before the Book Went to Press; and Whewell's Dialogue Rebutting His Critics, Reprinted from the Second Edition*, ed. M. Ruse (Chicago: University of Chicago Press, [1853] 2001).

in the plan of creation, we have a profusion of examples, where similar visible structures do not answer a similar purpose; where, so far as we can see, the structure answers no purpose in many cases; but exists, as we may say, for the sake of similarity: the similarity being a general Law, the result, it would seem, of a creative energy, which is wider in its operation than the particular purpose.[29]

On the other hand, Whewell stressed how very badly the world is designed anyway! What if the planets and stars are useless? Much of our world is useless. Hundreds of organisms are born that wither and die without success. "Of the vegetable seeds which are produced, what an infinitely small proportion ever grow into plants! Of animal ova, how exceedingly few become animals, in proportion to those that do not; and that are wasted, if this be waste!"[30] Just as well, because there would be nowhere for them to live anyway. Huge areas of our planet are arid and dry and worthless. "Vast desert tracts exist in Africa and in Asia, where the barren land nourishes neither animal nor vegetable life." I should say that all of this came out just a few years before the *Origin* was published. Without accepting the entirety of Thomas Kuhn's thinking on scientific revolutions, one is struck by how the pre-Darwinian paradigm was crumbling. All that confident stuff about God as a designer is starting to crumble.

What is not being suggested is that the inorganic world might show design of a kind yet more strongly than design in the organic world – hand, eyes, brains. Today, there are enthusiasts who propose precisely this! Their argument starts with what is known as "Strong Anthropic Principle."[31] The key idea here is that the universe had to be "fine-tuned," to get life going at all and sustain it. The various constants that govern the laws of nature could not be chosen at random but had to be very exact, within incredibly narrow limits. "There exists one possible Universe 'designed' with the goal of generating and sustaining 'observers.'" In other words, the lack of randomness implies a designer of some sort. What constants are we thinking of? Gravity, for a beginning. It is 1,039 times weaker than electromagnetism. Which is just as well, for if gravity had been only 1,033 times weaker than electromagnetism, the suns of the universe would be a billion times less big and burn a million times faster. Analogously, the nuclear weak force is 1,028 times weaker than gravity. If it had been slightly weaker, the hydrogen of the

---

[29] Whewell, *Plurality*, 221.   [30] Whewell, *Plurality*, 222.
[31] J. D. Barrow and F. J. Tipler, *The Anthropic Cosmological Principle* (Oxford: Clarendon Press, 1986).

universe would have been converted to helium, and that would have meant no water. Life as we know it would not be possible.

Expectedly, this kind of thinking has not gone unchallenged. It really does have a little bit of the odor of "think of a number, double it, and the answer you want is a half"! Suppose there really are multiverses, alternative universes, as many physicists believe. Wouldn't a universe like ours be bound to crop up if you tried enough times? Physics Nobel Prize winner Steven Weinberg writes:

> In any such picture, in which the universe contains many parts with different values for what we call the constants of nature, there would be no difficulty in understanding why these constants take values favorable to intelligent life. There would be a vast number of big bangs in which the constants of nature take values unfavorable for life, and many fewer where life is possible. You don't have to invoke a benevolent designer to explain why we are in one of the parts of the universe where life is possible: in all the other parts of the universe there is no one to raise the question.[32]

The fact that it is our universe or part of the universe in which there is life is no more improbable than that someone holds a winning lottery ticket. Given enough rolls of the dice or the drum, there was bound to be a winner eventually. The same with livable universes. Obviously, if we didn't hold the winning ticket, we wouldn't be around to tell everyone about it. That's no miracle, any more than that the person who won the lottery is the person who quits work and goes to live in the south of France.

Even in our universe, one gets the sense that often these anthropic arguments work from the alteration of just one parameter. Everything collapses, and the cry is that there must be more than chance. But what if you alter not just one constant but several in unison? It is less obvious now that life is impossible. Think of an analogy. You have a soccer team with a brilliant center forward. Your whole strategy is built on getting her and the ball up close to the opponents' goal while avoiding the offside rule. Then she breaks a leg. Does this mean you will never win another game? No! However, you probably aren't simply going to substitute for her, using someone else in the same role. You might, for instance, start to pay more attention to defense, hoping that the opposition will wear down and then collectively you can strike. As in physics. Pushing the analogy a bit, if your ultimate aim is to make a living by entertaining spectators, you might use your team's talents by switching from soccer to cricket or baseball, and

[32] S. Weinberg, "A Designer Universe?," *New York Review of Books* 46, no. 16 (1999): 46–48.

providing thrills there instead. Are we convinced that only the kind of life-form we know – carbon-based and so forth – is the only viable life-form? What about the Horta in Star Trek? Unlike some people I know, I am not that keen on sex with someone made from silicone; but if they can write music like Bach, I'm game. To go to the concert, that is.

Even if one gets past all of this, one still runs into the Humean problems – one designer or many, one instance or a chain of improving instances, and so forth. The trouble, of course, is that physicists think that their ideas are better than those of biologists. It ain't necessarily so. The resurrected argument from design is no more definitive than the other arguments we have considered in this chapter. So we seem to be at a bit of a draw. We turned to reason to help us because we did not find faith adequate. Let us be generous and say that the proofs tell us a lot about God, helping us to understand the entity we are to believe in if we can. But in the terms of this debate, they don't make it reasonable (in the sense of compelling) to believe in God.

Brian Davies

INTRODUCTION

Natural theologians have offered many arguments for it being true that God exists. These can be roughly divided into three kinds. Some hold that "God exists" is self-evident. Others claim that people have a direct and immediate "perception" or "experience" of God. Yet others amount to causal arguments. In what follows I shall say something about each of these kinds of argument. Some natural theologians have offered moral arguments for God's existence, but Michael and I shall defer discussion of those to a later chapter.

IS "GOD EXISTS" SELF-EVIDENT?

If I ask you to prove that George Washington was the first president of the United States, I assume that you would engage in some historical research. What, though, if I ask you to prove that all triangles have three sides? In that case, I suspect you would be likely to say "It's just *obvious* that any triangle *has* to have three sides since 'has three sides' is *included* in the meaning of 'triangle.'" And, so it has been argued, "exists" is included in the meaning of "God." Arguments to this effect are often referred to as examples of the "ontological proof" for God's existence.

The name "ontological proof" derives from Immanuel Kant (1724–1804). In his *Critique of Pure Reason* (1781), he discusses an argument for God's existence and gives it that title.[33] Yet he is unimpressed with the argument, which he associates with Descartes, who reasons as follows in the fifth of his *Meditations on First Philosophy*:

1. I have the idea of God in me; no doubt of that.
2. To think of God is to think of a supremely perfect being.
3. Existence is a perfection which must be had by a supremely perfect being.
4. So, the idea of existing is included in the idea of God, just as having three sides is included in the idea of a triangle.
5. So, God exists.

An argument similar to this is quoted by Aquinas. And just as Kant does not like the argument from Descartes that I have just summarized, Aquinas does not approve of the argument that he quotes, which runs as follows.

> A proposition is self-evident if we perceive its truth immediately upon perceiving the meaning of its terms.... For example, when we know what wholes and parts are, we know at once that wholes are always bigger than their parts. But once we understand the meaning of the word "God," we immediately see that God exists. For the word means "that than which nothing greater can be signified." So, since what exists in thought and fact is greater than what exists in thought alone, and since, once we understand the word "God," he exists in thought, he must also exist in fact. It is, therefore, self-evident that God exists.[34]

COMMENTS ON "GOD EXISTS IS SELF-EVIDENT"

Is the ontological proof successful? I think not. Kant knocks a big hole in the Cartesian version by noting that we add nothing to a description of anything by saying that it exists. I can note that my cat is black and agile, but I do not *describe* him by saying that he *exists*. My attempts to describe him take his existence for granted. As for the form of the proof quoted by Aquinas, that I think is nicely undermined by what he observes when evaluating it. For, as he says:

---

[33] See *Critique of Pure Reason*, A592/B620 to A602/B630. For an English edition of this work, see Immanuel Kant, *Critique of Pure Reason*, trans. and ed. Paul Guyer and Allen W. Wood (Cambridge: Cambridge University Press, 1998).

[34] Aquinas, *Summa theologiae*, 1a, 2, 1. Here and below I quote from Brian Davies and Brian Leftow, eds., *Aquinas: Summa theologiae, Questions on God* (Cambridge: Cambridge University Press, 2006).

Someone hearing the word "God" may very well not understand it to mean "that than which nothing greater can be thought." Indeed, some people have believed God to be something material. And even if someone thinks that what is signified by "God" is "that than which nothing greater can be thought," it does not follow that the person in question thinks that what is signified by "God" exists in reality rather than merely as thought about. If we do not grant that something in fact exists than which nothing greater can be thought (and nobody denying the existence of God would grant this), the conclusion that God exists does not follow.[35]

EXPERIENCE OF GOD AS A REASON FOR CLAIMING THAT GOD EXISTS

Accounts of direct awareness of God can be found in the Bible. In Genesis 32:30 the grandson of Abraham (Jacob) is reported as saying, "I have seen God face to face." In the book of Deuteronomy, the children of Israel cry out, "Behold the Lord our God has shown us his glory and greatness, and we have heard his voice . . . we have this day seen God speak with man and man still live" (Deuteronomy 5:24). And the prophet Isaiah writes: "In the year that King Uzziah died I saw the Lord sitting upon a throne, high and lifted up" (Isaiah 6:1). These texts seem to be saying that God has been directly encountered.[36] And that God has been directly encountered has been endorsed by a number of theologians and philosophers.

Consider, for example, John Baillie (1886–1960). In *Our Knowledge of God*, he declares: "There is no reality by which we are more directly confronted than we are by the Living God."[37] Baillie explicitly opposes the notion that knowledge of God is arrived at by inference. We must, he says, acknowledge God to be "of all realities, that by which we are most directly and immediately confronted."[38] According to Baillie, human beings have four "subjects" of knowledge: "ourselves, our fellows, the corporeal world, and God."[39]

Again, consider Professor Richard Swinburne. In *The Existence of God*, he appeals to what he calls the "principle of credulity." Am I justified in thinking that something is present just because it seems to me that the thing is there? Swinburne says, "Yes." It is, he suggests, "a principle of rationality

---

[35] *Summa theologiae*, 1a, 2, 1, ad. 2.
[36] Note, however, John 1:18 ("No one has ever seen God") and 1 John 4:18 ("No one has ever seen God").
[37] John Baillie, *Our Knowledge of God* (New York: Scribner, 1959), 166.
[38] Baillie, *Our Knowledge of God*, 175.   [39] Baillie, *Our Knowledge of God*, 178.

that (in the absence of special considerations), if it seems (epistemically) to a subject that x is present, then probably x is present; what one seems to perceive is probably so."[40] Swinburne says that this principle allows us reasonably to hold that God exists on the basis of direct experience of God. He writes: "If it seems to me that I have a glimpse of Heaven, or a vision of God, that is grounds for me and others to suppose that I do."[41] Professor William Alston (1921–2009) takes a similar line. In 1991 he published *Perceiving God: The Epistemology of Religious Experience*.[42] In this he argues that "people sometimes do perceive God and acquire justified beliefs about God."[43] In *Perceiving God* and elsewhere, Alston favors something like Swinburne's "principle of credulity." He observes:

> Any supposition that one perceives something to be the case – that there is a zebra in front of one or that God is strengthening one – is *prima facie* justified. That is, one is justified in supposing this unless there are strong enough reasons to the contrary. In the zebra case these would include reasons for thinking that there is no zebra in the vicinity and reasons for supposing oneself subject to hallucinations because of some drug. According to this position, beliefs formed on the basis of experience possess an initial credibility by virtue of their origin. They are innocent until proved guilty.... The main argument for the "innocent until proven guilty" position is that unless we accord a *prima facie* credibility to experiential reports, we can have no sufficient reason to trust *any* experiential source of beliefs. This is the only alternative to a thoroughgoing skepticism about experience.[44]

Alston is not saying that we are always right when convinced that we perceive something. He also recognizes that while millions of people claim to have perceived such things as dogs and cats, far fewer people have claimed to perceive God. In general, Alston is happy to concede that experience of God seems different in various ways from regular experience of objects in the world. Yet he does not think that we should therefore confidently dismiss it as giving us no knowledge of God. Some philosophers have rejected the notion of direct perception of God while holding (1) that claims based on sensory perception can often be confirmed by others or verified in some way

---

[40] Richard Swinburne, *The Existence of God*, rev. ed. (Oxford: Oxford University Press, 2004), 254. Note that by "epistemically" Swinburne just means "when it comes to knowing."

[41] Swinburne, *The Existence of God*, 260.

[42] William Alston, *Perceiving God* (Ithaca: Cornell University Press, 1991).

[43] Alston, *Perceiving God*, 3.

[44] William Alston, "God and Religious Experience," in Brian Davies, ed., *Philosophy of Religion: A Guide and Anthology* (Oxford: Oxford University Press, 2000), 284.

and (2) that this is not the case with claims to have perceived God. Yet Alston finds fault with this line of thinking. He suggests that there is no reason why experiences of perceiving God should be confirmable as sensory perception of things can be. Alston thinks that if someone cannot give a convincing reason for supposing that "the criteria available for sense perception constitute a necessary condition for *any* experiential access to objective reality," then that person is guilty of "epistemic *chauvinism*" in rejecting perception of God.[45]

COMMENTS ON THE ARGUMENT FROM EXPERIENCE OF GOD

I accept the "principle of credulity" praised by Swinburne and Alston. I think that, all things being equal, we should take what seems to us to be true to be true. If I seem to see a cat in my apartment, then I should assume that there is a cat in my apartment (unless someone can prove that I am suffering from dementia or illusions induced by alcohol or whatever). But I also think that there are reasons for being highly suspicious when it comes to claims to have directly experienced or perceived God. The strongest of these seems to me to turn on the notion of recognition. If I know that I have perceived such and such, must I not be in a position correctly to *identify* what I think I have perceived for what it *actually* is? Yet how can anybody be in a position to correctly identify what they think they have perceived as *God*?

Suppose I think that I've spotted a mouse in my apartment. If I am right, I must be able correctly to identify what I think I've spotted as a *mouse* rather than something else. Here I need some previous knowledge of mice. You can stick a mouse in front of the eyes of a newborn baby. But it will not realize that it is looking at a mouse. In the case of supposed experiences of God, however, the idea is that we might *just know* it is God that we have directly experienced or perceived or encountered. Yet I see no reason to think that this is so. "I know that" always invites the question "How do you know that . . . ?" Knowledge claims need more support than a mere repetition of them. If I claim to have been directly aware of X, you are surely right to ask me how I know that it is X of which I have been directly aware. What, however, could possibly enable anyone truly to declare that they have experienced/perceived/seen/directly encountered *God*?

Classical theists take God to be incorporeal, omniscient, omnipotent, and outside time and space. As I have noted, they also insist on the idea that God

[45] Alston, "God and Religious Experience," 386.

cannot be one of a kind, that God cannot be put in a list of things to be counted as we count the number of dogs and cats and so on. But if that is what God is (or is not), how is anybody able to know (in this life at any rate) that what they might take themselves to have directly encountered or seen or perceived *is* God? What could justify anyone appealing to direct experience to claim to know that what they have encountered or perceived or experienced is omniscient and omnipotent – let alone timeless? That, of course, is a rhetorical question to which I take the answer to be "Nothing."

Theistic personalists say that God is a person without a body who has lots of knowledge and power. But how could anyone by virtue of perception or direct experience be correctly able to identify something like this? Can one directly perceive what is incorporeal? Can one, just by perceiving something, see that it has lots of knowledge? Can one by perceiving it see that it has power to the degree that theistic personalists take God to have power? These are more rhetorical questions to which I take the answer to be "No." Traditional Christians (Roman Catholics at least) hope for a direct encounter with God after death (the "beatific vision"). But they take this to be a miracle of some sort and not something to be expected in this life.

With respect to the issue of correctly identifying God as an object of one's experience, Alston says: "To perceptually recognize your house, it is not necessary that the object even display features that are *in fact* only possessed by your house, much less features that, in this situation or in situations in which I generally find myself are sufficiently indicative of (are a reliable guide to) the object's being your house."[46] Alston goes on to say that this is how it stands with experience of God. For me to recognize what I am aware of as God, he says, all that is necessary is that God should "present to me features that are in fact a reliable indication of their possessor being God."[47] But I have problems with what Alston argues here.

For one thing, it assumes the truth of theistic personalism. That is because of the way in which Alston speaks of God having "features." Yet if classical theism is true, God has no *features*. By this I mean that on the classical theist's notion of God, it is false that God is something with attributes distinguishable from each other and from the reality that God is. The classical theist will say that there is no real distinction between the subject that God is and the attributes that we appear to distinguish from God and from each other when we say things like "God is omniscient" or "God is good" or "God is omnipotent." Alston's appeal to "features" that are

[46] Alston, *Perceiving God*, 96f.   [47] Alston, *Perceiving God*, 97.

"possessed" by God is not going to cut much ice with the classical theist. Such a theist will take what Alston says merely to apply to something like a human person, or a non-bodily human person (should there be one), or a purely material thing.

For the sake of argument, however, let us suppose that we are positively *bound* to think of God as a being possessing various properties or features as we *possess* or *have* them. Even if we suppose that, it is hard to see how we are in a position to recognize God on the basis of experience. Alston says that I might recognize that it is God I am perceiving if what I perceive has features that are "sufficiently indicative" of it being God. But what features? Could they be omniscience and omnipotence? But how can you know that something is omniscient or omnipotent just by perceiving it? Could one realize that one is perceiving God because the object of one's perception is eternal and perfectly good? Yet how can you know that something is eternal (as timeless or as everlasting) and perfectly good (by any standards) just by *perceiving* it? Someone might say that we can observe God making knowledge claims and being very powerful. To this, however, I can only reply that I have no idea of what I am now supposed to be thinking. I know what it would be for my friends to make knowledge claims to me. But people are things in the spatiotemporal world with whom I can have a conversation. Yet how am I supposed to conduct a conversation with a nonmaterial God? You may say that I can at least observe God being very powerful. But how can I do that? I can observe you being very powerful as I see you lifting weights that I could not even begin to imagine myself lifting. But that is because I actually observe you lifting the weights. What would be the parallel to this when it comes to perceiving God acting powerfully? I do not see that there can be any such parallel given that God is, by both classical theists and theistic personalists, taken to be incorporeal.

CAUSAL ARGUMENTS FOR GOD

Natural theologians have argued causally for the existence of God in two main ways. Some have reasoned that certain things in the world display *features* suggesting that nonworldly intelligence lies behind them. This is the big idea in versions of what is commonly called "The Argument from Design." Then there are natural theologians who focus on the *sheer existence* of the universe rather than on *features* that *some* things in the universe display. Having done that, they reason that the entire universe has a maker or creator. This is the main thought in versions of what is commonly called "The Cosmological Argument."

(A) Design Arguments: Some Famous Examples

Design arguments for God's existence can be divided into two kinds. First, there are arguments based on the notion of design, where "design" means what we take it to mean when thinking of *artifacts* as having designers – as when we say that the Eiffel Tower in Paris is named after Gustave Eiffel (1832–1923), whose company *designed* and built that tower. Second, there are arguments based on the notion of things in the universe being *goal directed*.

For perhaps the best-known version of the first kind of argument, the text to go to is chapters 1–3 of *Natural Theology, or Evidences of the Existence and Attributes of the Deity* written by William Paley (1743–1805). This book was published in 1802. It sold many copies, was reprinted twelve times between 1802 and 1822, and has been much commented on since then. For many philosophers, it offers the *classic* defense of the argument from design. For a famous version of the second kind of argument, a good text to consult is the fifth of the Five Ways offered by Aquinas in *Summa theologiae*, 1a, 2, 3.

Paley begins by asking what we would think should we happen to come across a watch on a heath. He suggests that, even if we have no previous knowledge of watches, or what makes them tick, we would have good reason to take what we have come across to have a designing agent behind it. Paley then argues that every manifestation of design present in a watch exists in what we find in the natural world. He suggests that our world is full of things that look as designed as any watch. In one place, for example, he writes at length about functioning eyes. These, he says, are complex things that consist of parts that enable them to work in a particular way. For Paley, just as a watch implies a watchmaker, eyes are mechanisms that imply a designer.

Aquinas argues differently. In his Fifth Way he does not compare anything in nature with mechanisms such as watches.[48] Instead, he notes that material objects in nature "act for the sake of an end." Why does Aquinas think this? Not because he thinks that material objects in nature are intelligent agents who can explain what they are doing as I might explain why I am rushing to the train station. He justifies his claim about material objects acting for an end from the fact that "they always, or usually, act in the same way so as to achieve what is best (and therefore reach their goal by purpose and not by chance)." But what does Aquinas mean when he says this?

---

[48] I am confident that Aquinas's Fifth Way is not an argument from design – if Paley's argument is taken as a paradigmatic "design" argument. Still, I discuss it as a kind of design argument since that is how it is frequently expounded or classified.

To begin with, note the "or usually" in the above quote. Aquinas is not saying that material objects always achieve what he calls their "end." Also realize that, when he speaks of material objects having an end, he is thinking of material things, all of which he takes to have distinct *ways of acting* and (barring interference) distinct *results of their acting*. He is thinking, for example, that whiskey, being what it is, will naturally leave you inebriated if you drink a lot of it in one sitting. Of course, drinking whiskey might not make you drunk since someone might kill you before you become inebriated. Yet we ought not to be surprised if you and I end up totally smashed having consumed two bottles of whiskey during an evening in my apartment with no assassins around. In his Fifth Way, Aquinas is noting that, all things being equal, material things in the world have ways of acting that cannot arise from chance. Aquinas believes that there can be chance events.[49] But he does not think that is by chance that whiskey tends to inebriate people (though not the bottles in which it is lodged before people drink it).

With that fact in mind, Aquinas seeks to account for it. To stick with the whiskey example, he does not think that whiskey makes me drunk because some intelligent agent in the universe is causing it to make me drunk. He thinks that whiskey is just whiskey and that it does what it does given what it *is*. He does not think that anything in the world is acting on whiskey as it goes about its business. But how should we account for this being so? How should we account for inanimate things consistently acting as they do? Aquinas thinks that there has to be an explanation for this, and he finds a clue to the answer in human practical reasoning, which employs material things for *ends* that people have *in mind*. Aquinas thinks that acting for ends is characteristic of rational agents. So, he reasons that the activity of non-intelligent material things acting regularly to produce the effects that they do has to derive from intelligence that is governing them.

(B) Comments on Design Arguments

It is seems to me that Paley's classic design argument is unconvincing for a number of reasons.

First, it rests on the premise that things in the world that look engineered must derive from something like human intelligence. Yet what is the evidence for that premise? You might say that we know the premise to be true because we know that what seems engineered always derives from intelligent

---

[49] Cf. *Summa theologiae*, 2a2ae, 95, 5.

people. But that is not the case. For what of things like spider webs and ant hills? These feats of engineering are not produced by human designers.

Second, while theists typically say that God has no beginning or end, Paley does nothing to show that the god to which he concludes is something that has not perished over the course of time. All human designers of mechanisms perish eventually. So, why should the cosmic designer postulated by Paley not be among them?

Third, Paley's argument does not get us to a creator of all things other than God. The best it gets us to is a being, like a watchmaker, who puts bits together to produce an artifact of some kind. Yet both classical theists and theistic personalists take God to have created the world without working on some preexisting stuff as do human designers.

Fourth, Paley's argument is that, just as a watch is clearly designed, so are things like eyes. They are designed by God. But while we might agree that watches are designed, watches and the like often come about because many people get together to produce them. Yet Paley assumes that what he takes to be designed in nature springs from a single designer, and he has no business doing that given his comparison between "designed" things in nature and objects such as watches. In short, Paley's argument leads as naturally to polytheism (belief in many gods) as it does to monotheism (belief that there is but one God).

Fifth, why suppose that living things in the world (which seem to be what Paley is most interested in) strongly resemble things such as watches? For they surely differ from human artifacts in many ways. Artifacts such as watches are all made of "hard stuff," so to speak. A watch is made of metal and glass. But many things in nature are not constructed out of material like that. You might reasonably say that the human eye resembles a camera. But it is also very different from a camera. It is not made of the stuff of which cameras are made. Again, what about my cat? What grounds could we have for thinking of it as being a machine in any serious sense? The talking droids in the *Star Wars* movies are machines. But my cat differs strongly from them. My cat was not made in a factory or workshop. It came to birth as a result of sexual activity between its parents. And it came to birth *slowly*, as it developed in the womb of its mother. It was not knocked out in a factory or workshop. Again, my cat is *organic*, which I take to mean that it is very much *not* like a watch or something like that. In short, why should we think of things in the natural world as being like artifacts in any serious sense? Are cats and the like so much bits of clockwork? Surely not. Human artifacts directly result from intentional actions. But this is not the case with living things in the world.

With all that said, however, I disagree with the view that design arguments akin to that of Paley have been refuted by what many people now think to be the best argument against them. Here I am referring to the claim that evolutionary biology shows that what Paley took to be designed can be accounted for *only* with reference to the notion of natural selection. This claim is (rightly or wrongly) most commonly associated with Charles Darwin (1809–1882). And I have nothing to say against Darwin on natural selection. I trust in Darwin as a scientist. And I look to Michael Ruse as one of his trusty prophets. But, while accepting what Darwin says about evolution, I do not think that it entirely rules out what Paley was driving at.

Darwin thought that geological evidence shows that many existing species came to develop over huge sections of time from things existing before them that resembled them in certain ways but not in others. He also argued that this history of species involved the survival of things favored by their environment, that species that ended up surviving did so because modifications in them and their most recent ancestors favored their survival in the circumstances in which they happened to find themselves. On the Darwinian theory of evolution, we do not have to invoke design to account for what we find in species that we can examine today. What we should be noting is that species appear to have evolved due to useful variations over time. On this account, what accounts for the appearance of design in living things is the disappearance of things unfit for survival. There are no hostile witnesses to testify against design. They have all been killed off in the struggle for survival and the coming into being of things more fit for survival given their development and the circumstances in which they existed. Hence, for example, Richard Dawkins observes:

> All appearances to the contrary, the only watchmaker in nature is the blind forces of physics, albeit deployed in a very special way. A true watchmaker has foresight: he designs his cogs and springs, and plans their interconnections, with a future purpose in his mind's eye. Natural selection, the blind, unconscious, automatic process which Darwin discovered, and which we now know is the explanation for the existence and apparently purposeful form of all life, has no purpose in mind. It has no mind and no mind's eye. It does not plan for the future. It has no vision, no foresight, no sight at all. If it can be said to play the role of watchmaker, in nature, it is the blind watchmaker.[50]

---

[50] Richard Dawkins, *The Blind Watchmaker* (Essex: Longman Scientific and Technical, 1986), 6.

Yet I find this conclusion to be premature. Here I agree with some remarks of Anthony Kenny. He writes:

> If the argument from design ever had any value, it has not been substantially affected by the scientific investigation of living organisms from Descartes through Darwin to the present day. If Descartes is correct in regarding the activities of animals as mechanistically explicable, then a system may operate teleologically while being mechanistic in structure. If Darwin is correct in ascribing the origin of species to natural selection, then the production of a teleological structure may be due in the first instance to factors which are purely mechanistic. But both may be right and yet the ultimate explanation of the phenomena be finalistic.[51]

By "teleological" and "finalistic" Kenny means "aiming at or tending to a goal." His point is that while Darwin may have explained in mechanistic terms why there are things that Paley took to be designed (because goal-directed), it does not follow that they are nothing but mechanistic in their origin. In short, if the structure of the human eye is evidence that it is geared to sight, the fact that the process that brought it into being is an unconscious one should not cause one to doubt that eyes can be thought of as designed. Or, as some defenders of Paley-like arguments say, there is no reason to suppose that God cannot produce what can be thought of as designed by means of a process in which design seems decidedly absent. I also think that, although natural selection might give us some true account of the emergence of teleological systems (things in nature with parts that seem to operate as goal directed), it cannot give us a full account. For, as Peter Geach remarks:

> There can be no origin of species, as opposed to an Empedoclean chaos of varied monstrosities, unless creatures reproduce pretty much after their kind; the elaborate and ostensibly teleological mechanism of this reproduction logically cannot be explained as a product of evolution by natural selection from among chance variations, for unless the mechanism is presupposed there cannot be any evolution.[52]

What, though, of Aquinas's argument from the noncoincidental operations of nonthinking things? If we understand it properly, I think that this makes more sense than what Paley has to offer as an argument for the existence of God. Paley is thinking that God exists since there is something "out there" that works as does a watchmaker. By contrast, Aquinas is thinking that there is something "out there" that is also *actively* involved

---

[51] Anthony Kenny, *The Five Ways* (London: Routledge & Kegan Paul, 1969), 118.
[52] Peter Geach, "An Irrelevance of Omnipotence," *Philosophy* 46 (1973): 330.

as anything in nature tends to its goal. While Paley is thinking in terms of efficient causation, Aquinas, though fully acknowledging the reality of efficient causation, is invoking the notion of what is sometimes referred to as final causation.

By "efficient causation" I mean what most of us have in mind when looking for a culprit. If I find my apartment ransacked, I want to know who or what caused it to become so. What turned over my lamps? What smashed my television? Here I am looking for one or more efficient causes. By contrast, I take final causation to be what we are invoking when saying that there is a goal-oriented explanation for some process. Why does John brush his teeth? Because he thinks that brushing his teeth is one way to maintain oral hygiene. What, though, should I make of goal-directed activity on the part of things in nature that, unlike John, cannot be doing what they do because they think it desirable?

That there is goal-directed activity in nonthinking things seems obvious since many naturally occurring things regularly tend to bring about effects that can be predicted once we understand what they are by nature. Whiskey regularly tends to inebriate people who drink it. Rocks regularly smash crystal goblets if flung at them. Natural objects other than people have tendencies to produce some particular effect or range of effects. They have ways of working that lead to results that do not come about by chance. As Edward Feser puts it: "A match, for example, reliably generates flame and heat when struck, and never (say), frost and cold, or the smell of lilacs, or thunder. It inherently 'points to' or is 'directed towards' *this* range of effects specifically."[53]

As Feser goes on to note, it is this phenomenon that Aquinas has in mind in his Fifth Way. He is not saying that things in nature have *functions*. He thinks that some of them do since some them are parts of things with a function within a whole – as, say, human hearts function so as to circulate blood. For Aquinas, however, every function is an instance of final causality, though not all final causality involves having a function. In his Fifth Way, Aquinas is thinking that directedness toward specific effects or a range of effects abounds in the natural world. Happy as he is with the notion of efficient causality, Aquinas thinks that we cannot make sense of this without recourse to the thought that such and such an efficient cause in the world can be invoked to account for something only because we understand how it is directed to producing certain effects (by nature and not by chance). Let me try to put this thought into a historical context concerning causality.

---

[53] Edward Feser, *Aquinas: A Beginner's Guide* (London: Oneworld, 2009), 17.

As I see it, all of us need help on causality from Aristotle and Aquinas, who famously insist on there being four kinds of cause: "material," "formal," "efficient," and "final." But that terminology rightly sounds odd to many people these days, partly because of translation issues. Aristotle's Greek word for "cause" is *aition*. Aquinas's word is *causa*. Yet I do not think that these words are best rendered these days as "cause." That is because when people today hear the word "cause" they think that a cause is always something that brings about a change. So, your typical cause is a hammer that gets a nail into a wall, or whiskey that makes you drunk, or the detergent that makes your clothes clean. These days, when people hear the word "cause," they think only of what Aristotle and Aquinas called "efficient or agent causes." So, no wonder they feel in a fog if someone goes on about material causes, formal causes, and final causes. Consider a rough parallel. Suppose that, for whatever reason, someone can make sense of the word "dog" only when taking a dog to be what Fido and Rover are. Such a person will be at sea if I talk about my having on my shelf six plastic dogs, two metal ones, and three glass ones.

In fact, however, a more reliable rendition into English of Aristotle's *aition* and Aquinas's *causa* is "explanation," where that word is taken to refer to mean what someone provides when asked, "*How come* this, that, or the other?"

How come the expensive crystal glass I just dropped on the stone floor smashed, while the cheap, plastic one just bounced around? *Answer from Aristotle and Aquinas*: Because the crystal glass was made of this stuff (glass) and the other one was made of that stuff (plastic). Hence "material causality/explanation."

Again: *How come* cats behave like *this* while comets behave like *that*? *Answer from Aristotle and Aquinas*: Because cats are things of *this* kind (mammalian mammals of a certain species), while comets are things of *that* kind (icy small solar-system bodies that, when passing close to the Sun warm and begin to release gases). Hence "formal causality/explanation" – explanation in terms of what Aristotle and Aquinas would have called a "substantial form," explanation in terms of what a naturally occurring thing is by nature.

Then again: Who pushed Brian in front of the car? *Answer from Aristotle and Aquinas*: Don't blame us; rather, look to someone else. Hence "efficient or agent causality/explanation."

Finally (no pun intended): Why does such and such display goal-directed behavior? *Answer from Aristotle and Aquinas*: Because it is acting for an end of some kind *given what it is by nature*. Hence "final causality/explanation."

Now, if I understand them correctly, Aristotle and Aquinas are not favoring one kind of "causality" over another. When it comes to what happens in the world, they seem to think that they are all there at the same time, as it were. At any rate, Aquinas (whom I know better than I know Aristotle) certainly thought that if I end up cooking a nice steak, there needs to be something to work on (material cause), something of a particular kind (formal cause), someone doing the cooking (efficient cause), and someone aiming at a juicy dinner before settling down to eat (final cause). As I read Aquinas, he is saying that one and the same phenomenon can be and needs to be explained in at least four different ways, for the sake of completeness. And it is the final cause/explanation of things that he has in mind in his Fifth Way.

Yet he is obviously not here arguing that unintelligent things consciously act with goals in mind. Rather, he is thinking that if I leave a bag of frozen french fries on my polished kitchen floor overnight, I should not in the morning be surprised to find a floor that has been water damaged.

This is where final cause/explanation becomes important for me, as for Aristotle and Aquinas. That is because it is here that you get to the notion that understanding how and why efficient causes act as they do, while producing the effects that they do, is *inseparable* from the notion of things acting for ends given what they are by nature. Here you get to the idea that everything material tends to or aims at an end (maybe many ends depending on circumstances).

Once again, therefore, what should I make of goal-directed activity on the part of things in nature that, unlike John, cannot be doing what they do because they think it intellectually desirable? You might say that this is a "brute fact" for which no account should be sought. But what would you mean by "brute fact" here? Presumably, you would mean "something that raises no causal questions." But the goal-directed activity that I am talking about now surely does raise causal questions. It does not exist of logical necessity. So, it might never have been there. But there it is. So, what could account for it? Surely, not something else in the spatiotemporal universe exhibiting the very activity with which we are now concerned. If not that, however, then what?

Here I would, as Aquinas does, appeal to the notion of practical reason as displayed by people. By "practical reason" I mean reason that we use so as to obtain something that we want. If I want to get quickly from New York to London, I might reason as follows. (1) A plane will get me to London more quickly than a boat. (2) So, I should catch a plane.

The main thing to note about practical reasoning is that it is goal-directed. When engaging in practical reasoning, we are not just performing a function. We are tending to an end by choice. And I think it reasonable to suppose that the tending to an end on the part of nonthinking things can derive only from something with knowledge and choice. For from what else could it derive? One might say that it derives from their nature. Yet the nature now in question (that referred to by Aristotle and Aquinas when they talk about material and formal causation) is not going to explain why we have so much goal-directed activity on the part of nonthinking things as we do. Logically speaking, the universe might have comprised nothing but an unmoving chunk of iron. But it does not. It amounts to something in which causal explanations can be given in terms of the natural and uninhibited tendencies of nonthinking things given their nature. So, I can make sense of Aquinas concluding his Fifth Way by saying that "there is a being with intelligence who directs all natural things to ends, and we call this being 'God.'" He is not here saying that once upon a time some being, possibly now defunct, set things up in nature so that they continue to act for ends. He is thinking of God as actively governing what continues to be God's creation as time goes on. He is saying that when you are presented by goal-directed activity in the natural world, you are presented by what can only be compared to what is going on when people act on the basis of practical reason, by acting with intention. Here I agree with Anthony Kenny when he says:

> It is essential to teleological explanation that it should be in terms of a good to be achieved; yet the good which features in the explanation, at the time of the event to be explained, does not yet exist and indeed may never exist. This is difficult to understand except in the case where the good pre-exists in the conception of the designer: the mind of the designer exists at the appropriate time even if the good designed does not.[54]

Still, Aquinas's Fifth Way does not show that God exists with all the "attributes" traditionally ascribed to God. Nor does it show that there is but one thing that accounts for nonthinking things tending to goals. As the fifth of five ways, it should, I think, be read as a kind of appendix to a set of arguments that Aquinas takes to show that there really is a cause of the continued existence of the universe. Aquinas's Fifth Way makes sense to me on that understanding.

(C) Cosmological Arguments: Some Famous Examples

Cosmological arguments can be divided into two kinds: (1) arguments holding that the universe must be created by God since it *began* to exist and (2) arguments holding that the universe must have a cause *whether or not* it had a beginning.

---

[54] Kenny, *Reason and Religion*, 82.

A contemporary defender of the first line of argument, which he calls "the *Kalām* argument," is William Lane Craig. According to him: (1) Everything that begins to exist must have a cause. (2) The universe began to exist. (3) So, the universe must have a cause. (4) We can speak of the cause of the beginning of the universe as God. Craig thinks that (1) is obviously true. He thinks that (2) is confirmed by scientific research and by philosophical arguments against the suggestion that the universe has existed for an infinite time. He thinks that (3) follows from (1) and (2). And he thinks that (4) is true because a being of great knowledge and power (as God is said to be) would explain the beginning of the universe. Or, as Craig himself puts it:

> Since everything that begins to exist has a cause of its existence, and since the universe began to exist, we conclude, therefore, the universe has a cause of its existence.... Transcending the entire universe there exists a cause which brought the universe into being.... But even more: we may plausibly argue that the cause of the universe is a personal being.... If the universe began to exist, and if the universe is caused, then the cause of the universe must be a personal being who freely chose to create the world.[55]

For a famous defender of the second kind of cosmological argument, we may again turn to Aquinas. He did not think it could be proved that the universe *began* to exist, but he did think that the actual existence of the universe at any time has to derive from something that causes it to exist from second to second. Ever keen on posing questions, Aquinas's view is that we should press our natural tendency to press causal questions to the limit. So, he thinks that, as well as asking what in the universe accounts for what, we should ask ,"What accounts for there being any universe at all?" or "Why is there something rather than nothing at all?" On the assumption that these are proper questions to raise, Aquinas holds that they can be answered only by referring to something distinct from the universe, something that is not a spatiotemporal individual, something that causes the very being of the universe from moment to moment, something that squares with the notion of God as Creator of the universe. Hence, for example, we find him saying this in *Summa theologiae* 1a, 44, 1:

> We are bound to conclude that everything that is at all real is from God. For when we encounter a subject which shares in a reality then this reality must needs be caused there by a thing which possesses it of its nature....

---

[55] William Lane Craig, *The Kalām Cosmological Argument* (London: Macmillan, 1979), 149–51. Craig calls his argument the *Kalām* argument since it finds notable supporters among medieval philosophers belonging to the Islamic *Kalām* school of thought (*kalām* is Arabic for "speech").

God is sheer existence subsisting of his very nature. And such being ...
cannot but be unique, rather as whiteness would be if it subsisted, for its
repetition depends on there being many receiving subjects. We are left with
the conclusion that all things other than God are not their own existence
but share in existence.[56]

Here Aquinas is basically claiming that nothing in the universe exists by
nature and therefore requires a cause of its mere existence, a cause the very
nature of which is to exist.[57] More precisely, he is saying that things in the
universe have it in common that they exist and that this existence common
to them all has to derive from what is not a sharer in existence, as they are.
They could exist only if there were something accounting for the existence of
things that have existence in common with other things, something that can
be thought of as pure and subsisting existence, something *positive* and *real*
whose nature it is to exist.

(D) Comments on Cosmological Arguments

Craig's *Kalām* argument is a valid one. Its conclusion follows from its
premises, which is something well worth stressing. Like Paley's design
argument, however, the *Kalām* argument defended by Craig does not, by
itself, rule out the possibility of the cause to which it argues having ceased to
exist some time after it did its causing. That is because of the argument's
focus on the *beginning* of the universe, not its *continued existence*. Craig
holds that God is timeless and began to exist in time as the universe came
into being, and if he is right, talk about God ceasing to exist is ruled out. But
I am not sure what Craig is committing himself to when conceding that God
entered time having brought about the beginning of the universe. In any
case, the *Kalām* argument does not rule out the possibility of the universe
beginning to exist by virtue of cooperation between a group of some kind.
For plenty of things that begin to exist depend on people or other things
working together.

Still, I find the thesis "Whatever has a beginning of existence must have a
cause" hard to shake off. I agree with Thomas Reid (1710–1796): "*That
neither existence, nor any mode of existence, can begin without a sufficient
cause*, is a principle that appears very early in the mind of man; and it is so

---

[56] I quote from volume 8 of the Blackfriars edition of the *Summa theologiae* (London: Eyre and
Spottiswoode and McGraw Hill Book Company, 1967), 7.

[57] This line of thinking emerges in many texts written by Aquinas. For example, it is present in the
second, third, and fourth of his Five Ways as found in *Summa theologiae*, 1a, 2, 3.

universal, and so firmly rooted in human nature, that the most determined skepticism cannot eradicate."[58] One determined skeptic who wrote against the principle (though he accepted it in practice) was David Hume. According to him:

> As all distinct ideas are separable from each other, and as the ideas of cause and effect are evidently distinct, 'twill be easy for us to conceive any object to be non-existent this moment, and existent the next, without conjoining to it the distinct idea of a cause or productive principle. The separation, therefore, of the idea of a cause from that of a beginning of existence is plainly possible for the imagination, and consequently the actual separation of these objects is so far possible that it implies no contradiction or absurdity.[59]

In reply to this argument, I can only agree with what Elizabeth Anscombe has said about it:

> If I say I can imagine a rabbit coming into being without a parent rabbit, well and good: I imagine a rabbit coming into being, and our observing that there is no parent rabbit about. But what am I to imagine if I imagine a rabbit coming into being without a cause?
> Well, I just imagine a rabbit coming into being. That this *is* the imagination of a rabbit coming into being without a cause is nothing but, as it were, the *title* of the picture. Indeed I can form an image and give my picture that title. But from my being able to do *that*, nothing whatever follows about what it is possible to suppose "without contradiction or absurdity" as holding in reality.[60]

When it comes to the *Kalām* cosmological argument, though, there is a problem with the claim that the universe began to exist. Some philosophers (Craig being one) have argued that the universe cannot have a history going backward to infinity since one cannot count down from infinity to arrive at the present. But that argument presupposes that there is some *starting point* from which to begin counting, which is precisely what someone who thinks

---

[58] Ronald E. Beanblossom and Keith Lehrer, eds., *Thomas Reid's Inquiry and Essays* (Indianapolis: Bobbs-Merrill, 1975), 330.

[59] David Hume, *A Treatise of Human Nature*, ed. L. A. Selby-Bigge (Oxford: Oxford University Press, 1965), 79f. I note that Hume did not subscribe to the principle *in practice* on his say-so. In a letter written in 1754, he remarks: "I never asserted so absurd a Proposition *as that anything might arise without a cause*: I only maintain'd, that our Certainty of the Falsehood of that proposition proceeded neither from Intuition nor Demonstration; but from another Source." See J. Y. T. Greig, ed., *The Letters of David Hume* (Oxford: Oxford University Press, 1932), 1:187.

[60] G. E. M. Anscombe, "'Whatever Has a Beginning of Existence Must Have a Cause': Hume's Argument Exposed," *Analysis* 34 (1974): 150.

that the universe is backwardly infinite is denying. Many scientists have argued that the universe has expanded from a "big bang" some 14 billion years ago. And for all I know, they are right. But then I wonder whether the big bang was an *absolute* beginning of the universe rather than a state of the universe with something before it that scientists have not yet detected. Being scientifically illiterate when it comes to cosmology, I am agnostic when it comes to the second premise of the *Kalām* argument. I also think that the argument as a whole moves too quickly to its conclusion. For even if we accept that whatever has a beginning of existence must have a cause, and that the universe had a beginning, why should we suppose that the cause of the beginning of the universe is what either classical theists or theistic personalists take God to be? As I asked above, why should we suppose that what accounted for the beginning of the universe still exists? Many things can account for the beginning of a thing's existence. My parents accounted for my beginning to exist. But they are both dead now. So, why presume that whatever caused the universe to begin to exist is still around in any serious way? I am not saying that defenders of the *Kalām* argument cannot have good answers to these questions. But the argument on its own (as I have presented it) does not incorporate any such answers.

I am, however, less agnostic when it comes to what thinkers such as Aquinas say as to why there is something rather than nothing *whether or not the universe had a beginning*. That is because I just am struck by the question "How come *something* rather than *nothing at all*?" This I think is a perfectly valid question to raise, though I also think that if we try to answer it by using the word "God," we do not understand what we are talking about.

I am now regarding "How come X?" as a question seeking an efficient cause (as explained above), and I am thinking that to take it seriously is, in a sense, to engage in an act of faith. Some philosophers have denied that there is any material world. Others have denied that causes are related to effects in anything but an accidental way. But your average scientist does not think in these terms. Scientists presume the existence of a material world and they think it proper to keep pressing causal questions while trying to arrive at explanations. They do not try to prove that there is a world to examine; nor do they try to prove that we can explain what we take to be effects as springing from the nature of their causes. They get on with the business of pressing causal questions. They presume (or have faith) in the validity of science. I share this presumption to the extent that I think it right to keep asking "How come?" unless our employment of this question is somehow absurd. I also think that the question can be pressed so as to ask how come science is possible at all. For why not ask, "How come any universe at all?"

while meaning not "What kick-started the universe in the past?" but "Why
does it exist from second to second?" I might wonder, "How come my cat?"
and be satisfied when referred to its parents. I might wonder how come cats
exist, and be satisfied when referred to an explanation concerning the
emergence of cats as a species and the conditions that allow them to survive.
So, why not keep pressing the "How come?" question so as to ask, "How
come the universe at all?" This is clearly not a scientific question, and its
answer cannot lie in anything we can note about how and why things in the
universe operate. Some philosophers have claimed that the existence of the
universe is a "brute fact," that the universe is "just there" and there is
nothing more to be said. Yet this claim seems to me as arbitrary as the
claim that cats *are just there* and we should not inquire why that is so.
Wittgenstein once said: "Not *how* the world is, is the mystical, but *that* it
exists."[61] If by this he meant that he had time for the question "How come
the universe rather than nothing?," I agree with him. You may suggest that
the question is an odd one just because it is not a scientific one that asks
what is doing what to what within the universe. But not all serious questions
are scientific ones. "Is there a material world?" is a question over which
many philosophers have anguished, and not without reason. But it is not a
scientific question. It cannot be answered by conducting experiments in a
laboratory, or something like that. For scientists presume the reality of the
material world whenever they are conducting experiments and so on. You
will not find any scientist trying to argue for the existence of the material
world while trying to say what in the world does what to what, and why.

Some people have suggested that "How come something rather than
nothing?" is a misguided question since *nothing* is not a serious *alternative*
to anything. You might think that there is sense in the question "Why is
John *sick* rather than *well*?" since it is asking us to explain why *this* state of
affairs obtains rather than *another*. And you might think that there being
nothing is not an alternative state of affairs in any sense. But natural
theologians who ask, "How come something rather than nothing?" are not
thinking of *nothing* as a state of affairs. They are not saying that *nothing* is
something that might have *been*. They are simply noting that we live in a
universe that might never have existed and that its mere existence from
second to second raises the question "How come?" Yet how can that claim
be defended? I have defended it above by suggesting that it coheres with our
practice of seeking causal explanations. If we don't feel happy with "Dogs are

[61] Ludwig Wittgenstein, *Tractatus logico-philosophicus*, trans. C .K. Ogden (London: Routledge &
Kegan Paul, 1922), 6.44.

just there," we should be equally unhappy with "The universe is *just there*."
But I think there is more to say than this when it comes to "How come
something rather than nothing at all?"

I think this because there is a distinction to be made between *what*
something is and whether or not it *exists*. As scientists get on with their
business, they aim to come closer and closer to an account of what various
things in the world are. So, experts on cats might well be able to deliver
learned (though maybe incomplete) accounts of what it is to be a cat. They
will not be telling us what the word "cat" means as a specialist in mythology
might tell us what "unicorn" means. They will not be giving us a dictionary
definition, for dictionaries often provide definitions of what does not exist
(e.g., "wizard" and "unicorn"). By examining cats in the world, they will be
telling us what *existing* cats are by *nature*. As Aquinas would have said, they
will be trying to get us closer and closer to understanding what actual cats
are *essentially*.

But having such an understanding does not guarantee the existence of any
particular cat (e.g., mine, known as "Sweetie"). Imagine a cat expert giving a
learned lecture on the nature of cats and then inviting questions. Also
imagine the first question being "*Which* cat were you talking about?" Our
expert will rightly reply, "I wasn't talking about any particular cat. I was
talking about what cats are by nature." And I take the rightness of that reply
to show that knowing what cats are by nature (knowing what is essential to
being a cat) is not something that comes with the knowledge that any
particular existing cat has to exist. We cannot know what cats *actually* are
if cats do not exist. So, we might say that all essences are actual – meaning
that to say what the essence of a cat is would be impossible if there were no
real cats to examine. We might define "wizard" as "someone who is able to
work magic." But this would be a merely *nominal* definition telling us
nothing but the *meaning of a word*. We can, however, contrast nominal
definitions with *real* definitions (as in "Cats, in the family Felidae, are a
species of mammal exhibiting features X, Y, Z, etc."). I take real definitions
to be telling (or trying to tell us) what actually existing things of certain kinds
are by nature. Yet such definitions will not entail that any existing individual
of the kind defined has to exist *by nature*. If to know what Sweetie is by
nature is to know that his essence includes existence, then Sweetie would
have *always existed* and would *never cease* to exist, which is not the case.

In this sense, the actual existence of anything in the universe is distinguishable from its nature or essence. In this sense, nothing in the universe
exists by nature, which has to mean that the universe as a whole does not
exist by nature since the universe is nothing but the sum of its parts. So, how

come the universe rather than nothing at all? I think that this is a sensible question to ask and that there must therefore be an answer to it. I conclude that there *has* to be (not that there *probably* is) something that accounts for there being any universe at all – anything that we can take to be the potential object of scientific inquiry. I mean that to think that there has to be an answer to "How come something rather than nothing?" is not to think that there is a scientific hypothesis to appeal to in order to account for the universe. It is to think that there *has* to be an efficient cause of some sort that accounts for science being possible *at all*.

But a cause of what kind? That is a question I shall be turning to in my part of Chapter 4. For now I leave you with the following suggestions. (1) One cannot establish the existence of God by attending to the meaning of the word "God." (2) There are problems with the view that we have reason to claim that God exists because some people have directly perceived God. (3) The argument from design presented by Paley does not give us good reason to suppose that God exists. (4) Aquinas's argument from non-thinking things in nature tending to ends works as an argument for the existence of God, but only if it supplemented by arguments showing that this end-directed activity derives from a single cause. (5) The *Kālam* cosmological argument does not show that the beginning of the universe (even if it had one) is explicable in monotheistic terms or in terms of something which continues to exist. (6) We should wonder why there is any universe at all and at any time, and the only possible answer to that question is that the universe continually derives from something that causes it to exist from second to second, something that exists by nature, something whose essence is to exist.

4

Against God

Michael Ruse

PROGRESS

I TAKE IT THAT, WHETHER OR NOT WE ARE NECESSARY EXISTENTS, within the Christian story we are necessary. Not much point in the creation if God did not make beings in his image. The trouble is that Darwinian evolution gives cause for worry about our necessity – within the scheme, that is. We have evolved. But did we have to evolve? There are reasons to think not. On the one hand, natural selection is relativistic. Having big brains has costs, not the least to have access to large chunks of protein – for example, the bodies of other animals. At once you run into the (Jack) Sepkoski problem, so named after an important paleobiologist of the late twentieth century. "I see intelligence as just one of a variety of adaptations among tetrapods for survival. Running fast in a herd while being as dumb as shit, I think, is a very good adaptation for survival."[1] On the other hand, against the necessity of humans, there is the randomness of new variation, mutation. This is not to say that mutations are not caused – they are – but that they don't appear to order. A new predator comes on the scene. Dark gray camouflage would be very helpful. As like as not, you will get pink or green. The only reason why this is not fatal to the whole process is that populations always carry much variation – so if the predator appears, although you might not have available the right camouflage colors, you may have variation to make you unpalatable, or difficult to find, including an urge to get away entirely. Again, though, big brains are not going to be the only or even the best option.

---

[1] M. Ruse, *Monad to Man: The Concept of Progress in Evolutionary Biology* (Cambridge, MA: Harvard University Press, 1996), 485.

So, no guaranteed humans. No Christianity? Not so fast! Many Darwinians, including the master himself, think you can get progress. It is certainly the case that many if not most think that there is progress. Herbert Spencer, Darwin's contemporary, adopted a criterion of progress (not so very different from Darwin's) that involved division and specialization, or, as he called it, a move from the homogeneous to the heterogeneous:

> Now we propose in the first place to show, that this law of organic progress is the law of all progress. Whether it be in the development of the Earth, in the development of Life upon its surface, in the development of Society, of Government, of Manufactures, of Commerce, of Language, Literature, Science, Art, this same evolution of the simple into the complex, through successive differentiations, holds throughout. From the earliest traceable cosmical changes down to the latest results of civilization, we shall find that the transformation of the homogeneous into the heterogeneous is that in which Progress essentially consists.[2]

In Spencer's eyes, everything obeys this law. Compared with other animals, humans are more complex or heterogeneous; compared with savages, Europeans more complex or heterogeneous; and compared with the tongues of other peoples, the English language more complex or heterogeneous.

In the early part of the twentieth century, by which time Mendelian genetics had appeared on the scene, Julian Huxley, the grandson of Thomas Henry Huxley (Darwin's great supporter) and older brother of Aldous Huxley (the novelist), argued that the key to understanding evolution lies in control and independence – basically the ability to manipulate one's environment and to break loose from its constraints. Thus judged, humans are clearly the winners in the race to the top. On the one hand: "It should be clear that if natural selection can account for adaptation and for long-range trends of specialization, it can account for progress too. Progressive changes have obviously given their owners advantages which have enabled them to become dominant."[3] On the other hand, Huxley saw an inevitability to the upward rise of humankind. "One somewhat curious fact emerges from a survey of biological progress as culminating for the evolutionary moment in the dominance of Homo sapiens. It could apparently have pursued no other general course than that which it has historically followed."[4]

---

[2] H. Spencer, "Progress: Its Law and Cause," *Westminster Review* 67 (1857): 244–67, 245.
[3] J. S. Huxley, *Evolution: The Modern Synthesis* (London: Allen and Unwin, 1942), 568.
[4] Huxley, *Evolution*, 569.

What about today? There are lots of thoughts of biological progress and claims that link it to modern evolutionary biology. Edward O. Wilson, already introduced as today's most distinguished living evolutionist, is open in his fervent belief in biological progress. "The overall average across the history of life has moved from the simple and few to the more complex and numerous. During the past billion years, animals as a whole evolved upward in body size, feeding and defensive techniques, brain and behavioral complexity, social organization, and precision of environmental control – in each case farther from the nonliving state than their simpler antecedents did."[5] Adding: "Progress, then, is a property of the evolution of life as a whole by almost any conceivable intuitive standard, including the acquisition of goals and intentions in the behavior of animals."

Why progress? Why progress in a Darwinian world? Darwin himself thought that natural selection really does make for upward change, because the winners overall will be better than the losers. And this ties in with the definition of progress.

> If we look at the differentiation and specialisation of the several organs of each being when adult (and this will include the advancement of the brain for intellectual purposes) as the best standard of highness of organisation, natural selection clearly leads towards highness; for all physiologists admit that the specialisation of organs, inasmuch as they perform in this state their functions better, is an advantage to each being; and hence the accumulation of variations tending towards specialisation is within the scope of natural selection.[6]

Today, like Wilson, Richard Dawkins is very much in favor of progress. "Directionalist common sense surely wins on the very long time scale: once there was only blue-green slime and now there are sharp-eyed metazoa."[7] Picking up on themes in Darwin, Dawkins argues that evolution often involves "arms races," where lines of organisms compete against each other, in the process getting ever-more refined adaptations. As the predator gets faster, so the prey gets faster. Dawkins points out that, more and more, today's arms races rely on computer technology rather than brute power, and – in the animal world – Dawkins translates this into bigger and bigger brains.[8] No prizes are given for guessing who has won. Rather unkindly

[5] E. O. Wilson, *The Diversity of Life* (Cambridge, MA: Harvard University Press, 1992), 187.

[6] C. Darwin, *Origin of Species*, 3rd ed. (London: John Murray, 1961), 134.

[7] R. Dawkins and J. R. Krebs, "Arms Races between and within Species," *Proceedings of the Royal Society of London, B* 205 (1979): 489–511, 508.

[8] R. Dawkins, *The Blind Watchmaker* (New York: Norton, 1986).

picking on the hippopotamus, Dawkins does some calculations to show that we humans are twenty-three times as intelligent as the hippo! It is just as well that its main occupation in life is wallowing in the mud of the Zambezi.

Is this enough? I am not sure you get around the Sepkoski problem. Sometimes you can be too clever by half and a simpler solution is better. I certainly don't see you get the kind of guarantee of humans that Christianity demands. I doubt that Dawkins really thinks that either. So here is another reason for the person without faith to wonder if they must necessarily accept Christianity. I suppose if the hypothesis of multiverses is correct – through time and space there are an infinite number of actual universes – then since it is possible for humans to evolve by natural selection – we humans show that – humans would necessarily evolve by natural selection, an infinite number of times in fact. A point that, I suspect, is a little rich for the Christian. Not to mention the worry about all of those near misses. Billions and billions of planets with creatures from science-fiction novels, like the Eloi and Morlocks in *The Time Machine* by H. G. Wells. Pity that the Bible doesn't give us more insight.

EVIL

We come to the big one, the problem of evil. Why Heinrich Himmler? Why the Lisbon earthquake? Start with faith. The problem of evil, at least in certain respects, is no problem for some religions. If we follow convention, dividing the problem into human evil – Himmler – and natural evil – Lisbon – then for a religion like Buddhism, natural evil is hardly an evil. Nasty things happen. That is the way of the world. I am not sure that moral evil, at least theologically, is an evil either. Humans just are as they are. Bad people are going to get it in their next incarnations – Hitler has a long future as a codfish – but overall there is no moral implication about the fact that people are evil. The moral or other implications are for individual people. For a religion like Christianity, however, evil is a problem. Why would a good God make evil people? Why would a good God make cancer and earthquakes? Have we another very good reason to reject the Christian God?[9] Start with moral evil.

Moral evil comes from free will. Himmler did not have to send literally millions of Jews to the gas chambers, but he did. How do you explain this? Philosophers are divided on this. Some, like David Hume, are *compatibilists*.

[9] M. Ruse, *Can a Darwinian Be a Christian? The Relationship between Science and Religion* (Cambridge: Cambridge University Press, 2001).

They believe in free will. They also believe in causal determinism. It is just that they don't think the two are opposed. The opposite of free will is constraint. If I am bound, then I have no control, no free will. They would probably say the same if one was hypnotized. One is not acting freely of one's own choice. They would point out that far from causal forces being a problem, they are essential. The person who is truly free is the person who decides to devote their life to others. The person who is not free is the one who is so much a tool of the emotions that they cannot think of others. Surely, education is a factor here – it had better be, otherwise my whole life is a waste! – and that education is a cause of my doing good. Lack of education, no discipline as a child, and I am spoiled and selfish. Moreover, to say that causes are unimportant leads to craziness, not freedom. If there is nothing leading to my actions, then I am a madman, not a responsible being.

Some, like Immanuel Kant, are *libertarians* – where it is understood that being a libertarian is not being like Ayn Rand, wanting no social constraints, but being in some sense outside the causal nexus.

> Since the conception of causality involves that of laws, according to which, by something that we call cause, something else, namely the effect, must be produced; hence, although freedom is not a property of the will depending on physical laws, yet it is not for that reason lawless; on the contrary it must be a causality acting according to immutable laws, but of a peculiar kind; otherwise a free will would be an absurdity.[10]

A popular way of going at this sort of thing is to distinguish between reasons and causes. We are all part of the causal picture; but, insofar as we are free, we are relying on something different: reasons. The reasons why Hitler attacked Russia were his felt need for more space – *Lebensraum* – his confidence after the conquer of France, and his sense of divine destiny. These are value notions, not causes.

There are huge debates on these matters, starting with the claim – to which I am sympathetic – that there is no argument why reasons should not be causes.[11] Why is Hitler's sense of divine destiny not a cause as well as a reason? The main point of importance here is that Christians are all over the place on free will, with some libertarians and some compatibilists. Kant, for a start, is a libertarian! I suspect many Catholics are likewise. It was the conservative Catholic convert Elizabeth Anscombe who made much of the

---

[10] I. Kant, *Foundations of the Metaphysics of Morals* (Indianapolis: Bobbs-Merrill, 1959), section 3.
[11] D. Davidson, "Actions, Reasons and Causes," *Journal of Philosophy* 60 (1963): 685–700.

reasons/causes dichotomy.[12] My feeling is that Quakers tend this way. They believe in the "inner light" or "that of God in every person," and if God is not Absolute Freedom, then I don't know what is. Calvinists, on the other hand, with their beliefs about predestination, tend to compatibilism. America's greatest theologian, Jonathan Edwards, was strong on this.

What this surely means is that the Christian cannot dismiss me as irrelevant whatever position I take on free will. Either way, I am in the tradition. As it happens, as a staunch Darwinian, expectedly I am on the compatibilist side. We are what we are because of the laws of nature, natural selection, and all of that. However, what is interesting is that as a Darwinian I want strongly to affirm the existence and importance of free will. I think people like Jerry Coyne, who deny we have any free will, are just silly.[13] As Dawkins feels able to generalize about philosophers, so I would say that the better the biologist, the greater the tin ear for philosophical problems. The whole point is that Darwinism insists on human free will – as Dan Dennett rightly says, we have all the free will that we need. Let us agree that plants don't have free will. Even if they do something, they cannot do anything except follow the laws of botany – a vine doesn't decide if it will climb the wall, a dandelion does not decide to cast its seeds on the air on a windy day. Move to humans and to the lower forms. Oysters and mussels are a bit like vegetables. So much so that Peter Singer eats them!

What about ants? They are what evolutionists call r-selected, meaning they have lots of offspring but don't put much effort into parental care. They don't learn what to do, they are programmed to do what they do. Take leaf-cutter ants. They send out foragers from the nests. They find leaves, cut them up, and head for home. How do they know where home is? Because they have left chemical – pheromone – trails. If it rains, and the trails are washed away, the foragers are stuck and don't get home. It doesn't really matter because the queen produces so many offspring that the loss of a few is simply the price of keeping the nest or hive functioning. Humans are different. We are K-selected. We have just a few offspring and raise them with massive parental care. That means we must have the ability to readjust as circumstances change. We cannot afford to lose two or three children every time it rains. As Dennett says, we are like a Mars rover.[14] It comes to a rock or a canyon. It doesn't just keep going. It reassesses and goes around. And the

[12] G. E. M. Anscombe, *Intention* (Cambridge, MA: Harvard University Press, [1957] 2000).
[13] J. A. Coyne, *Faith vs. Fact: Why Science and Religion Are Incompatible* (New York: Viking, 2015).
[14] D. C. Dennett, *Elbow Room: The Varieties of Free Will Worth Wanting* (Cambridge, MA: MIT Press, 1984).

point is that it does all this while being fully causally determined. The laws of nature are not suspended when a Mars rover meets a rock or canyon. In this very real sense, thanks to Darwinism, we do have free will.

Push now back to the theological issue of free will, given we are the creation of a good God. What now of Heinrich Himmler? The obvious question is why are we not good all the time? God is totally good. He is also totally free. We are made in his image. Why not us? The traditional answer is because we are tainted by original sin. That is why Jesus had to die as a sacrifice on the Cross: substitutional atonement. "For as by one man's disobedience many were made sinners, so by the obedience of one shall many be made righteous."[15] God made us free, which is a good thing, even though it has led to great evil. Some, like Alvin Plantinga, add – what is to me the totally incredible claim – that the subsequent death of God on the Cross was itself such a good thing that God, even though he knew we would sin, felt in the end the good outweighs the bad. *Felix culpa*. In the words of Augustine: "For God judged it better to bring good out of evil than not to permit any evil to exist."[16]

For a Darwinian, none of this will work. We have already dealt reasons for the implausibility of original sin. There simply was no unique Adam and Eve, first sinless and then sinful. At any point, humans were nice and nasty, as were their parents and children and everyone else in the species. And if you go back to when we were apes, they are not entirely chummy either. Some are really rough and nasty. So original sin, at least as traditionally conceived, is out. This is not to say that we don't have an innate tendency to sin. We do, and, as Himmler shows, some of us have more of a tendency than others. Likewise, as Sophie Scholl of the White Rose group shows, some of us have more of a tendency for noble acts than others. But it is not sin brought on by a deliberate act of disobedience. Hence, in tandem there was no point in Jesus making a sacrifice for us on the Cross. Quite apart, for the nonbeliever, why we should be tainted by the act of someone long ago. It is true that sometimes the sins of the parents are visited on the children – child-abusers often have horrific histories of having themselves been abused as children – but Vati and Mutti Himmler cannot take all the blame for the Holocaust. Sometimes good people have awful children. I feel a bit that way myself some days.

---

[15] Romans 5:19.

[16] St. Augustine, *The Augustine Catechism: The Enchiridion on Faith Hope and Charity* (New York: New City Press, 2008), chapter 11.

You can adopt the Incarnational theology of Irenaeus of Lyons, seeing the death on the Cross as the ultimate act of love, for us to follow. "He said, 'The one who showed him mercy.' Jesus said to him, 'Go and do likewise.'"[17] Knowing that we are not alone. "I am with you always, to the end of the age."[18] This is popular on the Orthodox side of Christianity. Quakers like it also. The fact remains that we are both nice and nasty and supposedly the creation of a good God in his image. Since we are now supposing that, whatever the ultimate role of God, at the more proximate level humans are part of the natural order of things – we are not the instantaneous, miraculous creation of a good God in his own image – perhaps we can turn profitably to the other limb of the discussion, natural evil. In a sense, we are saying that moral evil is part of the natural processes of the world. Is this a helpful move? It certainly starts to make sense of moral evil. The struggle for existence is not a particularly nice phenomenon. Darwin himself worried about this. "I cannot persuade myself that a beneficent & omnipotent God would have designedly created the Ichneumonidæ with the express intention of their feeding within the living bodies of caterpillars, or that a cat should play with mice."[19] The fact that humans are nasty as well as nice fits into all of this. Sometimes being nice pays good dividends. Darwin saw this.

> It must not be forgotten that although a high standard of morality gives but a slight or no advantage to each individual man and his children over the other men of the same tribe, yet that an advancement in the standard of morality and an increase in the number of well-endowed men will certainly give an immense advantage to one tribe over another.[20]

Sometimes being nasty pays good dividends. If you are attacked by another tribe, for instance. Or you might decide to cheat. A roll in the hay with a colleague's wife seems a lot more attractive than the feeling of virtue from exercising self-restraint. Or being nasty is the side-product of good intentions. Without in any sense condoning the behavior of Catholic priests, I can only say that any organization that makes a practice of taking impressionable late teenagers and raising them for a life without sex is really asking for it. For me, the real miracle is that sexual abuse is not more widespread than we think. Perhaps it is. Of course, no one denies – often thanks to culture – things get out of hand. One very much suspects that, at one point,

---

[17] Luke 10:37.   [18] Matthew 28:20.

[19] Letter to Asa Gray, May 22, 1860, in C. Darwin, *The Correspondence of Charles Darwin* (Cambridge: Cambridge University Press, 1985–), 8:224.

[20] C. Darwin, *The Descent of Man, and Selection in Relation to Sex* (London: John Murray, 1871), 1:166.

there was real biological advantage to being suspicious of strangers. The real threat to early bands of hominins was often other bands of hominins, looking for one's women and other goods. This hardly is a full explanation of Himmler's attitudes and actions toward Jews, but one can see how it might all have got started. One is certainly not now claiming that the Holocaust was justified by natural selection any more than that the tail of the peacock is a great aid to flying.

Two questions now arise. First, why did a good God choose such an awful way of making organisms, of making human beings in particular? Why not some warm and friendly manner like Lamarckism – the inheritance of acquired characteristics? Instead of countless giraffes starving to death because their necks were not long enough to reach the leaves, only the fit getting the food and then reproducing, giraffes just stretched and stretched, they got their food, and the good features were passed on without anyone suffering. Richard Dawkins answered this one.[21] Lamarckism is false. So is every other proposed mechanism, like jumps from one form to another – fox into dog. Jumps usually spell disaster, like dwarfism from typical-heighted people. It could well be that natural selection brought on by the struggle for existence is the only game in town – the only possible game in town. God could no more have created humans without natural selection – with the consequence that we are going to be nasty as well as nice – than he could have made $2 + 2 = 5$.

Agree that this is no real limitation on God's power, any more than that he cannot make $2 + 2 = 5$, although it is worth noting that Descartes thought that God could make $2 + 2 = 5$! Does this render Incarnational theology worthless? God's death on the Cross might make us feel guilty. It is not going to stop us from being sinners. Just as many Darwinians are convinced that there is biological progress, so many think there is cultural – including moral – progress. Steven Pinker, evolutionist at Harvard, is one such person. For all the inclination to violence, over the years we have restrained ourselves and today in fact we are a lot less violent than we used to be. "Believe it or not – and I know that most people today do not – violence has declined over long stretches of time, and today we may be living in the most peaceable era in our species' existence."[22] This has had significant consequences. "Daily existence is very different if you always have to worry about being abducted,

[21] R. Dawkins, "Universal Darwinism," in *Evolution from Molecules to Men*, ed. D. S. Bendall, 403–25 (Cambridge: Cambridge University Press, 1983).
[22] S. Pinker, *The Better Angels of Our Nature: Why Violence Has Declined* (New York: Viking, 2011), xxi.

raped, or killed, and it's hard to develop sophisticated arts, learning, or commerce if the institutions that support them are looted and burned as quickly as they are built." Pinker delves into various causes, ending by quoting his (and my) favorite author.

> As man advances in civilisation, and small tribes are united into larger communities, the simplest reason would tell each individual that he ought to extend his social instincts and sympathies to all the members of the same nation, though personally unknown to him. This point being once reached, there is only an artificial barrier to prevent his sympathies extending to the men of all nations and races.[23]

Perhaps Darwin and Pinker are right. I only wish I could feel more sanguine given the world today. To me it seems hopelessly naïve to suppose that in the next – let us say – 2,000 years, a moment in evolutionary time, no band of fanatics will ever get access to a nuclear weapon and let it off. I hope I am wrong. I shall not see but others will.

I have tried to be fair and to show that – although there are certainly major issues – Darwinism is not implacably opposed to all Christian thinking about evil. Why then should I conclude that evil is the problem that sinks Christianity? If I had faith, I doubt I would think that it does sink Christianity. I would refer to the mystery of the transcendent God. "For I know that my Redeemer lives, and that at the last he will stand upon the earth."[24] My position would be very much in the spirit of the God of Job. "Where were you when I laid the foundation of the earth? Tell me, if you have understanding. Who determined its measurements – surely you know! Or who stretched the line upon it? On what were its bases sunk, or who laid its cornerstone when the morning stars sang together and all the heavenly beings shouted for joy?"[25] I would follow this with a verse from my favorite chapter of the Bible: "For now we see in a mirror, dimly, but then we will see face to face. Now I know only in part; then I will know fully, even as I have been fully known."[26] And if more is needed, I would quote the poet Keats: "Call the world if you Please 'The vale of Soul-making.'"[27] Whatever the meaning of it all, God has his purposes and they are for our good.

Why should one assume that God's love is just like human love? That is the way of theistic personalism. A point, incidentally, that is pertinent to a

[23] Pinker, *Better Angels*, 671, quoting Darwin, *Descent of Man*, 1, 100–101.   [24] Job 19:25.
[25] Job 38:4–7.   [26] I Corinthians 13:12.
[27] From John Keats's letter to his brother and sister-in-law, George and Georgiana Keats, written on April 21, 1819.

topic, akin to the problem of evil, that, in recent years, has absorbed much time and attention: the so-called problem of God's hiddenness.[28] Supposedly, if God is good and loves us, he would never make a regular person ignorant of his existence. But there are such people – Michael Ruse! – and so God cannot exist. To which, on behalf of the Christian, I make the same response to that of the problem of evil. Christian tradition denies that God's love is necessarily identical to human love and so he should have made us know him as might be the case for humans. It may well be part of God's plan that some of us should labor in this life without knowing him.[29] I might add that, as a nonbeliever, I am not much myself inclined to invoke the divine hiddenness argument in support. As one who has declared himself an existentialist in the sense of Jean-Paul Sartre, meaning that whether or not God exists it is for us to create meaning to our lives, I find the thought that God would permit our ignorance quite to be expected.[30] My puzzle is more why he feels the need to expose himself to any of us! I would add, somewhat sourly, that the huge literature that this pseudo-problem has generated – literature that makes little or no attempt to look at Christian theology – suggests to me that analytic philosophers have altogether too much time on their hands.

Back to evil. In the end, sympathetic as I am to the Christian approach, one that stresses the ineffability of the Creator, my objections of Chapter 2 are decisive. For the believer, the thought that God's love can allow evil is possible – more than that, it is a central element of belief. For the non-believer, the thought that love can permit such happenings is simply not plausible. I don't have faith. Hence, in the end, I just don't see a God of any kind being prepared to create if he had thought through the consequences to the full. Harry Shaw was a five-year-old boy who loved motor racing and worshipped Lewis Hamilton, the current Formula One champion, so much so that Hamilton dedicated to Harry his 2019 victory in the Spanish Grand Prix and arranged that a Mercedes, Hamilton's team car, be sent over to

---

[28] J. L. Schellenberg, *Divine Hiddenness and Human Reason* (Ithaca: Cornell University Press, 1993).

[29] M. Rea, *The Hiddenness of God* (Oxford: Oxford University Press, 2018).

[30] "Existentialism is not so much an atheism in the sense that it would exhaust itself attempting to demonstrate the nonexistence of God; rather, it affirms that even if God were to exist, it would make no difference – that is our point of view. It is not that we believe that God exists, but we think that the real problem is not one of his existence; what man needs is to rediscover himself and to comprehend that nothing can save him from himself, not even valid proof of the existence of God" (J.-P. Sartre, *Existentialism and Humanism* (New York: Haskell House, 1948), 56, based on a lecture given in 1945).

Harry that he might see it and sit in the seat. Harry had Ewing's sarcoma, a rare form of bone cancer, and died on June 1, 2019. After Harry's death, the family posted:

> "Losing Harry means our happy family unit of 4 now becomes 3. We lose our firstborn child; our two-year-old daughter Georgia loses her brother who she will probably never remember; and the wider family lose their first grandchild and nephew.

> "We would like to say Harry died in peace and comfort; to an extent he did, dying at home in his own bed surrounded by his toys and the people he loved.

> "But the actual truth is the last few weeks of Harry's life were marked by terrible pain and suffering that no human, not least a 5-year-old boy, should endure."[31]

God, if such there be, is either inadequate, indifferent, or just plain malicious. I don't believe in God. I don't believe I should try to believe in God. I am not a blind man when all around me have sight. An element of self-deception is at work.

Brian Davies

INTRODUCTION

"How come the universe instead of nothing?" is a valid question to raise, and its answer has to be something that makes everything in the universe to exist for as long as it exists. But can we refer this something as "God"? And can we know what God is? What follows from me now is chiefly devoted to arguments against God's existence. Before I get to them, however, I need to say more than I already have concerning what I take God to be.

WHAT IS GOD?

It has often been said that God *explains* why things are as they are in the world/universe. Sometimes it is said that arguments for the existence of God should be arguments for a "best explanation." But I worry about this way of talking. For an explanation is something we understand *better* than *what we take it* to explain. Explanations dispel puzzlement. When we recognize that we have an explanation, we are thinking, "Of course; that *would* account for

---

[31] "Harry Shaw: Lewis Hamilton's 'Spirit Angel' Boy Dies," BBC News, June 4, 2019, www.bbc .com/news/uk-england-surrey-48506434.

such and such; that's what one would *expect* to account for such and such."
If we explain symptoms X, Y, and Z in terms of virus A, we are drawing on
our knowledge of A to account for what previously baffled us. In this sense,
an explanation is understood *better* than what we invoke it to explain. Yet to
say that God accounts for the existence of the universe surely cannot be
understood as a claim to understand God better than we understand things
in the universe. It is not as though we could think, "But *of course*: God is *just*
what we would *expect* to create a universe." I do not see how we can be thought
to understand God better than anything *in* the universe or the universe *as a
whole*. Not if God accounts for the existence of all the varied things that the
universe contains. So, I think that reasoning to God's existence has to begin not
with a grasp of what God *is*, but a grasp of what God has *produced*. The
existence of the universe presents a puzzle. How come it exists over and against
nothing at all? And I invoke the word "God" in this context because of the
familiar nominal definition of God as "that which accounts for the sheer
existence of the universe from second to second." But I am not claiming to
understand what God is in any serious sense. I am a Roman Catholic, but
I entirely agree with the Protestant *Westminster Confession of Faith* when it
says (7:2), "The distance between God and the creature is so great" that
reasonable people "could never have any fruition of him as their blessedness
and reward, but by some voluntary condescension on God's part."[32]

Is there, however, any reasonable way of trying to say what God is apart
from "voluntary condescension"? In one sense I do not think that there is.
That is because I think that knowing what something is amounts to grasping
its nature or essence. Experts on cats can say what cats are by nature. But
how did they get to the point of being able to do that? By long and careful
study of individual cats. By developing a science of cats. Yet there can be no
comparable science of God if God accounts for the sheer existence of the
universe. In this sense, we do not know what God is. But does this conclusion mean that we can say nothing *true* concerning God other than that God
makes the universe to exist? In response to this question, I think that we can
at least start by *truly* noting what God *cannot* be.

WHAT GOD IS NOT

For one thing, if God accounts for the existence of the universe from second
to second, then God cannot be a material object, for if God were that, God

---

[32] Here I assume that the *Westminster Confession* is referring to divine revelation.

would be part of the universe. So, God is an immaterial cause (hard though that is to make sense of; anyway, we cannot *picture* an immaterial cause).

In addition, and as I have previously suggested, God cannot be an individual subject sharing a nature with other things. For if God accounts for the existence of the universe, then God accounts for the existence of all that we can understand as individual things sharing a nature with other things. Were God to be like one of these, God would be one among many possibly nonexisting things, not that which accounts for there being any such things at all. If God is the immaterial cause of the existence of everything in the universe, God cannot be an individual *such and such* as my cat is an individual cat. As far we can figure out, there is no distinction to be made between God and God's nature. To think otherwise would be to think that we can place God in a collection of peers as we can place my cat among a collection of cats.

You might suggest that God belongs to the class of *beings*. Yet there is no such class as the class of things that *simply are*. We cannot group things together just by saying that they exist. Nor can we count things that *just exist*. We can count the number of Michael Ruse's children. But counting is out of the question if the things to be counted are supposed to be just *beings*, from which I conclude that the universe *plus* God cannot be thought to equal *two*. The question "Two what?" is looking for a count noun (like "dog" or "cat" or "person") that signifies something sharing a nature with other things in our world. Yet, so I argue, God is not an individual sharing a nature with other things. If God accounts for a universe in which things can be sorted out in terms of genus and species, then God cannot be placed in a genus or species since all things that can be so placed derive from God. If God is something that can be placed in a genus or species, then God would be something like the things in our world that should lead us to wonder why they exist at all.

If, however, God makes the difference between there being something rather than nothing, there can be no question of God failing to exist. If God accounts for the existence of things that might never have existed, we cannot place God among them as something that exists though it might never have existed. I have been arguing that we can press the question "How come?" when thinking of things that exist though they might never have existed. If God is not to be grouped among things such as these, however, then God is not something that might be thought of as able not to exist. I take this conclusion to mean that God is something the essence of which is simply to exist. I am not here claiming that existence is a property that God must possess. Existence is not a property to be added to a *description* of anything. What I am saying now is that while things in the universe might never have existed, God cannot be listed together with such things. I can understand what it takes for something to exist as a cat. I can understand what any cat is essentially or by nature. I can even get a decent grasp of what it is to be a human being. But this understanding does not tell me that any *existing cat* or any existing human *has* to exist. However, if God accounts for the existence of what exists, though not by nature, I think I have to conclude that God is the unique exception: something that exists by nature, something whose very essence is to exist, something that brings it about that there are existing things that do not exist by nature. And if I am right to say this, then I think that I would also be right to claim that God is omnipotent in a precise sense.

Some people have said that "God is omnipotent" means "God can do anything." Yet that view must be false since there are millions of things that God cannot do. I can catch a bus. If God is immaterial, however, then God cannot catch a bus. Nor can God vacuum a rug, put milk in the fridge, blow his nose, and so on.[33] When turning to God's omnipotence in his *Summa theologiae* Aquinas has no problem quickly agreeing that if God created the universe, then God can be said to be powerful.[34] Yet he is more cautious when turning to divine omnipotence. He says: "Everyone confesses that God is omnipotent. But it seems hard to explain just what his omnipotence amounts to since one might wonder about the meaning of 'all' when someone says that God can do all."[35] Yet Aquinas is rightly quite clear that one cannot take "God can do all" to mean that God can "do everything that created natures can do." Instead, he argues (correctly, I think), that God is omnipotent because God can make *to exist* anything that can be thought to exist.[36] His point is that if it is *possible* for something to exist, if there is no contradiction involved when saying that it exists, then God can *make* it to exist since God is what accounts for anything existing over and against there "being" nothing at all. Could God create a cat who is also a dog? Aquinas thinks not. Could God bring it about that something that *has* happened *has not* happened? Again, Aquinas thinks not. What he thinks is that if God accounts for the existence of what does not exist by nature, then God can

[33] Orthodox Christians writing in the conviction that God became incarnate in Christ would, of course, be happy to say that God could do something like catching a bus. On their account, since Christ is God incarnate, it is true to say that, for example, God walked around, was able to eat food and was even able to die. At the moment, though, I am talking about the divine nature without reference to anything that could be taken to be divine revelation concerning the doctrine of the Incarnation.

[34] Cf. *Summa theologiae*, 1a, 25, 1.

[35] Brian Davies and Brian Leftow, eds., *Aquinas: Summa theologiae, Questions on God* (Cambridge: Cambridge University Press, 2006), 273f.

[36] Cf. Davies and Leftow, *Aquinas*, 274.

make to exist anything that *could* exist without *having* to exist by nature. And I am at one with Aquinas on this conclusion.

I also agree with him when he argues that God cannot be a spatiotemporal individual. If God were that, then I would take God to be a member of what I think of as the universe, not its creator. So, I take God not to exist in time as you and I do while going through various changes. For me, God is immutable. In the sense that you and I have a life-story, God can have no life-story. Nobody could write a biography of God. For God to exist is for God to be different from things with memories or expectations. For God to exist is for God to be nonphysical and nontemporal. For how else could God account for there being a spatiotemporal world in which things move from their present to their future by going through several mundane changes?

WHOSE GOD? WHICH TRADITION?

As I have noted, we can distinguish between classical theism and theistic personalism. And you will by now have realized which of these theistic traditions I favor. My main worry with theistic personalism is that, as God is said to have made people in his image, theistic personalists have returned the favor by thinking of God as too much like a human being.

It is often said that God is a person since God knows and wills. But knowing and willing can be ascribed to my cat. It perceives things around it, and it acts while aiming at goals. In a serious sense, it knows where it is since it can figure out where its litter box is and where to find me when I am sleeping. My cat does not talk and is in no position to make claims to know something while giving reasons to support these claims. But I do not see why I should deny that my cat is something in which there is knowledge. Nor do I see why I should deny that there is will in my cat. My cat cannot verbalize arguments such as "I want X; if I do such and such, I shall obtain X; so, I should aim at X." But my cat acts on its own and is not being pushed around by anything (unless I lift it from my lap to the floor). When it is hungry and I wave some food before it, it homes in on the food rather than my desk. You may say that cats do not know and will as we do. But we need to remember that one and the same word can be used analogously when talking about things that seriously differ from each other.

If I say, "I keep my pigs in a pen" and "I keep my pen in my pocket," the word "pen" means something completely different in each sentence. If I say, "Mary is a human being" and "John is a human being," I am saying exactly the same thing about each of them. But what if I say, "I love my wife" and "I love my job" and "I love a hot curry"? Does "love" in these sentences mean exactly the same thing or something completely different? It does not mean exactly the same thing, but it does not mean something completely different either. Love can take different forms. And such is the case with knowledge and will. When I say that my cat knows and wills, I am not suggesting that there is knowledge and will in my cat as there is in me. But I do not think that I am talking metaphorically when ascribing knowledge and will to my cat. I think that I am talking *analogically* –meaning that when saying that I know and will and that my cat knows and wills, "know" and "will" have different but *related* meanings. So, I think that we have no compelling reason to suppose that God is a person, since all persons have knowledge and will. My cat has knowledge and will, but I do not think of it as a person. You might say that the Bible teaches that God is a person. Yet the formula "God is a person" *never* appears in the Bible. Not even *once*. To be sure, the Bible uses words we employ to refer to people when talking about God. Biblical authors speak of God as a creator, a king, a lord, a judge, a shepherd, an interlocutor, a husband whose wife has cheated on him, a builder, a gardener, a father, a mother, a nursing mother, and even a mother in labor. Yet the Bible also speaks of God in nonhuman terms. So, it tells us that God is a rock, a shield, fire, a sun, and a sanctuary. Rather than homing in on the sentence "God is a person," biblical authors present an array of nouns when referring to God.

Biblical attempts to compare God to creatures and to distinguish between them and God are well noted by classical theists, some of whom, as I have noted, comment at length on biblical texts (here I am especially thinking of Augustine of Hippo and Thomas Aquinas). Classical theists are perfectly aware of how and why biblical authors find it helpful to speak of God as if God were some creature. But they are equally aware of ways in which the Bible sharply distinguishes between God and creatures. By contrast, those whom I am calling theistic personalists seem to err on too close an assimilation of God to creatures, especially the human creature. When reading them, I turn with some relief to theists like Aquinas who continually remind us that we are much in the dark when it comes to understanding what God is. In texts such as *Summa theologiae*, 1a, 13, Aquinas spends a great deal of time trying to note what we can affirm of God *literally* (albeit analogically) and without simply saying what God is *not*. But he also argues that words that we use of creatures and God "signify imperfectly" when we use them to talk about God.[37] Among the more striking of his conclusions is that "God" is not a proper name (like "Michael" or "Brian"). It is, he holds, the name of the

---

[37] I elaborate on this point in chapter 3, "What God Is Not," of Jeffrey Hause, ed., *Aquinas's "Summa theologiae": A Critical Guide* (Cambridge: Cambridge University Press, 2018).

divine nature, as "mammalian" is the name of the nature shared by mammals.[38]

So, once again, when it comes to the question "Whose God? Which tradition?" my God is the God of classical theism and my tradition is that of people such as Augustine, Anselm, Aquinas, and the Roman Catholic Church. Henceforth, therefore, in this book I shall be writing from that perspective and using the word "God" exclusively to refer to the God of classical theism.

ARGUMENTS AGAINST GOD

Why should one believe that God does not exist? Some have argued that God does not exist since God is not an empirical object whose existence can be detected by sensory investigation. I said something about this view in my contribution to Chapter 2. Other philosophers not sympathetic to belief in God have argued that to believe that God exists is to believe something involving a contradiction. It has been argued, for example, that nothing can act if it is not in time. Again, it has been argued that nothing can be omnipotent since omnipotence is an incoherent notion. The idea here is that someone who believes that God is omnipotent faces the question "Can God make something too heavy for him to lift?" If God can do that, then there is something that God cannot do (i.e., lift the stone). If God cannot lift the stone, then again it would seem that there is something that God cannot do (i.e., make something too heavy for God to lift). So, given that reasoning, some have argued that omnipotence is an incoherent notion.

In reply to the claim that nothing can act if it is not in time, I say that while temporal things act in time, there is no reason why what accounts for the existence of the spatiotemporal world cannot be thought to act as making it to exist. This would be action of a unique kind. But it would surely be action since it amounts to X *bringing it about* that Y (central to the notion of efficient causation). In reply to the argument concerning omnipotence, I would say that God does not and cannot lift things (as we often try to do as physical beings), while adding that God can bring about the levitation of anything that can be thought of as able to rise.

Having said that, however, I am aware that various people have offered many more arguments against the existence of God than the two I have mentioned. Such arguments abound in books about God and in journals

---

[38] *Summa theologiae*, 1a, 13, 8.

devoted to the philosophy of religion, and I cannot even begin to try engaging with them in this book. But there is one argument against the truth of "God exists" that comes up again and again not only in academic disputations but on a day-to-day basis among people who would not even pretend to be philosophers or theologians. For many such people this is the ultimate and knock-down argument against the claim that God exists. It is usually referred to as "the problem of evil."

THE PROBLEM OF EVIL

One line of thinking holds that it is *contradictory* to accept both that evil exists and that God exists. Hence, for example, J. L. Mackie (1917–1981) famously argues:

> In its simplest form the problem is this: God is omnipotent; God is wholly good; and yet evil exists. There seems to be some contradiction between these three propositions, so that if any two of them were true the third would be false. But at the same time all three are essential parts of most theological positions: the theologian, it seems, at once *must* adhere and *cannot consistently* adhere to all three.[39]

Mackie concedes that "God exists," "God is omnipotent," "God is wholly good," and "Evil exists" do not, when affirmed together, *obviously* amount to the manifest self-contradiction of statements like "One and the same assertion is simultaneously both true and false" or "There is something that is both entirely red and entirely green." The contradiction, says Mackie, "does not arise immediately; to show it we need some additional premises, or perhaps some quasi-logical rules connecting the terms 'good,' 'evil,' and 'omnipotent.'"[40] Yet, Mackie thinks, we can supply such premises or rules. He writes: "These additional principles are that good is opposed to evil, in such a way that a good thing always eliminates evil as far as it can, and that there are no limits to what an omnipotent thing can do."[41] From these principles, says Mackie, "it follows that a good omnipotent thing eliminates evil completely, and then the propositions that a good omnipotent thing exists, and that evil exists, are incompatible."[42]

A less ambitious challenge to theism grounded in the reality of evil has contented itself with suggesting that evil renders God's existence *unlikely*

---

[39] J. L. Mackie, "Evil and Omnipotence," *Mind* 64 (1955): 200.
[40] Mackie, "Evil and Omnipotence," 200–201.   [41] Mackie, "Evil and Omnipotence," 201.
[42] Mackie, "Evil and Omnipotence," 201.

rather than *impossible*. Here I might mention William Rowe (1931–2015) and his paper "The Problem of Evil and Some Varieties of Atheism."[43] In general, Rowe allows that evil might be justifiable if it leads to some greater good, a good not obtainable without the evil in question. Yet he also holds that there is *unjustifiable* evil, which is evidence against God's existence. Or, in Rowe's own words:

1. There exist instances of intense suffering which an omnipotent being could have prevented without thereby losing some greater good or permitting some evil equally bad or worse.
2. An omniscient, wholly good being would prevent the occurrence of any intense suffering it could, unless it could not do so without thereby losing some greater good or permitting some evil equally bad or worse.
3. [Therefore] there does not exist an omnipotent, omniscient, wholly good being.[44]

For Rowe, the most controversial premise here is the first, which he admits might be false. Yet he thinks that we have *reason* to suppose that there *are* instances of pointless suffering even if we cannot definitively *prove* that there are such instances. For what of the many instances of seemingly pointless human and animal suffering that occur daily in our world? Turning to this question, Rowe maintains that the only reasonable conclusion is one unfavorable to the theist. He suggests:

> In the light of our experience and knowledge of the variety and scale of human and animal suffering in our world, the idea that none of this suffering could have been prevented by an omnipotent being without thereby losing a greater good or permitting an evil at least as bad seems an extraordinarily absurd idea, quite beyond our belief.[45]

COMMENTS ON THE PROBLEM OF EVIL AS REFERENCED ABOVE

(A) The Problem of Evil and Theistic Personalism

Are Mackie and Rowe right in what they say? I think that they are if we take their target to be what I have called "theistic personalism." For let us suppose that God is an all-powerful and noncorporeal center of consciousness: a

---

[43] William Rowe, "The Problem of Evil and Some Varieties of Atheism," *American Philosophical Quarterly* 16 (1979): 335–41.
[44] Rowe, "The Problem of Evil," 336.   [45] Rowe, "The Problem of Evil," 337.

mind with many and changing thoughts, something that is a person in the sense that you might be thought to be a person. If we suppose that, then we might think that if God is good, or perfectly good, then God will be what good people, or perfectly good people, are as they go about their business. God will act in accordance with the moral obligations or duties to which all of us should conform. Or God will exhibit the moral virtues praised by philosophers such as Aristotle. In that case, however, evil would seem to count against God's existence. For how could a perfectly good and all-powerful person subject to common moral evaluation fail to eradicate or prevent at least some evil in the world?

It has been argued that a morally good and omnipotent God might have reasons for permitting various evils to exist of which we are unaware. The idea here is that, for all we know, God permits evils that are necessary means to good ends – just as morally good parents might cause their children grief while trying to educate them. Yet if God is omnipotent, why suppose that God must depend on evils so as to bring about what is good? Why should God be unable to produce the goods directly?

Certain things we commonly take to be good seem logically to depend on there being certain evils. There can, for example, be no compassion without someone suffering. But why can a morally good and omnipotent God not merely permit goods that logically depend on evils of some kind? And if a morally good God can do that, would we not expect to find only those evils that logically depend on certain evils?

It might be said that there are invaluable goods that come about because of certain evils and that the existence of God and the reality of evil can be reconciled because of them. Yet this line of thinking is assuming that ends can always morally justify means, and one might wonder whether that is the case. We might morally absolve a dentist for inflicting pain on patients to relieve them from dental pain. But can we morally absolve an omnipotent God in a similar way given the history of evil? Might we not rather conclude that certain evils can never be outweighed by goods that happen to arise as a result of them? And might we not reasonably note that examples of such evils can be given?

(B) The Problem of Evil and Classical Theism

So, I have serious reservations with the idea that the problem of evil is to be solved on the assumption that God is to be thought of as theistic personalists suppose. Such a God seems to me to be dubious on the moral front. But I do not have this worry when trying to think about God and evil with an eye on classical theism, chiefly because of its approach to the proposition "God is good." Theistic personalists take it to be *obvious* that this proposition is asserting that God is *morally* good, that God is like someone who, if charged with a crime, can, given certain evidence and given certain doubts, be rightly declared to be "not guilty." But why should we think of God's goodness in this way?

One reason for not doing so derives from how we use the word "good" in general. For we do not always refer to things as being good because we think that they are *morally* good. We speak, for example, of good mountaineers and good opera singers. But we are not here passing moral judgment on them. The word "good" is one that we use when describing tons and tons of things without being concerned with any moral matters. And that is because "good" is what I would call a logically *attributive* adjective rather than a logically *predicative* one.

Suppose I say that I own a small cat. "I own a small cat" does not logically break down into "I own something small" and "I own a cat." If that were so, then, given certain premises, we might wrongly conclude that a small cat is, with respect to its size, the equivalent of a small elephant. "Small" is an adjective the sense of which we understand only when it comes to something of which are talking. "Small" is what I am calling a logically attributive adjective.

Now, though, consider the proposition "I have a green shirt." If you know that I have that, then when it comes to "green" you know exactly what my shirt is. "X is a green shirt" logically breaks down into "X is a shirt" and "X is green." "Green" is what I am calling a logically predicative adjective.[46] And, so I think, "good" is an adjective that is, when we commonly use it, always predicative. We do not know precisely what people are saying when they say that something is good unless we understand what it is that they are talking about (a good *nurse* or a good *opera singer*, and so on). There is content, of course, to the word "good" that kicks in whenever we use it since "good" is a general term of commendation. We are always *commending* something when saying that it is good. But things can be good for very different reasons. We might make this point by saying that while goodness can be perfectly objective (that it is there in something), it is also relative (since goodness takes different forms). Or we might say that there is no such thing as *just* being good or bad. In that case, however, it makes sense to ask why "God is good" should *automatically* be thought of as saying that God is a good *moral*

---

[46] For this distinction, see P. T. Geach, "Good and Evil," *Analysis* 17 (1956): 33–42.

agent. And if God is no such thing, does it not follow that there is no theistic problem of evil if that is taken to be a problem concerning God's lack of moral goodness?

The theistic personalist's answer to the first of these questions is "Because God is a good *person* and because goodness in persons is always moral goodness." As I have said, though, there are reasons for denying that God is to be thought of as we think of the persons of our acquaintance (i.e., human beings). If God accounts for the sheer existence of all spatiotemporal things, then, as classical theists maintain, God cannot be listed alongside any of them. If God is good, then God is *goodness*, not a good instance of something that can be classified in some serious way. While goodness in spatiotemporal things is an attribute *possessed* by them, goodness in God is not other than God's nature and from the subject that God is. It is as appropriate to say, "God is goodness" as it is to say "God is good." If that is so, however, the way is open to the conclusion that, considered as a problem concerning God's moral integrity, the problem of evil is not a genuine problem. We do not worry that tennis players do not score goals. Tennis players are not in the business of doing what players of football aim to achieve. So why should we agonize over whether or not God is a good moral agent? If God is not a moral agent at all, then worries about God being good or bad on the moral front do not arise.

This suggestion raises several questions and two of particular interest. For are not those in the Judeo-Christian tradition positively committed to holding that God is a morally good person? And if we do not think of God as a morally good person, what reason could we have to suppose that God is good?

GOD'S GOODNESS IN THE JUDEO-CHRISTIAN TRADITION

Judeo-Christians have always insisted on the goodness of God. Why so? Basically, because God's goodness is proclaimed in the Bible, not just because it has been argued for on philosophical grounds. The Bible makes a number of references to God's goodness (see, e.g., Psalms 107 and 119, and Matthew 19:16–17).[47] On the other hand, there is not a single biblical text that can be translated as "God is morally good." Biblical authors do not think of God as the best-behaved person around. They do not think of God as always acting in accord with moral obligations or as always displaying human

---

[47] Also see 1 Chronicles 16:34 and 17:26; 2 Chronicles 5:13 and 7:3; and Psalms 100:5, 106:1, 107:1, 118:29, 119:68, 135:3, and 136:1.

virtues. Biblical texts never come even close to asserting that God is morally good in the sense in which we typically understand "morally good." Even in Matthew 19:16–17 we find the claim that God's goodness is something not shared by anything else. In this passage Jesus is reported as saying that *only* God is good. In other biblical texts, the assertion that God is good appears to be saying that God provides good things for various human beings. God is said to be good to Israel and to the pure in heart (cf. Psalm 73:1). Again, in the letter of James we read "Every generous act of giving, with every perfect gift, is from above, coming down from the Father of lights with whom there is no variation or shadow due to change" (James 1:17).

In short, the Judeo-Christian tradition (at least when it comes to its seminal texts) does not propose to us the notion of God being a morally admirable person as we tend to think of morally admirable persons. The Bible commends God for good gifts coming from him. But it does not speak of God being *morally obliged* to provide them, just as it does not say that God is *morally dubious* for sending weal and woe on some people. In biblical texts, God is not presented as a person subject to a moral code. If anything, such texts take God to be the ultimate source of moral codes. And this biblical way of thinking is clearly at work in almost all post-biblical Christian authors from the earliest post-biblical times to the eighteenth century. To say that Christian theology presents us with a problem concerning God's moral goodness is demonstrably false. It depends on which self-identifying Christians you are talking about. Some of these insist that Christianity requires us (whether we are theists or atheists) to take it *for granted* that God is supposed to be morally well behaved. Many, however, do not.

WHY SAY THAT GOD IS GOOD?

In denying that God is morally good I am not, of course, suggesting that God is *submoral*, like a stone. Nor am I saying that God is *immoral*, like a rapist. My point is that God, the maker of all things, that which accounts for there being something rather than nothing at all, is not, like each of us, something to be graded morally. God is the Creator of such things. We may study moral philosophy and thereby get a sense of how we should or should not behave. But God is not a moral agent as we are. Our striving for moral perfection is an attempt to become something we are not to start with. But if God is no spatiotemporal individual, there can be no striving for perfection in the divine nature (which I am claiming *to be* God). God's goodness must be of another order from that of familiar, human goodness.

In trying to say how that can be so, it helps to reflect a bit more on the notion of goodness in general. I noted above that to call something good is not to say that it has a particular quality common to all good things (as, say, being made of wood is possessing a particular property common to trees and certain desks). Goodness comes in different forms in different things. What counts as goodness in a vaccine is not what counts as goodness in a doctor, and so on. Yet there *is* something we can say of anything we take to be good. Aristotle made the point by noting that "the good is what everything desires."[48] As truth is what is *known*, goodness is what is *wanted*. Goodness is what is aimed at or sought. Here I am not saying that anything we desire is good. I am thinking that we would not call anything good unless we thought it desirable in some way.

Hence, for example, to call someone a good doctor is to say that they match up to what we take to be desirable in a doctor. Or to speak of a car as good is to say that it has the features that we look for in cars. Again, to commend people to be morally good is to declare them to match up to what we take to be moral standards in people, to proclaim them to be just, prudent, temperate, and so on. And I want to suggest that it is this notion of goodness that gives us reason for thinking of God as good. It does not give us a comprehension of what goodness is in God since I do not think of God as something comprehensible. But it does give us a way of pointing to what I would call the mystery of God's goodness.

Here is what I argue:

1. All creatures naturally tend to their good.
2. The nature and tendencies of creatures are caused by God working in them.
3. In seeking and arriving at what is good for them, creatures are tending to what is in God before it is in them.
4. So, we can think of God as good.

But this argument needs some unpacking.

To start with, it is not saying that God is good just because God creates things that are good. That reasoning would commit me to supposing that since God causes plastic things to exist, then God is made of plastic. What I am suggesting gets its best human analogy from what someone is doing when trying to produce something good.

---

[48] *Nichomachean Ethics* 1, 1, 1094a3.

Suppose that I want to make a good apple pie. In that case I have something in mind that I want to make, and I want what I make to conform to my intention. I want my pie to match what I intend it to be. And if I am successful in my cooking, that is what it will do. As made, it will reflect what is in me before I even started to cook it. It will correspond to my idea of it as its maker. It will show forth what I have in mind when making it as good. It will come from me and tend to what I have in mind for it. At one and the same time it will have its goodness and fulfill my aim as its maker.

Now this, as I say, is just an analogy. But it allows us to get a sense of why we can think of God as good (apart from anything we might find in what we take to be divine revelation). For God is a maker. God creatively makes everything to exist and to act for as long as it exists and acts. Parents make their children by going through various physical operations. God creates all parents producing their children. Parents make children who might go on to produce children of their own; so no parent is the maker of all of its offspring, and no human parent accounts for there being any human parents. But God, as Creator, *is creating* (present continuous sense) everything involved in human generation and everything else in creation that can be thought to be good. So, when creatures display goodness, they are in a most serious way oriented to God as their maker. Every creature, just in naturally tending to its own goodness, is seeking God as what ultimately intends it, as its maker.

And that is a good reason to think of God as good. It is not a good reason to think that God would be good without having created. But it is a reason to think of God as good given that God has created. Given my classical theistic approach to divinity, I do not think that God must create in order to be God. So, I do not claim that God's being good depends on God creating anything that we can take as showing forth goodness in God. But I do think that from what God has made, we have reason (as distinct from revelation) on our side when saying that God is good. It is a philosophical reason, but a reason nonetheless. And it is one that in no way depends on the idea of God being morally good.

GOD AS LOVING

Yet does my philosophical account of "God is good" translate into the idea that God is loving or that God loves us (in particular)? Not if we insist on taking love always to be a matter of emotion. I have argued with classical theism for the view that God is incorporeal and immutable. Yet emotions come with physiological change and can be attributed to God only metaphorically. Still, I see nothing wrong in saying that one who loves another wills that person's good, which suggests that God can indeed be said to love creatures. For their goodness is willed by God. If God accounts for all creaturely good, then God is willing that good. And the more goodness there is in something, the more God can be said to love it. This argument does not show that God is by nature loving (that the divine essence involves God loving something other than God) since it is tied to the notion of God as creating, and I do not see reason to suppose that God has to create anything. Still, given that God *has* created, it makes sense to say that God loves creatures by willing what is good in them.

GOD, CAUSATION, AND EVIL

On the other hand, one might think that God wills a lot of evil. For evil is not an illusion and its occurrence has somehow to be due to God. So, should we not conclude that, if God exists, then God wills evil directly? With this question in mind I favor a response that has been made many times and criticized many times, but which still seems to me convincing. This is that evil or badness cannot be thought of as something created by God since its reality always consists in the absence of a due good. In other words, God cannot be said to *create* evil as a thing in itself while *directly* intending it as an end.

For what are we complaining about when we take something to be bad? We are surely worried that it is *not* exhibiting the goodness we expect of it. Its badness consists in the absence of a good we wish to be there. We can make sense of something being perfectly good considered as what it is. But we cannot, I think, make sense of something being nothing but bad. Badness can be said to exist only in the sense that there are things that lack goodness in various ways, that fail to live up to our expectations in some way. Yet a lack of an appropriate good is not anything substantial, not something existing with an identity of its own, from which I infer that badness, though no illusion, is not something created by God. It is what is "there" insofar as something is good to a certain extent, but not as good as it could or should be. And considered as such, it is not creatively caused to exist by God and does nothing to show that God is a bad thing that directly causes badness to be over and against there being nothing.

One might say that God could have made many things to be better than they are. One might charge God with neglecting to produce goodness of certain kinds. And I sympathize with that move since I do not think that God is unable to produce a world entirely lacking in badness. But nor do

I think that the Creator of the universe is under any obligation to create more good than there is in the world since I do not see how God can be under an obligation to create anything at all. It is the job of a dentist to make a patient's oral state as healthy and pain-free as the dentist is able. But I cannot see how it can be sensibly thought that it is God's job to make everything that exists to be as good as it could be. I would also add that when it comes to what philosophers call "naturally occurring evils" (e.g., sickness, the effects of earthquakes, and so on), we always have badness because something else is thriving in its own way. I mean that, when confronted by naturally occurring evils, we do not look for some malign being willing the evils just for the fun of it. We look for scientifically discoverable natural causes behaving in what, for them, is a good way. Naturally occurring evils always have a concomitant good: the good of the natural agents who bring them about. To put the point another way, all naturally occurring evil amounts only to the existence of what is good in that the predator (so to speak) is thriving in its action on its victim and in that the victim, just by existing, is good to some degree. This thought, of course, may be of small comfort to the victim. But I think that it is what we have to say when reflecting on what is going on when it comes to naturally occurring evils and the role that God plays when it comes to them.

CONCLUSION

In my contribution to this chapter I have briefly defended the following theses. (1) On the assumption that God accounts for the sheer existence of the universe from moment to moment, God is not to be thought of as an explanation of the universe. (2) On the same assumption, God is not something we can understand in anything like the way in which we can understand items in the universe and is not to be thought of as one individual among many of the same kind. (3) On the same assumption, God cannot be something material or something able not to exist. (4) On the same assumption, God can be said to be omnipotent and nontemporal. (5) On the same assumption, we have reason for denying that God is a person as people are persons (a conclusion that coheres with biblical accounts of God). (6) The problem of evil, which we can understand in two different ways, does not show that the God of classical theism cannot exist or is unlikely to exist since it relies on an unacceptably anthropomorphic view of God, one that biblical authors do not share. (7) There are sound philosophical reasons for claiming that God is good and that God loves creatures. (8) God cannot be thought to will (i.e., create) evil directly as an end in itself.

5

Morality

Michael Ruse

CHRISTIAN ETHICS

$\mathcal{M}$ORALITY IS ABOUT WHAT WE SHOULD OR SHOULD NOT DO, AS opposed to what we do or do not do. Its study by philosophers, ethics, generally assumes that the topic falls into two parts. What we should or should not do – normative or prescriptive ethics – and why we should or should not do – metaethics.[1] Christianity certainly has things to say at both the normative and metaethical levels. For all Christians – although some versions of the religion add on other sources, for example, Catholics having the Pope speak ex cathedra – the Bible is central to their understanding of normative ethics. Unfortunately, even if the Bible is central, still it would not be entirely true to say that all Christians agree on the normative dictates of their religion. The Bible has many books, reflecting different societies. Both sides in the American Civil War cited the Bible in their support.[2] Slave owners pointed to the story of Abraham and Sarah, and of Hagar, Sarah's slave girl. Although Sarah turned against Hagar when she had a child of her own, there was no discussion of the morality of Sarah turning over Hagar to Abraham for sexual/reproductive purposes. Critics of slavery turned to the preaching of Jesus. It is hard to imagine that someone who gave the Sermon on the Mount approved of humans owning other humans, as their property to do with them as they wanted. Treating a woman as a prize sow is simply not Christian.

This said, most Christians – and indeed, most members of other religions – would subscribe to something known as the Golden Rule. Treat

---

[1] M. Ruse, *A Meaning to Life* (Oxford: Oxford University Press, 2019).
[2] M. Noll, *America's God: From Jonathan Edwards to Abraham Lincoln* (New York: Oxford University Press, 2002).

others as you would be treated yourself. Thus, the Old Testament: "You shall not take vengeance or bear a grudge against any of your people, but you shall love your neighbor as yourself: I am the Lord."[3] Thus, the New Testament: "In everything do to others as you would have them do to you; for this is the law and the prophets."[4] "Do to others as you would have them do to you."[5] As Jesus pointed out, there is still room for discussion about the breadth of the applicability of all of this. Does it apply to everyone, or just to close neighbors and friends? On being asked, "Who is my neighbor?," Jesus gave the parable of the Good Samaritan, implying that all of humankind is one's neighbor, friends and foe. However, other parts of the New Testament – not to mention most of the Old Testament – do rather imply that neighborliness is somewhat restricted. There is a fair amount of honoring your mother and your father, as well as much on the obligations to one's children. Not that everything is that straightforward. "Whoever comes to me and does not hate father and mother, wife and children, brothers and sisters, yes, and even life itself, cannot be my disciple."[6] As you can imagine, that has led to 2,000 years of deconstruction! Perhaps, charitably, we can say that Jesus is telling us not to put others before him, which is not unreasonable if Jesus was the son of God, meaning for Christians that in some sense he was God.

What of Christian metaethics? I think it fair to say that most, if not all, Christians would want to tie the justification of substantive ethical claims to the will of God. God wants us to behave in a certain way, so we should behave in such a way. Speaking at a personal level, having been raised a Quaker in the years after the Second World War, I am much aware of the force of the appeal to God's will. Unlike the First World War, where to this day few can see any real justification for it – to be separated from reasons why it occurred – the Second World War seemed – seems – to have had more than enough justification. Hitler had to be stopped. Quakers, however, were (and are) pacifists. How can they justify standing aside? Ultimately, for all the arguments one might give about how nonviolence is pragmatically the better way, the case comes down to the will of God. God forbids violence and that is it. Usually the argument is put in an eschatological context, suggesting that, whatever happens, God is going to make things right again. But violence is forbidden. In the words of the Methodist Stanley Hauerwas against some of his coreligionists: "What the bishops fail to appreciate [American Methodists have bishops] is that the peace that sustains Christian pacifism is an eschatological notion. Christian pacifism is not

---

[3] Leviticus 19:18.   [4] Matthew 7:12.   [5] Luke 6:31.   [6] Luke 14:26.

based on the assumption that Jesus has given us the means to achieve a warless world, but rather, as John Howard Yoder suggests, peace describes the hope, the goal of which in the light of which the pacifist acts, 'the character of his action, the ultimate divine certainly which lets his position make sense; it does not describe the external appearance or the observable results of his behavior.'" Continuing to quote Yoder, "This is what we mean by eschatology: a hope which, defying present frustrations, defines a present position in terms of the yet unseen goal which gives it meaning."[7]

The appeal of the will of God raises the so-called Euthyphro problem, named after Plato's dialogue of that name. Does God want us to do the right thing because it is his will, or is his will something in conformity with a separate code of right and wrong? I am not sure that this is quite the devastating critique that many (philosophy undergraduates) take it to be. There is a respectable vein of Christian thought – one that relies heavily on the book of Job – that thinks God does have quite a hand in the nature of (substantive) morality. I am God. I am the Creator. I make the rules.

> Do you know when the mountain goats give birth? Do you observe the calving of the deer?
> Can you number the months that they fulfill, and do you know the time when they give birth,
> when they crouch to give birth to their offspring, and are delivered of their young?
> Their young ones become strong, they grow up in the open; they go forth, and do not return to them.
> Who has let the wild ass go free? Who has loosed the bonds of the swift ass?[8]

In short: "Who can confront it and be safe? – under the whole heaven, who?"[9] I am not sure that anyone thinks that God is capricious. But if God decrees pacifism, that is God's decision, not ours.

The other option is to subscribe to some form of Christian Platonism, where there are eternal rules, independent of the deity. But is this so very troublesome, theologically or philosophically? Remember, Descartes thought that God could make $2 + 2 = 5$; but most would argue that even God must accept that $2 + 2 = 4$ and that this is no true constraint on his omnipotence or omniscience. In fact, as we have seen, the standard response to the

---

[7] S. Hauerwas, "On Being a Church Capable of Addressing a World at War: A Pacifist Response to the United Methodist Bishops' Pastoral," in *In Defense of Creation: The Hauerwas Reader*, S. Hauerwas (Durham, NC: Duke University Press, [1988] 2001), 426–58, 436.

[8] Job 39:1–5.   [9] Job 41:11.

problem of natural evil is to say that God must work within the bounds of logic and mathematics, and in making this "best of all possible worlds" pain and suffering are bound to occur. The end result, plants and animals, up to and including humans, is worth it. So here, too, the Euthyphro problem is no real problem.

Does this kind of Christian ethics have any interesting implications? The now trendy, popular theologian C. S. Lewis – he of reluctant belief – rather thought it did. The only explanation is God! On the one hand, morality is not simply a matter of what we might want to do or not to do, what we like doing or not doing. It is laid on us as it were. "Consequently, this Rule of Right and Wrong, or Law of Human Nature, or whatever you call it, must somehow or other be a real thing – a thing that is really there, not made up by ourselves."[10] Hence, on the other hand, there must be something – or Some Thing – behind it. Modestly: "I am not yet within a hundred miles of the God of Christian theology." Less modestly: "All I have got to is a Something which is directing the universe, and which appears in me as a law urging me to do right and making me feel responsible and uncomfortable when I do wrong. I think we have to assume it is more like a mind than it is like anything else we know – because after all the only other thing we know is matter and you can hardly imagine a bit of matter giving instructions. But, of course, it need not be very like a mind, still less like a person."

Concluding with that buff heartiness that so delights his acolytes: "In the next chapter we shall see if we can find out anything more about it. But one word of warning. There has been a great deal of soft soap talked about God for the last hundred years. That is not what I am offering. You can cut all that out."[11] Hard soap: "God is quite definitely 'good' or 'righteous,' a God who takes sides, who loves love and hates hatred, who wants us to behave in one way and not in another."[12] More hard soap: Christianity

> thinks God made the world – that space and time, heat and cold, and all the colors and tastes, and all the animals and vegetables, are things that God "made up out of His head" as a man makes up a story. But it also thinks that a great many things have gone wrong with the world that God made and that God insists, and insists very loudly, on our putting them right again.[13]

---

[10] C. S. Lewis, *Mere Christianity* (New York: Harper Collins, [1952] 2015), 20.
[11] Lewis, *Mere Christianity*, 26.   [12] Lewis, *Mere Christianity*, 36.
[13] Lewis, *Mere Christianity*, 37–38.

Substantive ethics exists and is binding on us. The only metaethical justification is God. Hence, God exists!

EVOLUTIONARY ETHICS

In the 1960s, the decade of my twenties, the old foundations – God or society or whatever – no longer seemed adequate. The long nights spent discussing these issues and trying to find alternative answers – when one could have been having sex! Go back to the 1860s and one finds the same worries. Charles Darwin was entirely typical. When he wrote on humankind, in his *Descent of Man*, he gave short shrift to God, following Hume's line that it is all a matter of mistaken perceptions. Hume spoke of "human faces in the moon, armies in the clouds."[14] Darwin spoke in the same vein.

> The tendency in savages to imagine that natural objects and agencies are animated by spiritual or living essences, is perhaps illustrated by a little fact which I once noticed: my dog, a full-grown and very sensible animal, was lying on the lawn during a hot and still day; but at a little distance a slight breeze occasionally moved an open parasol, which would have been wholly disregarded by the dog, had any one stood near it. As it was, every time that the parasol slightly moved, the dog growled fiercely and barked. He must, I think, have reasoned to himself in a rapid and unconscious manner, that movement without any apparent cause indicated the presence of some strange living agent, and no stranger had a right to be on his territory.
>
> The belief in spiritual agencies would easily pass into the belief in the existence of one or more gods. For savages would naturally attribute to spirits the same passions, the same love of vengeance or simplest form of justice, and the same affections that they themselves experienced.[15]

So much for God. Morality, however, was a very different matter. Confining discussion here to those accepting the power and importance of evolution – something that gave an alternative world picture to Christianity – what did they have to say? Darwin devoted considerable space and thought to the issue. He was not a philosopher, but there are considerable hints and guidelines in his discussions to point the way to an evolutionary-based philosophical approach to morality. He was not the only person writing on this topic. Herbert Spencer was better known. It was he

---

[14] D. Hume, *A Natural History of Religion*, in *Hume on Religion*, ed. R. Wollheim (London: Fontana, [1757] 1963).

[15] C. Darwin, *The Descent of Man, and Selection in Relation to Sex* (London: John Murray, 1871), 67.

who was the father of the now infamous "Social Darwinism."[16] In a way, this paid off for Darwin because, to use a sports metaphor, it was Spencer who did the blocking. It was he who brought down huge amounts of criticism on any evolutionary approach to morality. And it was he who bore the brunt of the scorn. Still well known, and taken in many quarters as gospel, to use a metaphor, is G. E. Moore's withering critique in his *Principia Ethica*, where Spencer is highlighted as the most egregious offender with respect to the so-called naturalistic fallacy, a recycled version of David Hume's skepticism about deriving moral statements, "ought" statements, from empirical statements, "is" statements.[17] With some relief, we can ignore all of this here. My aim is not to give a full and disinterested history of evolutionary approaches to morality. Rather, it is to counter C. S. Lewis by showing that one can give a fully adequate analysis of ethics using Darwinian evolutionary theory instead of the will of the Almighty. The argument from morality is a species of what we have encountered already, an "argument to the best explanation." God is the only adequate explanation, so it must be the true one, or the one we hold until a better option becomes available. My aim is to show that, with respect to morality, a better option has become available.

DARWINIAN SUBSTANTIVE ETHICS

In Darwin's own writings and those of his contemporaries, there are certainly hints of it in the position about to be expounded, to the extent that we can properly speak of it as "Darwinian," but truly it has started to come into its own only since the growth, in the past half-century, of the study of social behavior from a Darwinian standpoint: "sociobiology."[18] Start with the empirical side of things, remembering that at some point we will need to introduce the difference between substantive ethics and metaethics.

It is now generally agreed that the key facet of human nature is our sociability. Talk about killer apes – popular in the years after the Second World War and during the Cold War – has fallen out of favor.[19] Biologically inclined students of human behavior – paleoanthropologists, primatologists, evolutionary psychologists – stress that our success comes not from our physical abilities – overall, we are not that fast or strong or protected from

[16] J. O'Connell and M. Ruse, *Social Darwinism* (Cambridge: Cambridge University Press, 2020).

[17] G. E. Moore, *Principia Ethica* (Cambridge: Cambridge University Press, 1903).

[18] M. Ruse and R. J. Richards, eds., *The Cambridge Handbook of Evolutionary Ethics* (Cambridge: Cambridge University Press, 2017).

[19] M. Ruse, *The Problem of War: Darwinism, Christianity, and Their Battle to Understand Human Conflict* (Oxford: Oxford University Press, 2018).

the elements – but from the ways in which we work together. This is obviously not a new finding.

> No man is an island,
> Entire of itself,
> Every man is a piece of the continent,
> A part of the main.
> If a clod be washed away by the sea,
> Europe is the less.
> As well as if a promontory were.
> As well as if a manor of thy friend's
> Or of thine own were:
> Any man's death diminishes me,
> Because I am involved in mankind,
> And therefore never send to know for whom the bell tolls;
> It tolls for thee.[20]

This is from the pen of the great, early seventeenth-century, metaphysical poet John Donne. We are all in it together. And it is here that morality comes in. If we are going to work together, there must be some biological reason behind this. Natural selection is all about "selfish genes," meaning not that either genes or humans are literally selfish all of the time, but that if an adaptation – including a social adaptation – does not benefit its possessor, then it is not going to be a great success in the effort to survive and reproduce.[21] The organism that grabs most for itself and leaves others hungry is ahead of the game. Except, of course, others are also in this game, and they don't much care for this. Often the best way to succeed in the game is to band together, and to share the proceeds – half a loaf is better than no loaf at all. There are various mechanisms that support this social behavior. One is kin selection, where close relatives cooperate. They have shared genes, so inasmuch as one reproduces, the other reproduces by proxy as it were. Another is reciprocal altruism. You scratch my back and I will scratch yours. There are hints of both of these in the *Descent*. Today, they have been worked through theoretically and been shown widely applicable empirically.

So, why morality? Why not just do things in a calculating way? Like in a store. I need the goods, you need the cash, so let us just exchange things. Nothing very moral about it, but it works. Kant saw the problems with this.[22] In theory, it is fine. In practice, it breaks down. Most obviously, there is the

---

[20] John Donne, Meditation XVII, Devotions upon Emergent Occasions.
[21] M. Ruse, *Darwinism and Its Discontents* (Cambridge: Cambridge University Press, 2006).
[22] I. Kant, *Foundations of the Metaphysics of Morals* (Indianapolis: Bobbs-Merrill, 1959).

question of efficiency. I see a child run into the road with traffic bearing down. I start to calculate. What are the chances of my being able to help the child? What statistics bear on this? What are the risks to me? What will happen if I do rescue the child? Will the parents reward me financially? Will society give me credit because I have done it? By the time you have made these calculations and come to a decision, the child is probably mown down and dead. You need a quick and dirty solution. Usually works, even if not always. Morality! Because of my moral nature, I dash across and pick up the child before the truck bears down on it. I might get injured or killed, but on balance it is better that I do this. If you like, not so much for my own good, but because I might well have a kid who is in similar danger. Of course, there are things other than morality that drive us. Love, for instance. But love has its bounds. I don't know that I feel much love for a grotesque beggar with hand outstretched. But I may feel a moral obligation to do something about the beggar's predicament.

Morality, then, is a good adaptation for organisms living, as do humans, in a social kind of way. Speaking now at the substantive level, I don't see – subject to points that will be made later – that the evolutionist is going to be terribly innovative here. The Golden Rule seems like a pretty good starting point. Interestingly, in that major work of ethics of the past half-century, *A Theory of Justice*, John Rawls argues that Darwinian evolution probably brought about his fundamental theorem of justice as fairness.

> In arguing for the greater stability of the principles of justice I have assumed that certain psychological laws are true, or approximately so. I shall not pursue the question of stability beyond this point. We may note however that one might ask how it is that human beings have acquired a nature described by these psychological principles. The theory of evolution would suggest that it is the outcome of natural selection; the capacity for a sense of justice and the moral feelings is an adaptation of mankind to its place in nature.[23]

One of the problems of a contract theory, such as is suggested by Rawls – and by others, for instance, Plato in the *Republic* – is that historically it never seems very plausible that a group of elders sat around and drew up the rules for proper conduct. Better to leave it to natural selection and the genes.

What does this add up to? At the substantive level, regular morality. Kantians would be happy. Treat people as ends, not as means. Utilitarians would be happy. Maximize happiness; minimize unhappiness.

---

[23] J. Rawls, *A Theory of Justice* (Cambridge, MA: Harvard University Press, 1971), 502–3.

DARWINIAN METAETHICS

But what now about the question of justification? Metaethics. One of the reasons why evolutionary ethics has such a bad reputation is that here it seems to jump right into philosophical quicksands. One is committing the error noted by Hume (and his sidekick Moore): one is going straight from talk about facts to talk about values and obligations. In the specific case here, it is assumed that evolution is progressive – that it follows a path from the simple to the complex, from the blob to the human, in short from the valueless to the valuable. Hence, what we should do is promote the evolutionary process and the products thereof. Already we have seen good reasons to doubt that Darwinian evolution is all that progressive. But even if we allow that it is, Thomas Henry Huxley, already introduced as Charles Darwin's great supporter – his "bulldog" – put his finger on the problem. Agreed: "Man, the animal, in fact, has worked his way to the headship of the sentient world, and has become the superb animal which he is, in virtue of his success in the struggle for existence."[24] However:

> For his successful progress, throughout the savage state, man has been largely indebted to those qualities which he shares with the ape and the tiger; his exceptional physical organization; his cunning, his sociability, his curiosity, and his imitativeness; his ruthless and ferocious destructiveness when his anger is roused by opposition.
>
> But, in proportion as men have passed from anarchy to social organization, and in proportion as civilization has grown in worth, these deeply ingrained serviceable qualities have become defects. After the manner of successful persons, civilized man would gladly kick down the ladder by which he has climbed. He would be only too pleased to see "the ape and tiger die."

We are going from "is" to "ought," and this you shouldn't do. You are going from this is the way that evolution works to the claim that we should cherish the methods of evolution, and Huxley shows that this is just not true. Let's not go down this road.

What road, then, are we to take? Perhaps we don't need to take any road! The problem is that of justifying substantive ethics. That's what the appeal to progress is supposed to do. What if you suggest that there is no justification for substantive ethics? In the lingo of the trade, what if you opt for a rather

---

[24] T. H. Huxley, *Evolution and Ethics*, ed. and with an introduction by Michael Ruse (Princeton: Princeton University Press, [1893] 2009), 51.

stringent form of moral nonrealism? No one can accuse you of illicitly going from "is" to "ought." You are not in that sort of business. In a way – in a very major way – your position is akin to the philosophical position known as "emotivism."[25] Morality is no more than an expression of feelings. I don't like pedophilia. Boo-hoo, leave little kiddies alone! I don't want you to like pedophilia. To be honest, this is not a very pleasing position to be in. When I joined philosophy, fifty or more years ago, emotivism was all the rage. I doubt I was the only one who thought it slick and dissatisfying to the point of immorality. Pedophilia is wrong, period. That has nothing to do with my feelings – or those of anybody else. Emotivism is a glib nonstarter. So, two questions. Why should one feel pushed in the direction of nonrealism? You, as a Darwinian, must give some reasons. Why should it not all be relative? I don't like the idea of sex with small kids. You do. Each to his own taste. If it feels okay, then it is okay.

Answering the first question, we seize on the nondirectionality of Darwinian evolutionary theory. (This is why the position is Darwinian, and not merely evolutionary.) There is no guaranteed end point for Darwinism. If it works, then it works. Suppose that there is an objective morality, existing in a kind of Platonic heaven filled with the Forms. Suppose it is our sort of morality, love your neighbor and that sort of thing. There is no absolute reason why we should find it out. Consider what I call the "John Foster Dulles system of morality," so named after Eisenhower's Secretary of State.[26] He hated the Russians with a passion. He thought he should hate them. He knew that they felt the same way about him. They compromised and got on. Suppose we evolved that way. We would have a different, functional morality, in ignorance of the real morality. And if that isn't a reductio of moral realism, I don't know what is. Darwin was onto this.

> If, for instance, to take an extreme case, men were reared under precisely the same conditions as hive-bees, there can hardly be a doubt that our unmarried females would, like the worker-bees, think it a sacred duty to kill their brothers, and mothers would strive to kill their fertile daughters; and no one would think of interfering. Nevertheless, the bee, or any other social animal, would in our supposed case gain, as it appears to me, some feeling of right and wrong, or a conscience.[27]

[25] A. J. Ayer, *Language, Truth and Logic* (New York: Dover, [1936] 1952); C. L. Stevenson, *Ethics and Language* (New Haven: Yale University Press, 1944).

[26] M. Ruse, *Taking Darwin Seriously: A Naturalistic Approach to Philosophy* (Oxford: Blackwell, 1986).

[27] Darwin, *Descent*, 1, 73.

Ladies! Instead of putting analytic philosophers up on a pedestal, when winter comes your greatest moral duty would be to kick them out of the house and let them freeze to death.

Note, incidentally, to counter the obvious objection, the situation here with morality is different from physicality. If a train is bearing down on you, then in the end there is but one solution – get out of the way. You might do this by different means – sensing the oncoming train via sight, hearing, radar, or whatever. But they must lead to the same end. In the moral case, there is no need to get to the same end. If the system of morality you have works – John Foster Dulles–style, for instance – then the existence of an objective morality is irrelevant. Which raises the relativism issue. If there is no controlling objectivity, doesn't this mean that anything goes? Which is hardly what we expect with morality. Fortunately, that problem is easily dealt with. Morality just wouldn't work if we could pick and choose our moral norms. Love your neighbor. Hate your neighbor. That is not to say we never do hate our neighbor – that damned dog again in the middle of the night! – but morality never says you will or will not think and act this way. It says you should think and act this way. However, morality must be more than that. Suppose it was just a question of eating spinach – I like it, you don't. Even if mother says you must eat it, it doesn't necessarily mean that you accept the rightness of eating spinach. You just do it because you are scared of mum. If we just knew that morality was merely emotion, then why not break it? Morality has no force. Like Raskolnikov in *Crime and Punishment*, you can do what you want.

In real life, as Raskolnikov started to realize, it's not that easy. The little tug of conscience starts to work away. The conscience might be yours, but it doesn't necessarily do or tell you what you want. It tells you what you should want. In other words, it "objectifies" – to use a horrible word employed by J. L. Mackie – your moral norms.[28] For morality to work, it has to seem objective – bigger than the both of us – even though it is really subjective. If we didn't think it objective, it would just collapse. And that, incidentally, is why you find so implausible what I am writing. Your genes are more effective than my arguments! (Now I have told you, why don't you go out and rape and pillage? Because you know that really you shouldn't. Your genes are telling you so. Giving good advice against doing what you really feel never works. I tell you not to have another drink. Good luck with that!)

---

[28] J. L. Mackie, *Ethics* (Harmondsworth: Penguin, 1977).

AND THE WORLD SAID

So where does this leave me, a Darwinian, against the Christian? For a start, C. S. Lewis's proof of the existence of God is in tatters. I have just given a perfectly adequate naturalistic account of morality – substantive ethics and metaethics – without bringing God into the discussion at all. I don't need God to explain morality. Second, I am not quite as hostile to the Christian as you might think. Suppose you do believe in God. You will not – certainly you will not, if you are in the Catholic natural-law tradition – think that God made up (substantive) morality capriciously. He is not a Jobean nightmare. God has guidelines. He is going to base morality on what is natural. Parents love their children, and feel a moral obligation to care for them, because if they don't, the kids will not survive. God expects and demands this of you. He doesn't say – "take babies out into the snow and let them freeze to death." For all the earlier-expressed worries about special obligations – Good Samaritan–like, we owe the same to everyone – Christians know that you have special obligations toward your own kids. The Apostle Paul was unequivocal on this issue – "And whoever does not provide for relatives, and especially for family members, has denied the faith and is worse than an unbeliever."[29] It is unnatural to have sex with small children, and God has pretty strong ideas on this too. Jesus said: "Let the little children come to me, and do not stop them; for it is to such as these that the kingdom of heaven belongs."[30] On the other hand, it does not take three people to reproduce, so God has not laid upon us obligations about having group sex. It is interesting how much time is spent by pagans and others, trying to persuade us – or themselves – that it is perfectly natural. (More memories of the 1960s!)

Of course, this is not to say that all problems are now resolved. Take (male) homosexuality. I suspect that most Darwinians would say that it must be natural. Nothing that remains relatively stable in a population at about 10 percent could possibly exist without the ongoing aid of selection. I suspect that most Roman Catholics would say that anuses are meant for defecation and not for sexual pleasure and so it must be unnatural. But differences like these are of a somewhat different order. The questions are more empirical than ethical. If you could show that being gay can be a good reproductive strategy – you help relatives to have way more children than you could have – then kin selection kicks in. Analogously, I suspect that most Darwinians would say that, given that women make up about 60 percent of the undergraduate population these days, it is a little bit silly to say that

[29] 1 Timothy 5:8.   [30] Matthew 19:14.

naturally – meaning selection-caused – women are less intelligent than men. St Paul apparently was of a different opinion.

> Let a woman learn in silence with full submission.

> I permit no woman to teach or to have authority over a man; she is to keep silent.

> For Adam was formed first, then Eve;

> and Adam was not deceived, but the woman was deceived and became a transgressor.

> Yet she will be saved through childbearing, provided they continue in faith and love and holiness, with modesty.[31]

The point is that we are now arguing about what is natural and what is nonnatural. Darwinians will differ among themselves as to what is natural, as do many Christians. The question is whether being natural is the basis of (substantive) morality, and the answer is that this is the position of both Darwinians and many, very traditional Christians.

Is this an end to things? Are Christian substantive morality and Darwinian substantive morality always going to be the same? Probably generally but not necessarily always. Take the virtue of meekness. Jesus doesn't mince words on the subject. "Blessed are the meek, for they will inherit the earth."[32] Darwinians recognize this sentiment. It's just that they don't much care for it. In Thomas Hardy's novel The Woodlanders, one of the main characters dies because, in bad weather, he gave up his cottage to someone (far less worthy) in need and as a result caught a chill. This, one should say, is the fitting climax of the loser's ongoing behavior. The one person who loves him consoles him with Jesus-based sentiments: "If ever I forget your name, let me forget home and Heaven! – But no, no, my love, I never can forget 'ee; for you was a GOOD man, and did good things!"[33] Well, yes – but! One is certainly not left with the feeling that the author agrees with any of this. If anything, Hardy's story is meant to show that Christianity is for dopes. And generally, those creative writers influenced by Darwin know the score. In Edith Wharton's Darwin-influenced world, losers are losers. "Every one knows you're a thousand times handsomer and cleverer than Bertha; but then you're not nasty. And for always getting what

---

[31] I Timothy 2:11–15.   [32] Matthew 5:5.
[33] T. Hardy, The Woodlanders (London: Macmillan, 1887).

she wants in the long run, commend me to a nasty woman."[34] The heroine gets what she deserves. She sinks lower and lower in society until she overdoses on chloral hydrate. Meekness is a mug's game.

In the real world, Darwin's bulldog, Thomas Henry Huxley, was the paradigm.[35] From a poor, lower-middle-class family, he pulled himself up via scholarships and nonstop hard work. He became a well-known biologist, a professor and then dean at the new science university (now Imperial College) founded on the profits from the great Exhibition of 1851, a writer of texts and brilliant essays for the general public, a consultant to the government, and one of the noted general speakers and debaters of his time. All this, despite the fact that he was subject to crushing depressions that would leave him lifeless and tragically unhappy. This was as far from meekness as it is possible to imagine. He was "a veray parfit gentil knight." Meaning not that he was gentle but that he was noble. He had earned such a description.

Huxley was not alone. In the medical world, there was the woman Florence Nightingale. In the political world, there was the Jew, Benjamin Disraeli. In the religious world, the founder of the Salvation Army, William Booth. And so many more earnest Victorians. Their creed was not "might is right," the motto of Thrasymachus in the *Republic*, and of the supposedly traditional Social Darwinian. But there is an appreciation of vigor and of a determination not to be fobbed off with second-rate alternatives. In this sense, Darwinian ethics did and still does differ from Christian ethics. In moral understanding and behavior, there is a real divide. And I know on which side of the divide I stand. With the person with guts and determination, rather than the wimp who gives way before things really start. Darwinian ethics not only replaces Christian ethics. It is better than Christian ethics.

Brian Davies

INTRODUCTION

Like the word "religion," the word "morality" is not neatly definable. We can say that a quadruped is an animal having four feet, and to say that is to offer a definition of "quadruped." But we cannot offer such a neat and definitive account of what "religion" or "morality" might be. And that is not surprising

---

[34] E. Wharton, *The House of Mirth* (New York: Dover, [1905] 2002), 34–35. See also M. Ruse, *Darwinism as Religion: What Literature Tells Us about Evolution* (Oxford: Oxford University Press, 2017).

[35] A. Desmond, *Huxley: From Devil's Disciple to Evolution's High Priest* (New York: Basic Books, 1997).

since "religion" and "morality" are not words that refer to naturally occurring things in the world, such as microbes and alligators. These words get their meaning from linguistic practice, from the ways in which people use the words "religion" and "morality." And people have used these words in different ways while often seeming to talk about very different things. So, if Fred says that he is concerned with religion or morality, we need to ask him, "Which religion?" or "Which understanding of morality?"

UNDERSTANDINGS OF "MORALITY"

Most typically, we think of morality as having *something* to do with *behavior*, and we distinguish between actions that are *moral* and those that are *immoral*. We also, of course, distinguish between moral and immoral *people*. So, if forced to say what *morality* is, I would suggest that it is what we have an eye on when trying to decide how we *should* behave simply considered as *human beings*. When people commend others for being *moral*, they are not applauding the fact that these others have skills when it comes to doing something mechanical, such as fixing a broken water pipe or engaging in brain surgery. They seem to be approving of them for being good *simply as* human beings.

This understanding of the word "morality" obviously has an evaluative notion built into it. I mean that if being moral is somehow to be *good*, then to say that people are moral is somehow to *approve* of them since "good" is a word implying commendation. For the same reason, to say that people are immoral is normally to *disapprove* of them. But in what ways and for what reasons? How should we think about what we are doing when approving or disapproving of people, considered as *people* and not just as good or bad given their ability to repair a computer or act as a tour guide?

Many philosophers these days advertise themselves as specializing in *moral philosophy*, and they tend to concern themselves with questions such as (1) "When we express moral approval or disapproval of people, are we saying something objectively true or false about them or merely expressing a subjective attitude toward them that we happen to have?" (2) "Can we defend moral judgements about people by means of argument?" and (3) "Do the words 'good' and 'bad' function as adjectives, or are they merely noises we make to register our approval or disapproval?" Moral philosophers raise many more questions than these, but they raise these ones very frequently. As a result, we find some moral philosophers typically favoring or disfavoring what is sometimes called "moral objectivism" – the view that there are moral truths that hold independently of anyone's personal likes or dislikes. Correspondingly, we find other moral philosophers embracing "moral subjectivism" – the view that there is no such thing as objective moral truth, that moral evaluations tell us only about the people making them (that they happen to have certain likes and dislikes). So, moral objectivists will say that statements such as "John is a bad man" are either true or false and, if true, tell us what John *really is* just as much as "Sarah is a biologist," if true, tells us what Sarah *really is*. By contrast, however, moral subjectivists will say that moral goodness or badness is only "in the eye of the beholder," as beauty is often taken to be. They will say that utterances such as "John is a bad man" are neither true nor false because they are not really statements at all but sentences expressing people's feelings, sentences that *look* like statements but are nothing of the kind.

An especially famous moral subjectivist is David Hume. He takes morality to be grounded or based on what he calls "sentiment." He thinks that we naturally warm to some things and are repelled by others. And he thinks that moral evaluations are *nothing but* expressions of feelings that we have. This view subsequently came to be embedded in what is now called the "emotive theory of ethics," which is associated with philosophers such as C. L. Stevenson (1908– 1979) and A. J. Ayer (1910–1989). This theory focuses on the *meaning* of statements such as "X is good" and "X is bad," and its proponents argue that what these "statements" *really* mean can be expressed by sentences such as "I approve of X, and I suggest that you do as well" and "I disapprove of X, and I suggest that you do as well." On this account, the notion of *objective* goodness or badness that *everyone* should acknowledge has disappeared.

MORALITY AS REASON FOR BELIEF THAT GOD EXISTS

It has been claimed that morality somehow depends on God. As far as I know, no moral subjectivist has defended this claim. But there have been many moral objectivists who have done so. And these people have reasoned in one of two ways. Some have argued that there could be no good moral reasoning if God does not exist. Others have argued that morality *implies* the existence of God.

The first conclusion here seems to me to be false if understood as meaning that there can be no decent moral philosophy of an objectivist kind that does not refer to God. Consider, for example, the moral philosophy of Aristotle and Kant. These two thinkers differ significantly when it comes to what morality is all about, yet they are both paradigmatic moral objectivists. They offer sophisticated accounts of morality that do not rely on the supposition that God exists, from which I conclude that it is possible to think well about moral matters without bringing God into the discussion.

Yet should we not suppose that belief in moral objectivism implies the existence of God, that moral objectivism ought to lead someone to suppose that God exists? Here, of course, we need to consider arguments to the effect that we *should* suppose this. There are many of these, but I shall now say something about what I take to be the best arguments presented so far for the conclusion that morality implies the existence of God. The first two come from H. P. Owen (1926–1996) and John Henry Newman (1801–1890). The third comes from Immanuel Kant.

OWEN AND NEWMAN

According to Owen, there are moral claims that "constitute an independent order of reality."[36] Owen takes these claims to be laws or commands objectively made on us. But then, says Owen, "It is impossible to think of a command without also thinking of a commander.... A clear choice faces us. Either we take moral claims to be self-explanatory modes of impersonal existence or we explain them in terms of a personal God."[37] According to Newman, "If, as is the case, we feel responsibility, are ashamed, are frightened at transgressing the voice of conscience, this implies that there is One to whom we are responsible, before whom we are ashamed, whose claim upon us we fear."[38]

In response to what Owen says, I agree that laws and commands often come from what we might call "personal agents." This is the case with laws that govern people in society. Take the United States. In that country, there are laws condemning murder and theft. And these laws come from human legislators. Again, consider university statutes. These amount to laws or commands governing the behavior of students and teachers. And they have been given out by personal agents promulgating them. Yet not everything we think of as a law is something that evidently comes from what we must take to be a personal source.

Consider, for instance, laws of logic such as the law of noncontradiction ("A proposition cannot be both unequivocally true and false,' e.g., "It is impossible for it to be the case that my cat is both a cat and not a cat") or the law of the excluded middle ("If a proposition is unequivocally true, then its contradictory is false,' e.g., "If it is true that my pet is a cat, then 'My pet is

---

[36] H. P. Owen, *The Moral Argument for Christian Theism* (London: George Allen & Unwin, 1965), 49.

[37] Owen, *The Moral Argument*, 49f.

[38] J. H. Newman, *A Grammar of Assent*, ed. C. F. Harold (London: 1947), 83.

not a cat' is false"). Most philosophers look to all people to abide by these "laws." But nobody, so far as I know, holds that they come from some personal being or beings as laws governing a country or university do. So, why suppose that moral laws come from some personal being or beings as do laws governing a country or university do? One might say that moral laws, unlike laws of logic, have *prescriptive* force (that they amount to imperatives or commands). And one might add that where we have imperatives or commands, there is always a personal source from which they derive. Yet while many laws or commands can be clearly traced to a lawmaker or commander, this does not seem to be the case with what Owen takes to be moral laws or moral commands. He thinks that these are things that we can just perceive to be there as binding on us. But even if he is right on this, it would remain that what he means by moral laws or commands are significantly different from laws and commands coming from people. Laws coming from people can be traced to the people giving them out. I mean, for example, that historians can explain how some US law got passed as binding on US citizens. Yet there does not seem to be any comparable history to be investigated when it comes to what Owen takes to be moral laws and commands. No historian is going to be able to trace these back to God.

As for Newman's argument, that is also answerable. Obviously, I might think that I ought to do such and such or refrain from doing such and such. And I might think this without having any human law to which I can appeal. I might also feel bad if I do such and such or fail to refrain from doing such and such. Yet why suppose that there is "One" before *whom* I feel bad? I might feel bad about myself if I make logical errors. But why should I think that there is "One" to whom I am accountable in making logical errors? Newman's account (addressed to a Christian audience) makes sense as a description of what people who already believe that God exists typically think when they take themselves to act against what they take conscience to demand. It makes sense considered as a sermon preached to a choir consisting of those who "feel responsibility, are ashamed, are frightened at transgressing the voice of conscience." But it does nothing to show that God truly exists. It is far too context-dependent to succeed at doing that. It amounts to more of a reminder to Christians who think as Newman did than it does to a reason to suppose that we can move from morality to the conclusion that God exists.

KANT

Kant is critical of several theoretical arguments for the existence of God. Yet in his *Critique of Practical Reason* (1788), he argues that our commitment to acting morally ought to lead us to *postulate* the existence of God. Kant held that there are moral obligations to which everyone should conform. He believed that there is a moral law and that there are moral duties of which all of us need to take account. In particular, he held that everyone ought to aim to promote what he calls "the highest good." He writes: "To bring about the highest good in the world is the necessary object of a will determinable by the moral law."[39]

But Kant thinks that to will the highest good means more than just willing what accords with the moral law. It means more than doing one's moral duty. It also means willing a proper return of happiness to those who pursue moral goodness. In Kant's view, willing the highest good means willing a correlation between moral rectitude and happiness. It means willing that those who do their moral duty should end up being in a good state. And yet, Kant goes on to note, we cannot ensure what he takes morality to require. Or as he puts the point:

> The acting rational being in the world is, after all, not also the cause of the world and of nature itself. Hence there is in the moral law not the slightest basis for a necessary connection between morality and the happiness proportionate thereto, of a being belonging to the world as a part [thereof] and thus dependent on it, who precisely therefore cannot through his will be the cause of this nature and, as far as his happiness is concerned, cannot by his own powers make it harmonize throughout with his practical principles.[40]

Kant here seems to be saying that, while it is rational to pursue the highest good, it seems impossible for us to bring it about. Kant does not think that we should be only seeking our happiness when acting morally. We should be seeking to obey the moral law that is binding on everyone. And Kant is open to the idea that acting morally might result in us being killed. But he thinks of the highest good as incorporating the well-being of all humans. And he therefore thinks that respect for the moral law includes wishing that all human beings should be happy. Yet, as I have noted, Kant recognizes that we cannot guarantee that all human beings are happy. Regardless of our obedience to the moral law, he thinks, we cannot ensure that the highest good shall come about.

Something else I should note is that Kant accepts the principle "Ought implies can." Suppose I say that you *ought* to get yourself from Paris to

---

[39] Immanuel Kant, *Critique of Practical Reason*, trans. Werner S. Pluhar (Indianapolis: Hackett, 2002), 155.
[40] Kant, *Critique of Practical Reason*, trans. Pluhar, 158.

Istanbul in under two minutes. My guess is that you would say that I am talking nonsense. For you obviously *cannot* get yourself from Paris to Istanbul in under two minutes. In that case, though, to say that X *ought* to do such and such is to *presuppose* that X *can* do such and such, which is what Kant thinks. So, he suggests that our aiming for the highest good should lead us to suppose that there is one who can ensure that this comes about – that is, God. He thinks that if we ought to aim at the highest good, then the highest good has to be something the existence of which can be guaranteed to come about. Hence, we find him saying:

> We *ought* to seek to further the highest good (hence this good must, after all, be possible). Therefore the existence of a cause of nature as a whole, distinct from nature, which contains the basis . . . of the exact harmony of [one's] happiness with [one's] morality, is also *postulated*. . . . The highest good in the world is possible only insofar as one assumes a supreme cause of nature that has a causality conforming to moral attitude. . . . The supreme cause of nature, insofar as it must be presupposed for the highest good, is a being that is the cause of nature through *understanding* and *will* (and hence is its originator), i.e. *God*. . . . It is morally necessary to assume the existence of God.[41]

Kant is saying that there are objective moral requirements that cannot be achieved unless God exists. The argument here is not intended by Kant to be a demonstration of God's existence based on morality. Kant's moral objectivism does not depend on belief that God exists. What Kant means by the moral law is something that he thinks reason can establish whether God exists or not. So, he is saying that to act in accordance with the moral law *implicitly* commits us to supposing (or "postulating") that the highest good, to which the moral law directs us, can be realized – this committing us to belief in God as ensuring that the highest good can be realized.[42]

Is that conclusion true, however? It is not if Kant is wrong concerning the objectivist approach to morality with which the conclusion is bound up in his thinking. Letting that point pass for now, though, there are problems with Kant's reasoning from morality to God. Kant is surely right to assume

---

41 *Critique of Practical Reason*, trans. Pluhar, 158.
42 Ad hominem arguments are often taken to be bad since they amount to mere abuse or ridicule. But that is not how I am understanding "ad hominem argument . . ." I am taking such an argument to be one that points out that if someone is committed to conclusion A, then they should not accept conclusion B which contradicts conclusion A. For the value of ad hominem argument, see P. T. Geach, *Reason and Argument* (Oxford: Basil Blackwell, 1976), 26–27.

that "ought" implies "can." It makes no sense for me to tell my cat that it ought to write a book or to tell paralyzed people that they ought to start walking. But why suppose that we are under any obligation to will the highest good if we do not know that it can or will come about?

In other words, why not presume atheism (or the impossibility or unlikeliness of the highest good coming about) to challenge Kant's claim that we ought to will the highest good? Or again, why not settle for a modified form of the obligation to will the highest good? Why not say this: (1) Unless we presume that God exists, we have no good reason to think that we can bring about the highest good in which virtue is rewarded; so we should not think that we ought to will the highest good. (2) Still, we might think that we ought to do whatever tends toward the highest good considered as a hypothetical if unachievable ideal. Notice that people often strive for what they take to be good without knowing that they can bring that good about. For example, people with cancer often struggle with chemotherapy without knowing that it will extend their lives to any serious degree. And people who work overtime for the cause of world peace do not seriously think that their efforts alone can guarantee that happy prospect.

These examples suggest that one might have a possibly unrealizable ideal, and that one might reasonably strive for that ideal – at least with the hope of bringing about something close to it. So, why not give Kant his claim that we ought to will the highest good *without* also conceding that the highest good can be brought about, or can always be brought about, by mere human effort? Or as J. L. Mackie once put it, "Even if, as Kant argues ... 'ought' implies 'can,' the thesis that we ought to seek to promote the highest good only implies that we can *seek to promote* it, and perhaps, since rational seeking could not be completely fruitless, that we can to some extent actually *promote* it. But this does not require that the full realization of the highest good should be possible. For example, it is thoroughly rational to try to improve the condition of human life, provided that some improvement is possible; there is no need to entertain vain hopes for its perfection."[43] In short, one might sympathize with Kant's notions of duty and the moral law without having to suppose that acting with an eye to what Kant means by duty and the moral law is going to result in the highest good coming about. And if I am right here, we do not need to postulate the existence of God for the reasons given by Kant.

---

[43] J. L. Mackie, *The Miracle of Theism* (Oxford: Clarendon Press, 1982), 109.

MORAL THINKING

So, I am arguing, we can think morally or ethically without appealing to God. I am not denying that there might be divine commands that people might rightly take to be binding on them. But moral philosophers rarely, if ever, appeal to divine commands when developing what they have to say. They usually try to explain how we should think about morals without benefit of divine revelation. And this strategy ought to be acceptable even to one who thinks that divine revelation communicates God's will concerning how someone or other should behave. For if there is philosophical sense to be offered concerning moral thinking, that sense cannot be canceled out by anything that God might reveal. Truth cannot contradict truth, so if we happen to arrive at some true understanding of what it is to be morally good, no *genuine* divine *revelation* could be at odds with that understanding. Yet can we arrive at some true understanding of what it is to be morally good – even some *general* understanding?

This question does not arise for people embracing a subjectivist view of ethics. They do not believe that there is any such thing as moral or ethical truth. But the question *does* arise for moral objectivists. And they have answered the question in different ways. Some have appealed to a sense of duty. Others have invoked the notion of moral *intuition*. Yet others have drawn on the notions of virtue and vice.

DUTY

What I have in mind by the "sense of duty" approach to moral goodness holds that the final answer to the question "Why should I do *this* or refrain from *that*?" is "You *just ought* to do this or refrain from that." The trouble with this line of thinking, however, is that it does not explain *why* I should do this or refrain from that. One can, of course, be convinced that one *just ought* to do this or refrain from that, convinced that one perceives oneself to have certain *specifically moral* duties. Yet people have been convinced that they were duty-bound to do all sorts of dreadful things, such as staffing the Nazi concentration camps. When saying this, I am, of course, presuming that these death camps were the result of the actions of people acting in morally bad ways, and you might reject this presumption. If you do not reject it, however, you will see what I mean by being suspicious of appeals to a "sense of duty," when it comes to what we *just ought* to do. People often appeal to what their "conscience" tells them to do – as if conscience were an inner voice directing us toward this or away from that. We might, though, worry about "inner voices" directing us one way or the other. For one thing, appeals to an inner voice of conscience report only what people *think* they should be doing. They do not tell us what they *should* truly be doing.

The word "ought" obviously has a use in our language. So, I might understandably say that if I want to get from New York to London quickly, I ought to take a plane rather than a boat. If I say that, however, I will be able to justify what I say by explaining why flying is a quicker mode of transport than boating. I will not assume that "I *just ought* to fly" is a rational answer to "Why ought I to fly?" By contrast, those who appeal to a uniquely *moral* sense of "ought" (an "ought" that *just ought* to be acted on, one that simply *binds* us of its own accord) seem to be invoking something truly puzzling.

In this connection I suspect that Elizabeth Anscombe was right to say that such an appeal is a holdover from a law conception of ethics according to which doing what we need to do considered as *human beings* (as opposed, say, to good *plumbers* or *logicians*) is to act in accordance with divine law.[44] In the context of such a law conception of ethics, "ought" talk is grounded in appeal to God's governing of the universe to good ends, and it makes sense. A hospital nurse might appeal to the decrees of her medical superiors as giving her reasons for what she should be doing for her patients. By the same token, someone subscribing to a law conception of ethics might make sense by elaborating on what is required by divine law. Yet what if God is taken out of the equation while talk of absolute "oughts" remains? Then, we might think, we would have "dangling oughts" that do not dangle *from anything* since the intellectual support needed for them has been removed. As Anscombe observes, it would be "as if the notion 'criminal' were to remain when criminal law and criminal courts had been abolished and forgotten."[45] Anscombe thinks that talk about the *moral* sense of "ought," where "You just ought" is taken as a final answer to "Why ought I?," is an interesting case of "the survival of a concept outside the framework of thought that made it a really intelligible one."[46]

INTUITION

When referring to the view that moral goodness is discovered by intuition, I am alluding to the claim that moral goodness is not some physical property

---

[44] Cf. Elizabeth Anscombe, "Modern Moral Philosophy," reprinted as chapter 4 in volume 3 of her *Collected Philosophical Papers* (Oxford: Basil Blackwell, 1981). Originally published in 1958, this essay has proved to be extremely influential among moral philosophers.

[45] Anscombe, "Modern Moral Philosophy," 30.

[46] Anscombe, "Modern Moral Philosophy," 31.

but a nonmaterial one that can be known directly and without reasoning from premises to a conclusion. Roughly speaking, the idea here is that people have an intellectual faculty that allows them to know what is morally good *immediately* in something like the way in which we see *straight off* and without argument that no circle can be a square or that two propositions cannot be simultaneously true and false. On this account, there are objective moral truths to be known, but moral goodness is not an empirical property shared by all morally good people. Rather, it is a nonempirical property grasped by an intellectual faculty that allows us to penetrate beyond sensory properties to a nonsensory one.

Yet can one know that someone is morally good *just* by *being convinced* that this is the case? I do not see how one can. Conviction that such and such is the case is not the same as knowing that it is the case. There was a time when people were (understandably) convinced that the sun moved around the earth. "I know that *p*" always invites the question "How do you know that?" And the reply "Because of my conviction" is not an adequate response.

Another problem with the grounding of moral objectivism in alleged intuition of moral goodness lies in the fact that "moral goodness," on this account, is supposed to be something nonmaterial or "nonnatural." We are supposed to perceive or apprehend or be aware of moral goodness, but not as we are aware of things in front of us, such as *this* cat or *that* dog. But why suppose that we have any faculty of literally perceiving or apprehending or being aware of what is not part of the spatiotemporal universe? We might immediately see that no circle is a square, but we cannot do that without learning what certain words mean, and words are part of the material world. The notion of perceiving or apprehending or becoming aware of what is not in any sense material seems curious in the extreme.

VIRTUE AND VICE

Moral philosophers who approach morality with an eye to the notions of virtue and vice do not think that reference to duties and obligations is silly. Indeed, they are typically happy to say that people can have many duties or obligations. But they think that people have duties or obligations in contexts in which they happen to find themselves. They think, for example, that Eleonore might have duties and obligations because of her status as a nurse or a teacher or the manager of a multinational corporation. Yet people such as Aristotle and Aquinas also think that, when considering what it is to be a good *human being*, we need to focus on the word "good."

As I have previously suggested, "good" is a logically attributive adjective. We understand what is being said when told that something is good only if we understand what it is that is being called good. It has been suggested that "good" is not an adjective at all but something like a whoop of approval or a verbal round of applause. Yet "good" is most certainly an adjective in indicative sentences such as "John is a good doctor" or "Elizabeth is a good mother." On the other hand, "good," taken by itself, does not pick out some single property had by all good things. In this sense, therefore, we do not describe anything just by saying that it is good – as we *do* describe something when referring to it as "black" or "wooden" or "organic." And for this reason, one might agree that "good" is not a straightforward descriptive term.

But "good" *is* descriptive considered as a logically attributive adjective tied to a noun. People who know what doctors, *as* doctors, are about will clearly understand what Mary is saying when she declares that Fred is a good doctor and that John is a bad one. And Mary will be understanding here with reference to *descriptions*. She will be thinking, for example, that, while John is hopeless at diagnosing medical symptoms, Fred's diagnoses are almost always correct. When it comes to the use of "good" as a logically attributive adjective, "good" can always be replaced by what we might think of as a more concrete adjective or a collection of more concrete adjectives. For example, instead of saying that Mary is a good lawyer, we can say that she is legally skilled or that she is learned in the law. Instead of saying that Henry is a good father, we can say that he is caring or devoted to his children.

You might reply, "But 'good' is an evaluative term and no description of Mary or Henry tells us that either of them is good." Yet now think about what that reply would commit you to. You would be saying that even though Mary is legally skilled or learned in the law, it does not follow that she is a good lawyer, or that even though Henry is caring and devoted to his children, that does not mean that he is a good father. Of course, in spite of her legal virtues, Mary might be morally bad considered as a human being since, having successfully navigated through some court proceedings, she always goes home to abuse her husband. Again, while Henry is a model father, he might also spend some of his time helping terrorists to prepare bombs intended to kill schoolchildren. But none of this means that we cannot descriptively and objectively capture what Mary's goodness as a lawyer amounts to or what Henry's goodness as a father involves. If anything, it would seem to suggest that we should be asking what is descriptively and objectively involved in being a good *human being* as distinct from being a good lawyer or father.

You might rightly say that there must be a significant difference between being good as a lawyer or a father and being good as a human being. You might add that, when it comes to being good as a human being, there is no skill to which we might appeal. But it would surely be strange if "good" in "good lawyer," "good mother," and "good human being" meant something *completely* different. And it would be extremely odd if "good father" could be explained in factual terms while "good human being" is merely an expression of someone's subjective feelings. In any case, though, there *is* something *common* at stake when things of different kinds are said to be good. A good X might indeed seriously differ from a good Y. But to call anything good is always to say that it is somehow desirable, that it somehow matches up to what we look for it to be considered as what it is. If I commend Mary for being a good lawyer, I am saying that she displays what it takes to succeed when it comes to being a lawyer. If I praise Henry for being a good father, I am saying that he matches up to being what it takes to succeed in being a father. So, why not think that to commend someone for being a good human being is to praise them for being successful as a human being?

When it comes to "good lawyer" or "good father," there are commonly agreed criteria for determining what goodness amounts to. This is not obviously so, however, when it comes to "good human being." On the other hand, though, human beings are things that can be examined and thought of as having various skills and dispositions that favor their well-being considered as what they essentially are. Someone who is lacking an ability to communicate with others is lacking something that they need to flourish considered as what they are by nature (human). We may not blame such a person for this lack, but we can still find it regrettable. And, as Aristotle and Aquinas argued, we can note lots of ways in which people would be better off than they are were they to display the famous cardinal virtues: prudence, justice, temperance, and courage. By "virtue" here I mean a disposition to act in certain ways that contribute to us being good as human beings, something that we might acquire by practice as someone who starts to learn a foreign language might end up speaking it without a second thought. It is in this sense that Aristotle and Aquinas think of cardinal virtues. They do not suppose that someone having these virtues is guaranteed a life without problems. They recognize, for example, that to be just might lead to one being killed by opponents of justice. On the other hand, they think that the cardinal virtues are what people in general need so as to flourish as people. And I agree with them. There is a vast and complex literature on why it is that people need the cardinal virtues. For now, though, I must leave you to think for yourself about the suggestion that there might be a properly *human* way of acting that is *properly* human because of what we are by nature.[47]

Having done that, however, you might say that knowing what this properly human way is does not mean that anyone *should* strive for it. Following David Hume, you might say that "is" does not imply "ought." You might ask, "What logical step can we rely on to move from the seemingly descriptive 'Boiling human babies is a bad human act' to 'One should not boil human babies'?" The sentence "You should not boil human babies" has imperative force. It does not look like a description of anything. So, what can one say to people who accept that "Boiling human babies is a bad human act" while asking why they should not boil human babies?

In my view, everything here depends on human needs. "Why should I do X, Y, or Z, or refrain from doing X, Y, or Z?" seems to me to be a perfectly reasonable question in any context in which it is raised. You might think that "Why should I do this or that?" is properly answered by the reply "You just ought." But I do not think that this answer provides any reasonable guidance when it comes to action. As I suggested above, it looks to be an imperative coming out of nowhere. But we can give each other reasons for acting in this or that way if we focus on what each of us needs to be successful in some way. People cannot fail to be choosing their manner of acting. I mean that if we are truly *acting* (rather than going through some bodily motion such as slipping on a banana skin), then we are always somehow choosing; we are acting voluntarily; we are doing what we *want* to do. And to recognize a manner of acting as being good is always to take it as objectively desirable in some way. So, one can certainly move from descriptive premises to conclusions with "ought" in them given that human beings have certain reasonable wants or desires.

Philosophers such as Aristotle and Aquinas tried to explain this point by distinguishing between what they thought of as *theoretical* reasoning as opposed to *practical* reasoning. By theoretical reasoning they understood reasoning concerning what is the case. They thought, for example, that I might reason: "If cats are carnivores, and if my pet is a cat, then my pet is a carnivore." By practical reasoning they understood reasoning as to what should be done. They thought, for example, that I might reason along these lines: "If I want to get from New York to London as quickly as possible while

[47] For books recommending this suggestion in detail and with clarity, I commend to you the following: Philippa Foot, *Natural Goodness* (Oxford: Clarendon Press, 2001); Herbert McCabe, *The Good Life* (London: Continuum, 2005); and P. T. Geach, *The Virtues* (Cambridge: Cambridge University Press, 1977).

being in London at 8 a.m. on July 8, I should take the only flight leaving New York with that arrival time promised." Theoretical reasoning does not contain any reference to "should" or "should not." But practical reasoning does, and we engage in practical reason on a day-to-day basis. But we do so, of course, because of what we take to be the case theoretically. Furthermore, theoretical premises can lead us to reject examples of practical reasoning, while such premises might make no difference to what we have argued at the theoretical level.

Suppose that I argue that if any cat is a carnivore, and if my pet is a cat, then my pet is a carnivore. My conclusion follows from my premises and no additional premises can show this not to be the case. My conclusion would follow even if I added premises such a "Paris is the capital of France" or "There are no such things as cats." But additional premises can make a huge difference when it comes to practical reasoning. Suppose I reason as follows: "If I want to get from New York to London as quickly as possible while being in London at 8 a.m., I should take the only flight leaving New York with that arrival time promised." That might seem like a good and motivating argument. But not if am told that this flight has been targeted by terrorists who intend on blowing it up. When it comes to practical reasoning, statements of fact play a serious role, but only given rational aims or desires that we have. Yet appeals to such aims or desires is part and parcel of practical as opposed to theoretical reasoning. So, to invoke a serious "is/ought" distinction seems just to miss the difference between theoretical and practical reasoning. Theoretical reasoning does not come with imperatives. Practical reasoning does, while relying on theoretical reasoning. It gives people grounds for how they ought to act given what they have reason to want. They might want well or badly, of course. But that does not mean that they cannot reason well when it comes to what it is objectively good for them to do or to try to do considered as human beings.

MORALITY AND THE WILL OF GOD

Let's suppose we all believe that God exists. Should we therefore think of morality as dependent on God's will? This question can be understood in two ways: (1) Can there be good moral thinking if God does not exist? and (2) Can God determine what, for us, is morally right or wrong? I have already said why I think that the answer to the first of these questions is "Yes." Now I want to turn to the second one.

Some people have said that what is morally right or wrong for us is settled by God issuing decrees as to how we should behave. On this view, how we should behave is to be judged by God *willing* that we should act in this or that way or avoid acting in some other way. But this view does not tell us what *is* morally right or wrong. I might order you to do such and such, but to know this fact is not to know what *is* morally right or wrong. Knowing what I have ordered you to do is only to know what I approve of or disapprove of. And so it must be in the case of "God wills that people should do X and refrain from Y." Even if this claim is true, it does not tell us anything about the nature of activities X and Y *in themselves* considered as *human* activities. To know that God approves of this kind of action and disapproves of that kind is no more to know what the kinds of action are in themselves than it is to know what cannibalism amounts to based on knowing that some people have approved of it while others are hostile to it.

Yet, of course, Christians typically say that certain kinds of action are willed or commanded by God and that certain kinds of actions conflict with God's will or contravene God's commands. And these thoughts have led some critics of Christianity to say that Christians are caught in a dilemma that has damaging consequences for any attempt to equate what is morally good and bad with what God wills or commands. For does God will or command a course of human action because it is morally good? Or is a course of human action morally good because God wills or commands it? It has been argued that if we say that God wills or commands a course of human action because it is morally good, we are committed to supposing that moral goodness and badness have nothing to do with God's will or commands – that God, like morally good people, wills and commands in the light of objective moral truths that are quite independent of God's will. On the other hand, so it has also been argued, if we say that a course of human action is morally good because God wills or commands it, we are committed to the erroneous conclusion that what is morally good or bad when it comes to human actions depends on someone's mere say-so.

In response to these lines of thinking, however, my attitude is rather like that of a child who, when asked to choose between cake and ice cream, says that they want both. For why not say *both* (1) that God wills or commands a course of action because it is morally good, *and* (2) that a course of human action is morally good because God commands it? The justification for (1) here is that if God is goodness itself, then in willing or commanding a course of action God will inevitably be willing what is objectively morally good for human beings. The justification for (2) is that what is objectively morally good for human beings depends on what they are as made to exist by God when considered as things of the kind that they are.

In speaking in favor of (1) here I am not taking God to be a morally good agent as you and I might wish to be. I am not thinking of God as subject to moral imperatives or as something to be judged virtuous or vicious as we can be thought to be. I am supposing that God is the unchangeable source of all creaturely goodness, this being something that reflects what God eternally and essentially is: the ultimately desirable, that which is good without qualification. Considered as such, God's creative action is always a willing of what is good, meaning, among other things, that God wills the moral goodness of morally good creatures. And it is this thought that leads me to accept (2). If we side with an Aristotelian approach to human goodness, as I have done above, then what is good for human beings, what makes for a genuinely good human life, depends on what people essentially are – things that need moral virtues of different kinds. But there being things like this depends on God's creative will, which is not a matter of whim. It amounts to God genuinely willing the world in which human beings can truly flourish and can become good considered as what they are by nature. In effect, what I am saying now is that good moral thinking is part of what God brings about as Creator of all things "visible and invisible." On this account there is no good and quick inference from "Gordon acts morally" to "God exists." We can make sense of the idea that, even if God does not exist, Gordon can be a fine human being. Good moral philosophy and the acting on its findings do not depend on belief that God exists. In this sense, ethics can be separated from religious belief. In another sense, however, there would be no good human beings and no good moral philosophy were it not for God making the universe to be from second to second. In this sense, the good life for people, the morally good life for them, crucially depends on God, as does everything that exists other than God.

CONCLUSION

In this chapter I have tried to give you a sense of some significant answers to the question "What is morality?" I have briefly argued in favor of an objectivist view of ethics while denying that there can be no good moral thinking if God does not exist. I have also rejected some arguments for the conclusion that morality somehow implies the existence of God. I have also said why I think that one way of thinking about human moral goodness is superior to some other ways, and why moral philosophy and natural theology can be brought into alignment with each other. What I have not been able to do is speak to disagreements that people have when it comes to such particular moral questions as "Can there be a just war?," "Is abortion always wrong?," and "What good account can we give when it comes to sexual ethics?" Christians and atheists often differ in their answers to these questions, and many Christians differ among themselves when it comes to them. Something else that I have not been able to do is to reflect on whether there might be virtues displayed by people that go beyond what philosophers such as Aristotle had in mind when talking about cardinal virtues. Aquinas thought that the classical cardinal virtues can be acquired by people on the basis of their natural abilities. But he also thought that people can come to possess virtues going beyond the cardinal ones, virtues that depend entirely on the grace of God. A discussion of that thesis, however, would need a book to itself.

6

Christianity

Michael Ruse

MANY FAITHS: THE PROBLEM OF PLURALISM

I WAS RAISED A QUAKER. AS I EXPLAINED EARLIER, MY GOD WAS ethereal, in major respects unknowable. To be approached in negative terms – what he is not.

> By homely gift and hindered Words
> The human heart is told
> Of Nothing –
> "Nothing" is the force
> That renovates the World – [1]

This is known as "apophatic" theology. The ninth-century theologian John Scotus Erigena wrote: "We do not know what God is. God Himself does not know what He is because He is not anything [i.e., "not any created thing"]. Literally God is not, because He transcends being."[2] Not surprisingly, Quakers are much attracted to mysticism. And many Christians are not! Many would react in horror at such a conception of the Christian God as I have been articulating, especially those who focus on personhood. Their God is a father and they know fully what that means. Stern, perhaps; wise, certainly; and loving, overwhelmingly. "Our father who art in heaven, hallowed be thy name. ... Give us this day our daily bread, and forgive us our sins, as we forgive those who sin against us." In my neck of the woods, the American South, God has rather strong views on such topics as homosexuality and abortion.

---

[1] Emily Dickinson, *The Complete Poems* (New York: Little, Brown, 1960), 1563.
[2] W. Franke, *On What Cannot Be Said: Apophatic Discourses in Philosophy, Religion, Literature, and the Arts, vol. 1: Classic Formulations* (South Bend, IN: University of Notre Dame Press, 2007), 186.

This is just regular Christianity. God knows – perhaps he does – what happens when we get to the Jehovah's Witnesses, the Christadelphians, and the Latter-Day Saints (Mormons). What about the Trinity? The Apostles' Creed. One: "I believe in God the Father Almighty, Maker of heaven and earth." Two: "And in Jesus Christ his only Son our Lord." Three: "I believe in the Holy Ghost." You cannot get much more central to Christian belief than this. But all three of the groups just mentioned – Jehovah's Witnesses, the Christadelphians, and the Latter-Day Saints – deny the Trinity. The Mormons believe that Jesus is separate from God and only one of God's sons (another is Lucifer).

We move beyond to the Jews and Muslims. At least they believe in one God, the same God as do the Christians. But they too deny the Trinity. They differ in other respects too. For Christians, the hereafter is all-consuming. "In my Father's house there are many dwelling places. If it were not so, would I have told you that I go to prepare a place for you?"[3] For Jews, although it does pick up somewhat as we approach the Christian era, the hereafter is very vague and not that exciting. The big issue is God's promise to Abraham that the Jewish people would keep going. Islam is another kettle of fish. If Richard Dawkins's views of the afterlife in Islam are anywhere like correct, even Donald Trump will find himself busy. Christianity, to the contrary, is a bit deflating on the subject. "For in the resurrection they neither marry nor are given in marriage, but are like angels in heaven."[4] I take it that this is not a suggestion that heaven is an eternal Playboy Club.

It continues. Buddhists famously have no Creator God, although it is true that they do have orders of gods. At one with the Mormons here, I guess. And then what about the pagans? They worship the Earth itself.[5] "The blue whale and the redwood tree are not the largest living organisms on Earth; the ENTIRE PLANETARY BIOSPHERE is." Individual organisms are the cells of Terrabios (now known as Gaia). The deserts and the forests and the prairies and the coral reefs (the "biomes") are the organs. "ALL the components of a biome are essential to its proper functioning, and each biome is essential to the proper functioning of Terrabios." Not only do you worship this super-organism; it has moral implications. "You can't kill all the bison in North America, import rabbits to Australia, cut or burn off whole forests, or plow and plant the Great Plains with wheat without seriously disrupting the ecology. Remember the dust bowl? Australia's plague of rabbits? Mississippi

---

[3] John 14:2.   [4] Matthew 22:30.
[5] M. Ruse, *The Gaia Hypothesis: Science on a Pagan Planet* (Chicago: University of Chicago Press, 2013).

basin floods? The present drought in the Southwestern U.S.? Terrabios is a
SINGLE LIVING ORGANISM, and its parts are not to be removed,
replaced, or rearranged."[6]

Scientists differ, sometimes bitterly, over theories and purported facts. But
they have justifiable confidence that there is an end and someday that will be
reached. I simply do not know how you could possibly hope to reconcile all
these faith-derived positions. Either Jesus is the Son of God, or he is not.
Either there is a heaven or there is not. Either the world is alive or it is not.
Either you, pagan-like, need to practice polyamory (group sex in a kind of
sanctified way) or you do not. John Hick did his best to answer this problem
of "pluralism." He writes:

> Let us begin with the recognition, which is made in all the main religious
> traditions, that the ultimate divine reality is infinite and as such transcends
> the grasp of the human mind. God, to use our Christian term, is infinite. He
> is not a thing, a part of the universe, existing alongside other things; nor is
> he a being falling under a certain kind. And therefore, he cannot be defined
> or encompassed by human thought. We cannot draw boundaries around
> his nature and say he is this and no more. If we could fully define God,
> describing his inner being and his outer limits, this would not be God. The
> God whom our minds can penetrate and whom our thoughts can circum-
> navigate is merely a finite and partial image of God.[7]

We are all like the blind men and the elephant. We describe different parts of
the elephant as we feel it, but in the end, it is all one elephant, and our
knowledge is limited.

With reason, Hick had a truly saintly reputation. I have mentioned his
efforts to bring together people of different faiths, in the British Midlands
industrial city of Birmingham. I wish I could see him as offering the route to
a successful end. I agree fully that if the Christian is to get out of the
pluralism mess, one must take an approach along the lines taken by Hick.
And indeed, one can see reasons for so doing. Given the world as it is – or
rather, as it was before the internet – one has people living in different,
essentially isolated cultures. What knew the Ancient Jews of the religious
developments in India or China? Little wonder that different peoples came
up with different world views. But, I ask, "Is there any underlying shared,

---

[6] O. Zell-Ravenheart, *Green Egg Omelet: An Anthology of Art and Articles from the Legendary Pagan Journal* (Franklin Lakes, NJ: New Page Books, 2009), 93.

[7] J. Hick, *God and the Universe of Faiths: Essays in the Philosophy of Religion* (New York: St. Martin's Press, 1973), 139.

core-belief system to the various religions, and is it one that a Christian
would find acceptable?" Hick certainly thinks there is and – surprise!
surprise! – it seems remarkably like the belief system he has always endorsed.
He writes of an "eschatological unity" that is shared. He draws our attention
to "St John's vision of the heavenly city at the end of the Christian scrip-
tures." For the heathen, let me quote the relevant passage.

> Then one of the seven angels who had the seven bowls full of the seven last
> plagues came and said to me, "Come, I will show you the bride, the wife of
> the Lamb."

> And in the spirit he carried me away to a great, high mountain and showed
> me the holy city Jerusalem coming down out of heaven from God.

> It has the glory of God and a radiance like a very rare jewel, like jasper, clear
> as crystal.[8]

Well, yes, all very nice. At the least, it seems that Hick sees a future of
meaning culminating in the possibility of something good. But is this
necessarily the underlying message of all religions? My interactions with
pagans have, somewhat to my surprise, been rather refreshing. These days
I am not so sure about polyamory – I am nigh eighty years old and my long-
past experience was that half of the fun of illicit sex was that it was illicit –
but I came away convinced of their deep commitment to the environment
and its well-being. And yet, I had no sense that we are going anywhere
eschatologically, as it were. Their thinking, perhaps not surprisingly, was
much more in tune with Greek thinking – no beginning, no end, no overall
direction. There was no sense that we are trying to accumulate Brownie
points to get into heaven. (To be fair, Christians would deny that they are
into that either. It is the Pelagian heresy. To which I can only reply that what
people proclaim and what they really believe are often not the same.)

Of course, even if there is a shared under-belief, that does not make it
true. Before that, however, I fear that Hick has somewhat underestimated
the possibility of getting to a shared belief, whatever its nature. If I were a
person of faith, I would say that all will be revealed in the end, and, for the
present, I am not at all surprised that peoples of different cultures have
different conceptions of ultimate reality. It is part and parcel of the
transcendent God picture I have endorsed. To which I make the same
reply as before. I am not a person of faith. I just cannot see the end
resolution. Either the Catholics are right or the Mormons are right.

---

[8] Revelation 21:9–11.

They cannot both be right. Either the Pope is the representative of Peter and what he says goes, at least when he is speaking ex cathedra. Or this is an illusion. Either Joseph Smith found and translated those golden plates, or the Mormon religion is the biggest con game of the nineteenth century. Except for the Seventh-Day Adventists and the Christian Scientists and the Jehovah's Witnesses and the Christadelphians and the Plymouth Brethren and . . . Turning from belief to activity, either God is okay with group sex – I guess King Solomon with 700 wives and 300 concubines would qualify here – or God is not okay. I suspect God is not okay, since they turned Solomon from God. Either way, I just don't see how you – or God – can resolve these dilemmas. A believer will say that they know the truth. A nonbeliever, like myself, armed only with reason and for whom faith is a nonstarter, can only wonder.

MIRACLES

Let us start to dig into the claims of Christians. Three seem overwhelming. There is a Creator God. Humans are special, we are made "in the image of God." We got into a mess, so God sent his son Jesus down to Earth to put things right. We have looked at the standard proofs for the existence of this God, as well as at counterarguments. I want now to look at one more argument, which covers not just God but Jesus also. This is the argument from miracles. The world is law-bound. It is "natural." Miracles are violations of law. There must be some reason. This reason cannot be natural, hence it must be "supernatural." That of course does not prove the existence of the Christian God, but the nature of the miracles is going to give hints if not significant information. Miracles that are helpful or worth having in some way are pointing to a benevolent deity. Miracles that go the other way point to an unfriendly, perhaps even malicious deity. Presumably, the magnitude of the miracle is also relevant. A God who can part the Red Sea and let the Israelites pass is clearly one up on the God of the dermatologist who is good at cleaning up pimples on noses. Happily would I bow down before a God who could get my graduate students to finish their dissertations on time.

What do we say about this? I am a bit of a Humean on these matters. It is more likely that the stories are made up than that they are true.

That no testimony is sufficient to establish a miracle, unless the testimony be of such a kind, that its falsehood would be more miraculous, than the fact, which it endeavours to establish; and even in that case there is a mutual destruction of arguments, and the superior only gives us an assurance suitable to that degree of force, which remains, after deducting the inferior.[9]

I don't take this to deny the possibility of miracles. Logically, it is quite possible for the molecules of a dead person to rearrange themselves so the person is again living. I am not a Cartesian dualist, so I have no big problem with the mind and thought coming back as a consequence of the rearrangement. It is just that I don't think them reasonable.

I am not saying that you should never use the term "miracle." When I was growing up in the 1940s, almost everyone in England spoke of the evacuation of the British Army from Dunkirk, at the end of May and beginning of June 1940, as a miracle. In fact, it was known as the "Miracle of Dunkirk." First, for whatever reason, Hitler ordered his troops not to enter the town and deliver the coup de grace. Then the channel, so often stormy (think of the storms after D-Day in June 1944) was like a mill pond. All sorts of little ships and boats were able to lift men off the beaches. But if you had asked people if this was a direct intervention by God or just a fortuitous combination of events, I suspect most would have looked at you as if you were queer in the head. It was the meaning of the event that counted. God made it possible for the British to go on fighting the evils of the Nazi regime. That was the miracle. I very much doubt that many thought that God had entered Hitler's vile mind and manipulated it.

In any case, miracles and their purported evidence so often seem so tawdry. I am all in favor of the miracle at Cana, turning water into wine, but it seems so much more meaningful if the host is moved by Jesus and recognizes the moral thing to do, rather than by something done by the magician David Copperfield. I worry too about the big miracles, particularly the resurrection. It really does sound forced to claim that, because the first reporters were women, and because it was so unlikely back then that anyone would take seriously reports from women, the only explanation is that it must be true that women were the first reporters. No one would have made it up. If everything about the Christian religion depends on this sort of thing, no thanks. For me, it is far more meaningful if the disciples are down and depressed, and then, suddenly, they know in their hearts that their Redeemer liveth. If you tell me that it is all mob psychology, my response would be that

---

[9] D. Hume, *An Enquiry Concerning Human Understanding* (Oxford: Oxford University Press, 2007), chapter 10.

I would expect this. It is no less a miracle than that Dunkirk was made possible by a quirk in the weather.

Finally, today's miracles. Pope John Paul II was made a saint on the basis of this sort of thing.

> The late pontiff was credited with curing Floribeth Mora, a woman from the town who had a severe brain injury. Her family prayed to the pope's memory and says she was cured on May 1, 2011.

> Mora's neighbor Cecilia Chavez voiced the community's feelings. "How can it be that in a small country such as Costa Rica, in this poor small neighborhood, this miracle took place? It's amazing! There are no words to describe it," she said.

> Floribeth Mora had walked into a hospital in Costa Rica's capital San Jose complaining of a headache. Neurosurgeon Alejandro Vargas Roman, who diagnosed her with a brain aneurysm, says the question of why it disappeared without surgical intervention is without explanation. "I have never read about this anywhere around the world," he said.[10]

Yes, indeed! And note what God was willing to do to bolster the standing of a man who consistently turned a blind eye to the horrendous sexual abuse by his priests, who were causing untold agony for small children. Not to mention his continued support and friendship for the charismatic Mexican founder of the Legion of Christ, Fr. Marcial Maciel Degollado, a man with a truly disgusting personal record. Enough said.

THE TRINITY

With respect to miracles, I am not saying that neither God nor Jesus is divine. I am saying that I don't think the biblical miracles do the trick. And I am even less enthused by non-biblical miracles. Move along. Jesus came down to Earth to help us. Now, if he is just a prophet – like Elijah or Elisha, or even like Mohammed – at one level, there is no big problem. God is God is God. And only he is God. However, generally for the Christian – acknowledging that some slipped off the edge into Unitarianism – this is not enough. The whole point is that Jesus is not just a good fellow. He is himself God, whatever that means. And since, following Judaism, Christians are totally committed monotheists, that means that Jesus must himself be the God – the God of the Old Testament. Worse than this, Jesus gets killed and

---

[10] Henry Ridgwell, "Pope John Paul II to Become Saint after Miracle Approved," *VOA News*, July 5, 2013, www.voanews.com/europe/pope-john-paul-ii-become-saint-after-miracle-approved.

although supposedly he returns for a while, it is temporary. But we cannot be abandoned, so in a sense he cannot leave. He stays in the form of the Holy Ghost, to speak archaically, or Holy Spirit, to use a more modern term. In other words, we have three gods, but since there is only one God, they all must be part of the same God. The Trinity.

Christians are backed into this whether they want to be or not. Unlike the Jews, they do have a Messiah. Unlike the Muslims, they do have a divine presence among them – for a while at least. If you are going to go with the Jesus story, then you are stuck with two Gods or one God, two-in-one, and really it is hard to avoid a third God, or one God, three-in-one, if you are not going to leave us stranded and alone after the drama of the Gospels. Leaving for a moment the question of what exactly Jesus was up to in his time down here on Earth, the nineteenth-century theologian Friedrich Schleiermacher has a very good take on things.

> Unless the being of God in Christ is assumed, the idea of redemption could not be thus concentrated in his Person. And unless there were such a union also in the common Spirit of the Church the Church could not be the Bearer and Perpetuator of the redemption through Christ. Now these are exactly the essential elements in the doctrine of the Trinity.[11]

Well, you might need something like this to make sense of the whole Jesus story, but you are not going to find much biblical evidence to back you up on this. Perhaps not so much of a worry to people like the Quakers, who have always relied more on the Holy Spirit than on the written word. But horrendously troublesome to more conventional Christians who do turn to the Bible for guidance, and a nightmare for Protestants who are into *sola scriptura*. Luther and Calvin really wriggled on this one, and a number of Reformers went all of the way and denied Christ's divinity. Charles Darwin's wife Emma used to attend the village Anglican church. Raised a Unitarian, during holy communion she turned her back on the altar. For her, it was heretical to believe that Jesus was divine.

This is just a start. What does it all mean and how does it work? To be honest, for all that for 2,000 years some very bright people have tried to make sense of all this, you are trying to square the circle. It just can't be done. You patch up the container on one side, and a leak appears on the other. Generally, you fall into one of two corresponding heresies. On the one side, you have Ebionitism, where you keep God, Son, and Spirit separate but then have trouble with the One. On the other side, you have Docetism, where you

---

[11] F. Schleiermacher, *The Christian Faith* (Edinburgh: T and T Clark, 1928), 147.

have the One but trouble with seeing how God, Son, and Spirit function apart.[12] How, for instance, do you make much sense of the cry from the Cross – "And about three o'clock Jesus cried with a loud voice, 'Eli, Eli, lema sabachthani?' that is, 'My God, my God, why have you forsaken me?'"[13] – if you have one and the same person on both sides? The very point is that Jesus is in terrible physical and psychological stress. That is what makes the moment of realization and acceptance – "Then Jesus, crying with a loud voice, said, 'Father, into your hands I commend my spirit.' Having said this, he breathed his last."[14] – so very powerful. Luther tended a bit toward Docetism – "God in his own nature cannot die; but now that God and man are united in one person, it is called God's death when the man dies who is one person or substance with God." Calvin a bit towards Ebionitism – "The Son of God descended miraculously from heaven, yet without abandoning heaven."[15]

The Cappadocians, three saintly pals, writing in the fourth century, were hugely influential on later understandings of the Trinity. They wrote of one substance, or *ousia*, and of three persons, or *hypostases*. Showing obvious Platonic influences, where individuals in this world get their nature by "participating" in the Form, they argued that the three – God, Son, and Spirit – get their nature by participating or relating to the one divine substance.

> I shall say that essence (*ousia*) is related to person (*hypostasis*) as the general to the particular. Each one of us partakes of existence because he shares in ousia while because of his individual properties he is A or B. So, in the case in question, ousia refers to the general conception, like goodness, godhead, or such notions, while hypostasis is observed in the special properties of fatherhood, sonship, and sanctifying power.[16]

Thus, just as Wilbur (*Charlotte's Web*), Piglet (*Pooh*), and Napoleon (*Animal Farm*) are all pigs because they participate in the Form of Pig (for all that Napoleon is trying to wriggle out of it), so God, Son, and Spirit – *hypostases* – share in the same substance – *ousia*.

Also influential is – as one would expect – Augustine's thinking on the Trinity. He was more inclined to the psychological, arguing that we humans, being made in the image of God, would be expected to show or echo the Trinity. He argued that mind has three parts – memory (*mens*),

[12] A. E. McGrath, *Christian Theology: An Introduction*, 2nd ed. (Oxford: Blackwell, 1997).
[13] Matthew 27:46.   [14] Luke 23:46.
[15] D. Marmion and R. V. Nieuwenhove, *An Introduction to the Trinity* (Cambridge: Cambridge University Press, 2011), 140.
[16] Basil the Great, *Epistle*, 214.4.

understanding (*notia*), and will (*amor*). Less proof and more expansion on earlier thinking, Augustine made much of the way in which the will functions as loving – the importance of which is underlined by the great prayer, ending: "And now faith, hope, and love abide, these three; and the greatest of these is love."[17]

One could continue with historical exposition. Particularly significant was the controversy over the question of the role of Jesus in making or creating the Trinity – the *filioque* question. Did the Holy Spirit come straight from the first person of the Trinity, God, or was the Spirit created through Jesus from God? The Cappadocian position seems to imply that the Spirit comes straight from God, whereas Augustinian thinking seems to imply that memory and understanding lead to the will, to love. The Spirit comes from God through Jesus. Augustine backed this with biblical evidence. Jesus comes to the disciples after the Resurrection.

> When it was evening on that day, the first day of the week, and the doors of the house where the disciples had met were locked for fear of the Jews, Jesus came and stood among them and said, "Peace be with you."
>
> After he said this, he showed them his hands and his side. Then the disciples rejoiced when they saw the Lord.
>
> Jesus said to them again, "Peace be with you. As the Father has sent me, so I send you."
>
> When he had said this, he breathed on them and said to them, "Receive the Holy Spirit."[18]

One should say that this is no small matter. It was one of the root causes of the split of the Eastern and Western Churches. The former, the Orthodox, go for spirit straight from God, and the latter, the Roman and Protestant churches, for spirit from God through Christ. It is still a matter of controversy when reciting the Nicene Creed. Does one say, "I believe in the Holy Spirit, the Lord, the giver of life, who proceeds from the Father and the Son"? Or does one leave the son out of this?

So much for exposition. I am much tempted to leave discussion as an exercise for the reader. Only a believer could believe in any of it. Let us leave Augustine's somewhat dicey psychologizing out of this – although one cannot forebear noticing that anyone who takes seriously Hume's distinction between "is" statements and "ought" statements is going to have questions about moving from memory and understanding straight to love, apart from

---

[17] 1 Corinthians 13:13.   [18] John 20:19–22.

the fact that there are many clever people who are not very loving – and turn to the Cappadocian analysis. All the problems of Platonism are right there, and more of their own. What is the status of the Forms, and are they really needed? A nominalist would say that you can get the similarities without positing a hypothetical entity in the rational world, which, when it comes down to it, doesn't seem to do much anyway. And what is it to "participate" in a Form? These are just words. What really is the relationship between Jesus and God? If Jesus participates in God, does this make him part human and part divine or wholly divine in some sense? Apart from anything else, the particulars exist in our world of becoming – neither truly real nor truly nonreal. Even if this is good enough for Jesus, is this good enough for the Spirit let alone God? And obviously hovering over everything is the Docetism/Ebionitism division. If you might say that Augustine tends a bit toward Docetism – everything is really different aspects of one functioning mind – the Cappadocians clearly tend toward Ebionitism. Wilbur, Piglet, and Napoleon really are three different porcine persons. Could one not equally say the same of Father, Son, and Holy Ghost? They are three different divine persons? Assuming, that is, that being part of this world does not preclude being divine in some sense.

What does one say? If ever there was a case of preaching to the converted, this is it. Christians are committed to something like the Trinity. It comes with the religion. But if two such fundamental figures as Luther and Calvin – both *sola scriptura*, both responding to the problems of the medieval Catholic Church – can come to such very different positions on the nature of Christ – man or God? – then what are the rest of us to make of it? For a nonbeliever like me we make nothing of it. We have a made-up story. Fiction.

ORIGINAL SIN

Finally, what about the need for and role of Jesus? Why did he have to come to Earth? Why did God have to get involved? Because God wants us to be saved, able to spend eternity in bliss with Him – we are, after all, made in his image – and at the moment this is impossible. We humans are not perfect, we are sinners, and therefore not suitable material for heaven. This is prima facie odd, since we are the creation of a good God, in his image. One would expect us to be perfect. The Christian answer – that is to say, the answer of those within the Augustinian tradition, one eschewed by many Protestants like the Quakers, not to mention the Orthodox Church in toto – is our old friend, original sin. Note that original sin is a theological doctrine and is not what we normally mean by sin. Or rather, it is more than what we mean by sin. Cain killed Abel and that was a sin. Why did he, the creation of a good God, do such a thing? Because of original sin. According to Augustine, who was drawing heavily on Paul, the sin of Adam – eating that apple – tainted us all and that is why we are sinners. We may not be born sinners, but we have inclinations that way. According to Augustine and Paul before him, the death of Jesus on the Cross was a blood sacrifice that wiped out or made null our sins. First the sin, Adam's disobedience; then the sacrifice and its consequence. Eternal salvation – or at least the possibility thereof.

> Therefore, just as sin came into the world through one man, and death came through sin, and so death spread to all because all have sinned – [19]

However:

> For just as by the one man's disobedience the many were made sinners, so by the one man's obedience the many will be made righteous.[20]

It is through belief – "justification by faith" – that we can get off the hook.

> the righteousness of God through faith in Jesus Christ for all who believe. For there is no distinction, since all have sinned and fall short of the glory of God; they are now justified by his grace as a gift, through the redemption that is in Christ Jesus.[21]

A host of worries come gushing up, starting with revulsion at the idea that blood sacrifice, of the most barbaric kind, is necessary for the cleansing of our sins. This is truly pagan, although I suspect that most of today's pagans would be horrified at the very thought. Could not the sins be eradicated in another way, for instance, by a marijuana-induced love-in, involving lots of group sex? Less excitingly, why cannot we save ourselves, perhaps through good deeds? That, as noted, is the Pelagian heresy; but, why should it be a heresy? Should a decision made more than 1,500 years ago be binding on us?

Then, there is the worry about the nature of Jesus, God and/or man, in all of this. The usual reason for Jesus' being on the Cross is that only God can pay the debt needed to wash away our sins. However, there is a line of theological thought that denies God can suffer or feel pain. Whatever is the personhood of God, it simply cannot be like ours. Thus Anselm: "For when thou beholdest us in our wretchedness, we experience the effect of compassion, but thou dost not experience the feeling."[22] Thus Aquinas: "To sorrow,

---

[19] Romans 5:12.   [20] Romans 5:19.   [21] Romans 3:22–24.
[22] St. Anselm, *Anselm: Proslogium, Monologium, an Appendix on Behalf of the Fool by Gaunilon; and Cur Deus Homo*, trans. S. N. Deane (Chicago: Open Court, 1903), 13.

therefore, over the misery of others does not belong to God."[23] God, it is said, is "impassible." Which means that at best one is left with a kind of Calvin position, where it is Jesus-as-man suffering on the Cross, not Jesus-as-God. Which rather destroys the whole point of the Crucifixion and makes one wonder why it had to be a God in the first place. Would not Sophie Scholl's death on the guillotine for opposing Hitler do just as well, if not better?

To a nonbeliever, original sin is starting to look as much in a pickle as the Trinity. No one is denying that we are sinners. There is no doubt about that in an age that saw Heinrich Himmler in action. The question is why we are sinners. There are all sorts of theological conundrums with the Augustinian position, and that is before we get to uncomfortable empirical questions about the actual existence of Adam and Eve, and their supposedly sinless nature before that unfortunate fruit eating. The human species may have gone through bottlenecks, but (as noted earlier) the population was never less than 10,000 or so. And the parents would have been as nice and nasty as their offspring.[24] Sin did not suddenly come into the world, one sunny afternoon in a nice garden somewhere in the Mideast. Moreover, original sin has some rather unpleasant applications. Apparently, it is this original sin that is at the root of the nonbelief of Michael Ruse and Richard Dawkins and Uncle Tom Cobley and all. Thus, Saint John Paul II:

> According to the Apostle, it was part of the original plan of the creation that reason should without difficulty reach beyond the sensory data to the origin of all things: the Creator. But because of the disobedience by which man and woman chose to set themselves in full and absolute autonomy in relation to the One who had created them, this ready access to God the Creator diminished.[25]

Frankly, it is condescendingly ad hoc to suggest that I and Dawkins and the others are differentially smeared with original sin in a way that believers are not. In 2018, Cardinal Theodore McCarrick relinquished his red hat after accusations of sexual abuse, dating back to at least the early 1970s, of young men, some of whom were mere children, not yet teenagers. His behavior was well known, and several times substantial sums of money had been paid out in compensation and to hush things up. I very much doubt that Richard Dawkins is as pure as driven snow. I know that I am not. But neither of us

---

[23] St. Thomas Aquinas, *Summa theologiae*, I (London: Burns, Oates and Washbourne, 1952), I, 21, 3.

[24] M. Ruse, *The Philosophy of Human Evolution* (Cambridge: Cambridge University Press, 2012).

[25] John Paul II, *Fides et Ratio: Encyclical Letter of John Paul II to the Catholic Bishops of the World* (Vatican City: L'Osservatore Romano, 1998).

have used our power so to degrade our status and to inflict such awful harm on young people. I simply do not know what to say to someone who says that Dawkins and I, through no fault of our own, are tainted in a way that McCarrick, through no merit of his own, is not.[26]

THE DARWINIAN DIVIDE

I don't want to end this discussion of Christianity on a high horse of indignation. Why am I so far from someone like my coauthor, a thoroughly decent, extremely intelligent and learned person? The simple fact is that he and I are on opposite sides of the Darwinian Revolution. He believes that humans are special. We are, uniquely in the animal and plant kingdoms, made in the image of God. From that, everything follows. Our nature, the need of a Redeemer, the ultimate purpose of it all. I believe that although humans are certainly distinct, unique in our physical nature, our thinking, and our behavior, so are all other animal and plant species. Most importantly, we humans are part of the tree of life that connects us all. Ultimately, we are not that special. Or, rather, we are special, because everything is special. We don't need or merit special treatment. There is no Redeemer of humans any more than there is a Redeemer of warthogs. If I had faith, then presumably I would think otherwise. I don't, and that is an end to it.

Brian Davies

INTRODUCTION

I have concentrated on what I think we can know of God independently of divine revelation. I have suggested that we have reason to suppose that God exists as that which accounts for there being something rather than nothing. Yet I have also said that our knowledge of God's nature is extremely limited. If God is the Creator, then God is not part of the universe. To think that God is anything like an item in the universe leaves us with the puzzle I have concerning the universe as a whole: What accounts for its sheer existence? The more one tries to conceive of God as like *anything* in the universe, the further away one is from grasping what God is.

---

[26] In using the example of Cardinal McCarrick, I am not trying subtly – or not so subtly – to imply all organized religion is evil. The enforced celibacy on the priests of the Roman Catholic Church leads to great wickedness. The eighteenth- and nineteenth-century campaign of Quakers and Evangelicals to abolish slavery was morally humbling.

As I have also said, this does not mean that we cannot make true statements about God. We can, for example, speak of God as acting (as Creator). We can also speak of God as omnipotent, as good, and as willing goodness to creatures. In addition, we can intelligibly deny certain things of God – that God is bodily, mutable, or able to be causally acted on by anything. As I have also argued, however, to speak of God in these ways cannot be to single out God as a spatiotemporal thing with a set of distinct "attributes." I have been claiming that all that is *in* God *is* God and that God is not an individual belonging to a natural kind who happens to have a set of distinguishable features. It is this kind of thinking that has led me to stress that, in a *serious* sense, we do not know what God is. You may think that in saying all this I am suggesting something theologically unusual or even radical. But I am not. What I have so far been arguing about our ignorance of God is commonplace for authors such as Aquinas. It is also clearly proclaimed as true in the 1994 *Catechism of the Catholic Church*, according to which:

> God transcends all creatures. We must therefore continually purify our language of everything in it that is limited, image-bound or imperfect, if we are not to confuse our image of God "the inexpressible, the incomprehensible, the invisible, the ungraspable" – with our human representations. Our human words always fall short of the mystery of God.[27]

MYSTERY AND THE DOCTRINE OF THE TRINITY

I have just reiterated what I have previously suggested about God because of the topic of the present chapter. For I want to make it clear that I do not view the doctrine of the Trinity as an attempt to explain *what* God is so as to leave us with an *understanding* of God. Catholic priests and clergy of other denominations often dread trying to preach on what Christians refer to as "Trinity Sunday" (which celebrates the doctrine of the Trinity). Why so? Often because they feel that they know where they are when thinking about God as Creator but are confused when it comes to the "mystery" of the Trinity. But why should they feel so confused? Why should they think that the Trinity is more mysterious than God considered as the maker of all

---

[27] *Catechism of the Catholic Church*, 18. The first quote in this text comes from the Anaphora in the *Liturgy of St. John Chrysostom* (Archbishop of Constantinople in the fifth century). The second comes from the fourth Lateran Council of the Catholic Church (1215). The third comes from Aquinas (*Summa contra Gentiles*, I, 30).

things "visible and invisible"? If to say that God exists is to say that there is something we cannot comprehend, why should we think that to preach the doctrine of the Trinity is to preach about something less comprehensible than the nature of God? To assert the existence of God is to draw attention to a mystery that defies the human mind. To assent to the doctrine of the Trinity is not to embrace a mystery more incomprehensible than what we are saying when holding that God exists at all.

It has been suggested that the Trinity is not really all that mysterious. Here I refer to what is called "Social Trinitarianism," according to which the Trinity amounts to three centers of consciousness (Father, Son, and Holy Spirit) united by their divinity while individually providing a fine model of how we should be with each other (caring and loving and so on).[28] Yet this thought is at odds with the doctrine of the Trinity in its traditional form as ratified by Church Councils such as the First Council of Constantinople (AD 381) and the Council of Chalcedon (AD 451). According to this, there is but one God who exists as three "persons." But "persons" here does not mean "centers of consciousness." In Latin formulations of the doctrine of the Trinity, the Father, the Son, and the Holy Spirit are commonly each referred to as a *persona* (a word that is naturally translated into English as "person"). In Greek formulations, however, each is referred to as a *hypostasis*, with later Latin writers preferring the term *suppositum*. In using these words, theologians were stressing that Father, Son, and Spirit are somehow *distinct* without being three gods. The orthodox doctrine of the Trinity affirms a distinction of "persons" in God while insisting on the unity of the divine nature. It is not asking us to think of God as a committee of like-minded people with good moral sense working with a good and common aim for human beings. In one sense, but only in *one* sense, the doctrine of the Trinity is not concerned with human beings at all.

I say this since the classical doctrine of the Trinity is defended by people who typically distinguish between the "immanent" Trinity and the "economic" Trinity. "Immanent" here has the meaning "existing only in" and derives from a distinction to be made between action that is only in one thing and action of an agent insofar as it has an effect outside the agent. If I kick you, I act on you, so my action amounts to me producing some change in you. But what if I fall in love with you without ever acting in a way that shows that I have done so? Then my loving you remains in me. Hence, in

---

[28] For a description and critique of social Trinitarianism, see Brian Leftow, "Anti Social Trinitarianism," in Thomas McCall and Michael Rea, eds., *Philosophical and Theological Essays on the Trinity* (Oxford: Oxford University Press, 2009).

theological discussions of the Trinity, "immanent" is flagging what the Trinity is *regardless* of its creating the universe. By contrast, "economic" (a word derived from the Greek *oikonomia*, which literally means "household management") is applied to the Trinity to signify how God acts to draw people into union with God and all that God wills.

This distinction, which is an ancient one, is not implying that there are two divine trinities as there are two major political parties in the United States. Indeed, a commonplace among contemporary Christian theologians is that the immanent Trinity *is* the economic Trinity.[29] The idea here is that the one true God can be considered (1) for what God is apart from creatures (immanent Trinity) and (2) for what God has revealed himself to be in history by acting as that which is triune (economic Trinity).

On this account, the doctrine of the Trinity is revealed in the New Testament and the teachings of the Church, and it can be thought of in terms of how God in time has acted so as present what God eternally is. Talk about the economic Trinity rests on thoughts about what the eternal God has revealed himself to be during time. Conversely, those concerned only with the immanent Trinity are conscious that God as revealed in history is not different from what God eternally is. This immanent/economic distinction naturally prompts two questions: (1) How can we think of God as Trinity from eternity? and (2) How can we think of God as Trinity given that God is the Creator of all things? You might say that God is as God does. And the immanent/economic Trinitarian distinction arises as theologians reflect *both* on what God is from eternity *and* on how God has freely produced a spatiotemporal universe without being a spatiotemporal individual.

CHRISTIAN SCRIPTURE AND THE DOCTRINE OF THE TRINITY

You will not find the formula "God is a trinity of persons" anywhere in the Old or New Testament. This formula emerged over time as Christians came to reflect on certain New Testament texts. Some of these texts are ones in which Jesus is portrayed as referring to God as his father in an intimate sense, not just that in which pious Jews took God to be the father of Israel (cf. Mark 14:36, Matthew 26:42, and Luke 23:46). Again, Jesus talks to his disciples by distinguishing between "my father" and "your father" while also seeming to claim to speak with divine authority (as in the Sermon on the Mount, with its refrain to the effect of "You read such and such in the Old

---

[29] Cf. Karl Rahner, *The Trinity* (New York: Crossroad, 1998).

Testament, but I say to you . . ."). Famously, of course, at the outset of John's gospel Jesus is identified as "the Word," which was "with" God and "is" God from "the beginning." At the end of that gospel one of Jesus' disciples addresses him as "My Lord and my God." John's gospel is often said to present a view of Jesus that goes beyond what we find in the synoptic gospels (Matthew, Mark, and Luke). But there are strong parallels to passages in John in the synoptic gospels. Compare, for instance, John 8:15–16 and Matthew 11:27. In the first of these Jesus declares, "You judge by human standards; I judge no one. Yet even if I do judge, my judgment is valid; for it is not I alone who judge, but I and the Father who sent me." In the second passage we find Jesus saying: "All things have been handed over to me by my Father; and no one knows the Son except the Father, and no one knows the Father except the Son and anyone to whom the Son chooses to reveal him." At the end of Matthew's gospel we have Jesus saying: "All authority in heaven and on earth has been given to me. Go therefore and make disciples of all nations, baptizing them in the name of the Father and of the Son and of the Holy Spirit, and teaching them to obey everything that I have commanded you. And remember, I am with you always, to the end of the age" (Matthew 26:18–20).

In short, the New Testament clearly has the idea of Father, Son, and Holy Spirit as all divine from everlasting to everlasting. I mean that there is good New Testament warrant for the notion of the immanent Trinity.[30] Indeed, it was that warrant that led Church councils to end up with their formal declarations of the doctrine of the Trinity. Some say that Christians should believe only what is explicitly taught in the New Testament and not by Christians living later than New Testament authors and reflecting on the New Testament. Yet the New Testament is a set of texts presenting the earliest theology written by Christians, which ought to allow for the possibility of the New Testament being reasonably commented on by later Christians striving to adhere to and interpret its teaching in circumstances in which they found themselves. And if one thinks that Christ gave authority to his disciples to teach in his name (as seems to be implied in various New Testament texts), the way is open to the possibility of their successors having grounds for trying to interpret New Testament texts as time goes on and as circumstances demand. One might also bear in mind that what is now called the "New Testament" is nothing but a set of texts sanctioned

---

[30] For an especially clear elaboration of this view, I recommend Declan Marmion and Rik Van Nieuwenhove, *An Introduction to the Trinity* (Cambridge: Cambridge University Press, 2011), chapter 2, "The Trinity and Its Scriptural Roots."

as authoritative by Christians living much later than the time when these texts were written.[31]

Yet the formal declarations of the doctrine of the Trinity raise questions. I suspect that for most people they raise philosophical ones concerning consistency. For how can God be *both* one *and* three? Three cats are three cats, not one cat. So, how could *three* persons be *one* God? Well, many have tried to explain how it is possible to assert the truth of the doctrine of the Trinity without resorting to self-contradiction, and I shall now try to give you my attempt, while noting in advance that it is not one that comes only from me. In presenting it I am drawing heavily on Aquinas.[32] Also, like Aquinas, I aim only to indicate why the doctrine of the Trinity can be thought to be not self-contradictory, to be *thinkable* even if not *understandable*. Someone saying that three fish are one fish would be talking nonsense. But I do not take the orthodox doctrine of the Trinity to be doing that.

THE IMMANENT TRINITY

I begin from the perspective of classical theism as I have tried to explain it in previous chapters. So, you will not now be surprised when I say that there can be nothing in God that amounts to a change that God undergoes, as, for example, I change when cooking a curry or brushing my teeth. To say that God creates the universe is not to say that God goes through some kind of process of making (as does the painter of a painting). It is to say that God makes things to be from nothing and not at some time in God's life history (a perfect example of how we can use words to talk about God that we also use when talking of other things, while stretching these words to their limits so as to end up imperfectly striving to talk about God). To put things another way, if God is what accounts for there being something rather than nothing, there can be no *accidents* in God and therefore no question of God undergoing change.

By "accident" I mean a feature that something can acquire or lose without ceasing to be what it is by nature. I happen to be sitting in a chair now. But I could get up and walk around without this change in me causing me to cease to be human. As human, I have the *potential* to be different in various ways, the ability to change without this affecting what it is that I am by nature. Yet, if God is what accounts for there being something rather than nothing, there cannot in God be anything corresponding to a distinction

---

[31] For much more on this, see Bruce Metzger, *The Canon of the New Testament: Its Origins, Development, and Significance* (Oxford: Clarendon Press, 1987).
[32] Cf. *Summa theologiae*, 1a, 27–32.

between God and God's nature. God is not something capable of undergoing change. In this sense, God just *is* the divine nature.

Yet people often talk *as if* God undergoes change while taking themselves to be speaking *truly*. I do this a lot. So, I will, for example, happily say that God *became* my creator at such and such a time. Or I will say that God once *came* to arrange for me to be friends with Michael Ruse. But I am not here referring to changes in God. I am referring to what can be called "notional changes" rather than "real" ones. I am saying that at such and such a time I came to be born as a creature of God and that at such and such a time I came to be friends with Michael by virtue of God. You might think that if X is related to Y, then X changes if Y comes to be related to it in a different way. You might think that my cat changes if I have come to be to the left of it just because I have walked around it. But this kind of change is not a *real* change in my cat. I am the thing undergoing *real* change as I walk around my cat. My cat sleeps undisturbed as I walk around it. For a comparable example, think of falling in love with someone. Does it follow that X falling in love with Y implies some change in Y? Obviously not. For Y might not even know who X is. Think here of stalkers who track the objects of their attention without these objects being remotely aware of the tracking and of what is going on in the stalker.

So, we can think or talk of God being related to creatures in ways that do not imply any real change in God. If we do that, we will be thinking that true relational statements can be made about God without them implying that God undergoes any accidental change. Reference to God creating this or that will not be telling us anything about God's nature. It will be telling us something about a creature: that it owes its being and its changes to God. It will be telling us about God bringing things forth without being something changeable and temporal.

But now entertain the thought (critical to the doctrine of the Trinity) that, though God is not something changeable, there *might* be a *coming forth* in God that has nothing to do with God having any effect on something other than God.[33] And when trying to entertain this thought, note the difference between what goes on with us as we act causally on the world and what goes on in us even though we are not doing that. If I stroke my cat, I have an effect on it. I bring about a change in it. Here we have me acting, where "acting" means "having an effect on something other than me." Yet things

---

[33] In classical accounts of the Trinity, a coming forth in God is commonly referred to as a "proceeding.." The Son is said to proceed from the Father and the Holy Spirit is said to proceed from the Father and the Son (or, for Eastern as opposed to Western Christians, from the Father *through* the Son).

can be thought to be acting (to be doing something) where there is no external effect implied. I can come to understand what something is (this amounting to a change in me) without thereby acting on anything. And I can pine with love for someone without acting on my inclinations. In other words, there can be a *doing* or a *bringing about* that remains *in* me, albeit that I am a changeable creature of God. Nothing outside me is affected by my coming to understand. If I grasp what it is to be a cat, no cat suffers the slightest change. Similarly, of course, nothing outside me is automatically or necessarily affected by my being drawn to it, loving it, or delighting in it.

Now, of course, if God creates, then God produces effects that come from God and are different from God. But *what if* God eternally and without undergoing change understands what *God* is? What if God, just by being God, forms a *concept* of God? That will not amount to God *creating* anything and it will not amount to a *change* in God. It will be as internal to God as our thoughts can be internal to us should we choose not to act on them. But a concept of God that God has when understanding what God is surely has to be thought of as something *coming forth* in God, albeit eternally. So, it is something *real* in God without being an *accident* that God acquires. So, it must *be* God *if* all that is in God *is* God. And this thought allows us to say that if God knows what God is, then there is in God a conception of God that can be said to derive from God while being God (which is what classical defenders of the doctrine of the Trinity have in mind when they say that God the Son proceeds from God the Father from eternity).

I do not think that we have philosophical reason to suppose that God forms a concept of himself. We have no philosophical reason to think that God acquires concepts as we do or that a concept in God would be what a concept would be in us. Yet I do not think that we have philosophical reason to think that God *cannot* from eternity do something comparable to us forming a concept. And if it is possible that God somehow forms a concept of God, then there is *in* God something to which God is related by *nature*, not just something we can think of as being related to God because we can relate God to creatures by saying that Mary came to exist by virtue of God or that Moses did what he did because God was acting through him.

Aquinas makes this point by starting with the assertion in John's gospel that in the beginning was the Word, and that the Word was God. He suggests that when we form concepts, there arises in us something by which we understand and which we express in language (words). On Aquinas's view, we can think of understanding in terms of us forming a "word in the mind" corresponding to what we say as we try to express what it is that we understand. "Word" in this context does not mean some English or French or German word. Speakers of various languages can express the same thoughts in different words. When they do so, however, they are employing concepts common to all of them. Drawing on this truth, Aquinas (correctly, I think) invokes the notion of a "word in the mind" while suggesting that such a word could exist in God without it being different from God (on the assumption that all that is in God is God).

The classical doctrine of the Trinity is stated with use of the word "proceed." It says that the Son *proceeds* from the Father. And when speaking of the Son's "proceeding," it speaks of the Son as "generated" or "begotten" by the Father. I take this teaching to mean that God the Son comes from what God the Father is eternally. And I take this thought to mean that God the Son and God the Father are distinct, not as two centers of consciousness with attributes peculiar to each of them, but as what God is as, so to speak, God *thinks* himself and thereby has one, in God, to which he is related. But this obviously has to mean that God the Father and God the Son are distinct only because of the fact that there is *in* God a real relation between what comes forth from eternity in God and what God *is* from eternity. It means that God the Son is distinguishable from God the Father only in terms of real relation in God based on proceeding. The Son derives from or proceeds from the Father as what the Father eternally knows when understanding himself. *Just that.* And the Father is just that from which the Son proceeds. It cannot be that the Father is something that creates another God and it cannot be that the Son is something that God creates.

Like many theologians, Aquinas here invokes the idea that in God there is distinction that rests only on *relation*. He thinks that God the Father can be taken to be distinct from God the Son since each is something at opposite ends of a real relation, that each of them exists as different from each other just because their very existence amounts to them being *subsisting* relations, realities that exist as separate only insofar as they are related to each other.

You might say that the notion of a subsisting relation is logically objectionable, that there is a contradiction involved in it. Yet, whether we realize it or not, we work with the notion of subsisting relation even when thinking mathematically. The number six is *nothing but* the successor to the number five and the predecessor to the number seven. Insofar as we think of numbers as real, we do so with an eye on their identity in terms of relation.[34]

---

[34] This point is nicely made in C. J. F. Williams's essay "Neither Confounding the Persons nor Dividing the Substance," which is chapter 10 of Alan G. Padgett, ed., *Reason and the Christian Religion: Essays in Honour of Richard Swinburne* (Oxford: Clarendon Press, 1994).

You might think that there can be no such thing as a relation that *subsists* as one real thing as opposed to another. But, as I have argued, it makes sense to deny that God has knowledge and power or whatever as *accidents*. It makes sense to say that God's knowledge *is* God and that God's power *is* God and that God's knowledge and power exist, not as knowledge and power exist as shared by creatures, but as something that *is* God, considered as Creator of the universe.

Another way of making this point is to say that God is *subsisting* knowledge and power, which leaves room for saying that in God there are subsisting relations, on the premise that all that is in God is God. I have no idea what knowledge and power would be considered as what something *just is*. I cannot *imagine* what it would be. But I do not think that I subscribe to a logical contradiction when saying that God is subsisting knowledge and power. By the same token, I do not think that I subscribe to a logical contradiction when saying that, in God, there can be subsisting relations that do not compromise God's simplicity.

Yet what about God the Holy Spirit, the third person of the Trinity? Here, like Aquinas, I say that if the Spirit is God as is the Son, and if the Spirit is other than the Father and the Son, that can be only because of its relation of origin. There must be some sense in which the Spirit eternally proceeds or comes forth. And here, also like Aquinas, I turn to the notion of love as providing a clue.

As I have said, love can remain in me without leading to some process outside me. So, what if God's knowing God comes with God loving God? What would then be eternally arising in God would not be a concept of God that is like God (as the Son is like the Father) but something in God springing from the Father and the Son – not so much a similarity (as between concept and thing conceived) but a movement toward or an impulse. Yet if there is such a thing in God, and if all that is *in* God *is* God, this movement or impulse *is* God.

I might say that God loves me by willing my good. But to say that is to try to flag only what is real in me: that I happen to have some good and that this is brought about by God. Yet if there is love in God for God, this is not an accident in God. It belongs to God's very being as God. On this account, there is no suggestion that the persons of the Trinity are three distinct centers of consciousness. For on this account, the "consciousness" of the Son is that of the Father and the Spirit. It is simply the consciousness of God. As Herbert McCabe observes: "There are not three knowledges or three lovings in God. The Word simply is the way in which God is self-conscious, knows what he is, as the Spirit simply is the delight God takes when knowing it. If we say that there are three persons in God, in the ordinary sense of person, we are tritheists."[35]

We might, and I think we *should*, consider whether there are better ways to talk about the immanent Trinity than I have been using. One way might avoid talk about God the *Father* and God the *Son* since it seems to confirm the illusion that God has a human gender or that God is sexual in any way. The doctrine of the Trinity speaks of God the Son proceeding from God the Father. And that language coheres with New Testament ways of talking about God since these refer to God being the father of Jesus. But there is nothing to stop us talking about God the mother eternally conceiving that which is equal to her. Masculine nouns abound in classical Trinitarian theology. But they can hardly be taken literally unless we focus on their claim that God the Son is eternally *generated* from God the Father while supposing that this claim is asking us to think that human generation is what Aristotle and medieval theologians took it to be: what happens because a man generates a son by putting his son into a woman without her contributing to the process of generation. We now think of human generation with an eye to the splitting of chromosomes and the sharing of genes. So, why not God the Mother and God the Daughter? I even think that when it comes to God the Father, it might even be appropriate to speak of God *the parents* rather than God the *Father*. I say this since I do not see that the plural "parents" is any more misleading than is the sexual connotation of "Father." Each of these terms conjures up helpful images when trying to think about the mystery of the Trinity.

That said, however, I am certain that all attempts to talk about the Trinity will fall badly short if they do not most emphatically stress that the Trinity is not something we understand any more than we understand what God is considered as Creator of the universe. When saying this I am echoing what orthodox Christians have been teaching for centuries.

THE ECONOMIC TRINITY

Yet what does the doctrine of the immanent Trinity imply when it comes to Christian faith? Is it just talk about notions such as relation and subsistence and nature? Is it just an exercise in holy arithmetic? Critics of the doctrine of the Trinity sometimes conclude that it is, which now brings me to talk about the "economic Trinity." I have previously been referring to what God is from

---

[35] Herbert McCabe, *God Still Matters* (London: Continuum, 2002), 52.

eternity. Now I aim to say something about what the triune God is in *our* story and why this might be thought to matter to people (any people). And I want to start by talking about what God is thought to be in the Old Testament.

Here God is the Creator of the universe. God in the Old Testament is not a creature and not even one of the gods. "Who is like you, O Lord, among the gods? ... Now I know that the Lord is greater than all gods.... Do not invoke the names of other gods; do not let them be heard on your lips" (Exodus 15:11, 18:11, 23:13). For Old Testament authors, God is not a local god. God is the incomparable lord of the universe. As I have noted, these authors explore this thought by means of many images, some much appealed to these days by theologians with feminist interests. So, we find references to God carrying Israel "from the womb" (Isaiah 46:3), groaning "like a woman in labor" (Isaiah 42:14), and being a midwife (Psalm 22:9–10). But references such as these are clearly intended metaphorically since Old Testament authors most certainly do not think of God as something literally physical – not even when speaking of God as lord, king, or father. For them God is first and foremost an inscrutable mystery to be feared and worshipped. In this sense, the God of the Old Testament is very much *other* and seriously remote from us (though making us to exist and having a most serious role when it comes to human history).

And that, you might think, is an important thought if it is true. Yet while this thought is affirmed in orthodox accounts of the doctrine of the Trinity, it is added to by theologians focusing on the Trinity in the light of what they take to be divine revelation concerning God's action in the world (the economic Trinity). For given the doctrine of the Incarnation (from which the doctrine of the Trinity cannot be separated), God is not totally *other* since Christ is the Word of God born in our world. Or as 1 Corinthians 8:6 has it:

> There is for us one God, the Father, from whom are all things and for whom we exist, and one Lord, Jesus, through whom are all things and through whom we exist.

In this text, God and Jesus are clearly being put on the same level. The thought seems to be that, in Jesus, God has bridged the gap between divinity and humanity for purposes of human redemption. And this is part and parcel of what theologians have meant when talking about the economic Trinity as that which, so to speak, projects into time what God is from eternity – one who wants to draw people into union with God.

But orthodox reflections on the economic Trinity go further than this. For what they are driving at is that the Trinity is at work in the created order so as to raise people to a sharing in God's life. In a striking sentence in 2 Peter 1:4 we are told that God aims to make people "participants of the divine nature." And, so we might think, this is just what is effected by the Incarnation in that it shows that God from eternity loves us as the Father loves the Son. Or as Herbert McCabe says:

> Surely there could not be between the creator and his creatures the kind of love which we sometimes find between grown-up human beings for each other, for that love demands equality. It would be a mutual self-giving which it would be absurd to picture between God and his creatures. But this is the love that, Jesus says, the Father bears *him*. He is not a servant, a slave of God, not even a well-treated servant: he is one of the family of God, related to him by love.... With Jesus we come to a new vision of God, of the same God who was the God of Moses. Now, though, God is not seen primarily as making, acting, doing, not primarily as holding the universe in being, but primarily as eternal lover of Jesus. The life of God is not primarily the life of sustaining the existence of all creatures: the life of God within the Godhead is ultimately the life of love between Father and Son, and this life of love and delight we call the Holy Spirit.... The Christian gospel, the astounding good news, is that God's love is not confined to the eternal love between Father and Son, between these divine equals, but that God extends this same love – not just his kindly creative power but his love to us human creatures. All so that in the Son become man he loves us too as equals. Because of the Son become man we are taken up to share into the love between Father and Son, we are taken up into the uncreated Holy Spirit: our life becomes divine. As St Thomas Aquinas put it succinctly, "God became man so that man might become God."[36]

Here Trinitarian reflection moves well beyond an account of what God changelessly is from eternity.

THE INCARNATION

As I have said, the orthodox doctrine of the Trinity is tied to the (orthodox) doctrine of the Incarnation, according to which Jesus was literally *both* human *and* divine. But how are we to think about this doctrine?

We might proceed by trying to rationally prove that the doctrine is true. Yet I do not see how that could be done. For one thing, the doctrine is tied to

---

[36] McCabe, *God Still Matters*, 235–36. I assume that, when citing Aquinas, McCabe is referring to *Summa theologiae*, 3a, 1, 2, where Aquinas is approvingly quoting from St. Augustine of Hippo. Cf. also *The Catechism of the Catholic Church* 460: "The Word became flesh *to make us 'partakers of the divine nature.'*"

the doctrine of the Trinity insofar as it takes Jesus to be God the Son incarnate, and, as I have previously said, I do not see how the doctrine of the Trinity can be philosophically proved. Then again, I do not see how the doctrine of the Incarnation could be proved on the basis of some inspection of Jesus. Suppose that we could step into a time machine and get ourselves back to the days of Jesus to subject him to minute scientific examination. Even on that scenario, we would not be able to establish that Jesus is divine, for all we would be able to examine is a human being. One cannot determine that something is divine by putting it under a microscope – not if to be divine is to be what accounts for there being a universe rather than nothing at all. Some Christians have argued that the divinity of Jesus is shown by the fact that he performed miracles. Yet if a miracle is something that only God can perform (which is a pretty common understanding of "miracle"), there seems to be no way of showing that a miracle associated with some historical individual is proof that the individual in question is divine. At best, it is evidence that God is somehow at work in that person's career. Some people try to ground belief in Jesus' divinity in his recorded resurrection from the dead. But it is one thing to say that Jesus rose from the dead and quite another to say that Jesus was therefore divine. The gospels provide accounts of more than one person rising from the dead. In Luke 7:11–17 the son of a widow at Nain rises from the dead, as does Lazarus in John 11. But Luke does not infer that the widow's son was divine, and John does not infer that Lazarus was God. And, of course, Christians believe that all people shall be raised from the dead without for a moment supposing that this means that all people are all that God is.

Another way of trying to think about the doctrine of the Incarnation would be to reflect on the life and death of Jesus and what it might be taken to have achieved – by, for example, developing something like my brief comments above on the economic Trinity. Yet many people would say that we can spare ourselves the trouble of doing any such thing since the orthodox doctrine of the Incarnation is a logical absurdity to begin with. So, I shall now simply focus on that idea while arguing that the doctrine of the Incarnation is not a logical absurdity.

WHY SHOULD THE DOCTRINE OF THE INCARNATION BE THOUGHT TO BE LOGICALLY ABSURD?

I take the orthodox doctrine of the Incarnation to be found in teachings of the Council of Nicaea (AD 325) and the Council of Chalcedon (AD 451). According to this teaching, Jesus was (and will forever be) "one person with two distinct natures." On this account Jesus is literally human and literally divine. Talk about Jesus employing the words "person" and "nature" belongs, of course, to post-biblical theology. You will not find it in the New Testament. You will find passages such as the prologue to John's gospel, in which Jesus is said to be the Word that was God from the beginning. The notion of Jesus being divine, and therefore worthy of worship, pervades the New Testament.[37] But it is with Nicaea and Chalcedon that the Christian Church (responding to what it took to be wrong interpretations of Scripture) began to speak of Jesus considered as a *single* subject having both a human nature and a divine nature.

Is there a better way of expressing what Jesus is without *denying* what Nicaea and Chalcedon affirm? I do not know. Perhaps there is or will be as time goes on.[38] But it is one thing to look for a better way of saying what Nicaea and Chalcedon taught and another thing to deny what they teach. Yet it is their affirmations concerning Jesus that are now often taken to be logically incoherent. So, we might ask why we should think that this is so.

Those who have said that it is so typically insist that no single thing can have two distinct natures. My cat cannot also be a dog, and so on. In the natural world we have things of different kinds, and differences of kind when it comes to things in nature cannot be squeezed into one thing having the properties of both. A lizard and an elephant cannot each be lizard and elephant. Hence, for example, in a book called *The Myth of God Incarnate*, John Hick says: "To say, without explanation, that the historical Jesus of Nazareth was also God is as devoid of meaning as to say that this circle drawn with a pencil on paper is also a square."[39] That is the kind of argument I face when attempting, as I am about to do, to suggest that there is no logical absurdity in the orthodox Chalcedonian doctrine of the Incarnation.

TALK ABOUT JESUS

All cats are carnivores. When saying this, however, we are not talking about any particular cat. We are noting what we take all cats to be given their nature. But we often speak of one particular thing when saying something about it. So, we might say that John is Egyptian. When doing that, we are singling out a subject and saying (predicating) something about it. So, I take

[37] Cf. Matthew 14:33, 28:9, 28:17; Luke 2:37; John 9:38; Philippians 2:6–11; and 1 John 1–4.
[38] Cf. Gareth Moore, "Incarnation and Image of God," *New Blackfriars* 64 (November 1983).
[39] John Hick, ed., *The Myth of God Incarnate* (London: SCM Press, 1977), 178.

it that statements about Jesus first single him out as something to which we are referring. Then they say something about him. And as far as logic goes, we can single him out in different ways, sometimes by phrases that we would normally use when saying what something is. I might say that the current Lucyle T. Werkmeister Professor of Philosophy (i.e., Michael Ruse) is taking a shower. But I could just as well say that Michael is taking a shower. Here I would be presuming that Michael is the current Lucyle T. Werkmeister Professor of Philosophy. Logically speaking, the two propositions are equivalent. They single out a subject and say something about it.

Now according to the orthodox doctrine of the Incarnation, that is what all true statements about Jesus are doing. They are picking out a subject and then predicating something of it. And they affirm of the subject in question that it is various things. If Chalcedon is right, then what we can truly affirm of God can be affirmed of Jesus and what we can truly affirm of a human being can also be affirmed of him. So, for example, we can say that Jesus is omnipotent, and that Jesus was able to die. Or we can say, "The Son of Mary died" and "the Son of God died" (on the assumption that the subject of these propositions is the second person of the Trinity). For Chalcedon, what is important is *the subject* we are talking about. The idea here is that since Jesus is God the Son, we can speak of him both as being what God is and as being what a human being is. The question, of course, is, Do we clearly contradict ourselves when talking like this?

To start with, you might think that we *clearly* do so. You might instinctively embrace one of the arguments that Aquinas discusses when talking about the Incarnation. According to this, God and people are vastly different from each other, and it makes no sense to say that some human being is divine. No more sense than saying that some cat is also a reptile.[40] But I resist that conclusion.

In doing so, I assume that sentences of the form "X is Y" can sometimes tell us what something is by nature and are not always identity statements like "The Morning Star (Venus) is the Evening Star (Venus)." And I think of something having a nature because it has what it needs to exist as what it is. So, I would say that "Michael Ruse has human nature" gives us notice that we can say of him things such as "Michael is a mammal," "Michael is a rational animal," "Michael is mortal," and "Should Michael cease to be any of these things, then Michael would cease to exist." In taking this line I am not suggesting that we have a complete knowledge of the essence or nature

---

[40] Cf. *Summa theologiae*, 3a, 16, 1 objection 1.

of everything, including Michael. I am just claiming that we know enough to
be able to say with respect to some things what naturally belongs to them,
what they have to be so as to be what they are by nature, how they should
be described, and what their abilities are in general. And I draw on this
thought when turning to the incarnation in the light of the Council
of Chalcedon.

I understand Chalcedon to teach that Jesus is one divine subject (the
second person of the Trinity) who can be truly spoken of as we might
speak both of what is divine and of what is human. So, I think that of
Jesus we can truly say things such as "Jesus walked around," "Jesus was
incorporeal," "Jesus was born in time," "Jesus is eternal," "Jesus is
human," and "Jesus is divine." In short, I hold that both "Jesus is human"
and "Jesus is divine" are both literally true. I think that the incarnation
really amounts to there being one subject or individual with two
distinct natures.

As I have noted, an obvious objection to this conclusion runs along the
line: "Nothing can simultaneously be both able to eat and incorporeal, or
both born in time and eternal, or both human and divine." And I agree with
this objection if it is understood as criticizing the attempt to ascribe to
something with one nature attributes or activities that cannot simultaneously be had by things possessing only that single nature. I have no problem
conceding that a cat, say, cannot be both corporeal and incorporeal. In line
with Chalcedon, however, I do not think of Jesus as having only one nature.
I think that he is one subject with two distinct natures. I think that we have
two ways of speaking about Jesus, based on the two distinct natures he
possesses, both of which ways are true since they can both be used when
referring to one subject – Jesus, considered as the Second Person of the
Trinity. I take "Jesus" to be a proper name that refers to the second person of
the Trinity. I do not mean that the man Jesus preexisted the Incarnation.
Some theologians refer to the "preexisting Jesus" as if Jesus of Nazareth,
considered as a human being, existed before he was born. What I am saying,
however, is that "Jesus" names the one who is God incarnate, and what we
truly predicate of Jesus is what we can predicate of him given that he has
both a divine nature and a human nature.

So, I will say, for example, that with respect to his divine nature, Jesus was
incorporeal, while with respect to his human nature, he was able to eat. Or
again, I will say that, with respect to his human nature, Jesus was born in
time, while with respect to his divine nature, he is eternal. I do not think of
the two natures of Jesus as being like two essential attributes of one thing or
two properties that something with one nature might have while able to

acquire or lose them while not ceasing to be what it is by nature. I take them to be completely distinct natures had by one subject. In doing so I am not saying that humanity is divine or that divinity is human. I am saying that when it comes to the Incarnation, we have one subject with two natures. As Aquinas writes in *Summa theologiae*, 3a, 2, 2: "The Word has a human nature united to itself, even though it does not form part of the Word's divine nature . . . [and] . . . this union was effected in the person of the Word, not in the nature." In accordance with this conclusion, Aquinas argues that, since Jesus is God, everything truly said of Jesus with respect to his humanity can be attributed to God. So, for example, we can assert that God died since Jesus died, or that God was born since Jesus was born. Correspondingly, Aquinas thinks, everything truly said of Jesus with respect to his divinity can be attributed to the man Jesus. So, for example, we can assert that Jesus is omnipotent, omniscient, and eternal since God is omnipotent, omniscient, and eternal.

Once again, the key to thinking about the orthodox doctrine of the incarnation is the idea that Jesus is *one* subject with two *distinct* natures. Insofar as this subject has a divine nature, it is all that God is. Insofar as it has a human nature, it is all that is required to be essentially human. *As divine* Jesus is all that God is essentially. *As human* he is all that a human being essentially is. When it comes to Jesus, "we have two ways of speaking about him – only one of which we understand. In virtue of his human nature we speak of him in the same way that we would speak of any other human being. In virtue of his divine nature we can also say more enigmatic and mysterious things such as that he forgives sins or is our redeemer."[41] When it comes to the subject term "Jesus," I find no problem in saying things such as "Jesus rode on a donkey." Since I also think that "God" can be substituted for "Jesus" in this sentence for purposes of signifying a subject (the second person of the Trinity), I also have no problem in saying "God rode on a donkey." I would, however, have a problem saying, for example, "Jesus, *insofar as he is divine*, rode on a donkey" or "Jesus, *insofar as he is human*, is omnipotent."

In short, since both "Son of God" and "Son of Mary" can be used to refer to Jesus (given the teaching of Nicaea and Chalcedon), I say the same thing if I say "The Son of God died" or "The Son of Mary died." Also, given Nicaea and Chalcedon, if we can say (1) "The Son of God died," we can also say (2) "God died." Though "God" in (2) signifies the divine nature, it does not in

---

[41] McCabe, *God Still Matters*, 107.

the subject place refer to that nature. It refers to *what* has that nature – the man Jesus. And though I do not understand how this can be so, I do not see that to say that it is so is flatly to contradict oneself. Divinity and humanity do not exclude each other as do two created natures since divinity and humanity do not occupy the same universe. Indeed, as I have been stressing in previous pages, the divine nature does not occupy *any* universe.

7

Reflections

Michael Ruse

THE IMPORTANCE OF FAITH

T O MY GREAT SURPRISE, AS I LOOK BACK ON WHAT I HAVE WRITTEN AND what Brian Davies has written, I find that I learn more about myself than I do about Brian.[1] I knew I had been raised a Protestant. I knew that I am a nonbeliever. What I did not know was quite how Protestant a nonbeliever I am! What do I mean by this oxymoron? How can a nonbeliever be Protestant or Catholic or Mormon or whatever? What I mean is that I take faith to be absolutely central to the Christian position – no surprise here and no arguments with Catholics on this – and I am with Kierkegaard and others like Karl Barth in thinking reason in some significant sense corrosive of faith – surprise here and arguments with Catholics and others, including a whole tradition from the Elizabethan Settlement with members of the Church of England. I take what Jesus said to Thomas – "oh yes, you believe now, but it would have been better if you had believed without empirical evidence" – to be definitive and fundamental. I think that in some sense reason undermines faith. Faith means taking risks, a leap into the absurd.

Which now brings me round to Brian Davies's arguments in favor of faith. As I understand it, he argues that all of us must make ultimately unjustified claims or beliefs. So why not include faith in that category? "The giving of reasons or the appeal to evidence really does depend on believing without reasons or evidence; it depends on taking certain things for granted, things that are not themselves conclusions inferred on the basis of what we might

---

[1] Many people, notably my late father, would doubt that this was at all a surprise. Wherever my journey starts, it ends with me.

grandly refer to as 'reason.'"[2] Well, yes, I agree that all the time we make and
use assumptions that are not ultimately justified. I cross the road believing
that it is not the case that, through some kind of quantum entanglement, a
truck speeding along in Sydney, Australia, is going to materialize and mow
me down. Logically, this could happen. I have no definitive proof that it will
not happen. But I live my life happily assuming it will not happen. In short,
like it or not, we all depend on faith, so why not allow a bit of slack to the
Christian?

I have tried to deal with this in Chapter 2. I argue that there is a logical
divide between empirical claims – naturalistic claims as we find in science –
and religious claims. Without being an ardent Popperian, I argue that
naturalistic claims – no truck will materialize – are always up for empirical
grabs. Nature could show us wrong. This is not the case with religious
claims. Nature cannot show wrong religious claims about the ultimate
reason or cause of existence. The metaphorical nature of science – of
naturalistic thinking generally – precludes asking or answering such questions. Even the body–mind problem. Science can tell a lot about the working
of the brain and how we might expect related mind experiences. But the
machine metaphor of modern science precludes a solution to the body–
mind problem. I am with Leibniz on this. So my position is that a religious
faith claim – like "a good God created the universe, made us in his image,
and intends eternal bliss with him" – is simply not the same kind of thing as
"trucks in Sydney are not going to be transmitted to downtown Tallahassee
just at the moment I am crossing the road." I just don't accept the move that
Brian Davies makes. I see faith, and presumptively I argue that the Christian
sees faith, in a way different from those get-on-with-everyday-life claims that
get us through this vale of soul making.

Brian in Chapter 2 then goes on to defend the possibility and practice of
natural theology – getting at God through reason. Paradoxically, I agree! I do
think natural theology, in principle, is a viable enterprise. But note that my
reasons for thinking this are not Brian's. He wants natural theology to be a
partner with revealed theology or religion, as given in faith. I argue that faith
gets you nowhere. Hence, it is reason or nothing. Natural theology is based
on reason, so as such I have no objection to someone pursuing it. Brian,
expectedly, is not very keen on the Kierkegaardian approach I take to faith.
That way, for a person of faith, leads to no natural theology. We differ. I am
interested to note that the Kierkegaardians he quotes seem to base their

[2] This volume, p. 23.

position in large part because of the nature of their faith objects. As he says: "For both Barth and Gunton, natural theology amounts to a wrongheaded attempt on the part of reason to pass judgment on God (and on divine revelation) using human, philosophical categories."[3] I am inclined to give faith its special position because of its nature rather than because of its objects. I don't think there is any big mystery here. I don't have faith so I don't really know what the objects are. If I did, I would be with Kierkegaard and followers. As I have said in Chapter 6, I am into apophatic theology. I know what God is not, rather than what God is! If I were a Christian, this is the route I would take – as John Hick takes – when faced with different faiths. The Catholics believe one thing, the Anglicans another, and then there are the Mormons and all the others, not to mention non-Christian religions like Islam and Buddhism. I would simply say I have faith in God and leave it at that. I don't have faith in God, and so I cannot leave it at that.

INCOMPATIBLE IDEAS OF GOD

Apophatic theology? As I noted when I introduced this idea, that puts me in opposition to many Christians, especially Protestants. They know what God is. He is a person! Theistic personalism! I have been, at least I have intended to be, witheringly dismissive of this sort of stuff. Perhaps I should not have been quite so quick. In the analytic philosophical world, it has distinguished supporters. Noted Christian philosopher Richard Swinburne – actually, for more than twenty years now he has been Orthodox – is categorical. "Theism claims that God is a personal being – that is, in some sense *a person*. By a person I mean an individual with basic powers (to act intentionally), purposes and beliefs."[4] And that means we can know some things about God. Take his relationship with Abraham. "I am God Almighty; walk before me, and be blameless. And I will make my covenant between me and you, and will make you exceedingly numerous."[5] God is a bit of a deal maker. Do what I ask, and I will reward you accordingly. "And I will give to you, and to your offspring after you, the land where you are now an alien, all the land of Canaan, for a perpetual holding; and I will be their God."[6] But you have got to recognize me and show your commitment. "You shall circumcise the flesh

---

[3] This volume, p. 46.
[4] Richard Swinburne. *Is There a God?*, rev. ed. (Oxford: Clarendon Press, 2010), 5. Alvin Plantinga is another into this sort of stuff. See his *Does God Have a Nature?* (Milwaukee: Marquette University Press, 1980).
[5] Genesis 17:1.   [6] Genesis 17:8.

of your foreskins, and it shall be a sign of the covenant between me and you."[7] Same in the New Testament. God is a loving father. Jesus gets baptized. "And a voice from heaven said, 'This is my Son, the Beloved, with whom I am well pleased.'"[8]

I suspect I am not the only nonbeliever who gets a bit frustrated here. Some good and respectable (and respected) Christians tell us that we cannot speak of God in direct terms. We can say only what he is not. Some good and respectable (and respected) Christians tell us that we can speak of God in direct terms. He makes deals, he gives but expects something in return. He is a loving father. And more. Christians! Make up your minds! Tell me what it really is that I am missing. As we know, things are even worse than this. There is a whole philosophical tradition that is happy to tell us about the nature of God. It's just that he is not a person. He is a necessary being, unchanging and eternal, outside time and space. Remember St. Augustine. "Thy years neither go nor come; but ours both go and come in order that all separate moments may come to pass. All thy years stand together as one, since they are abiding."[9] This is the God like $2 + 2 = 4$. And I simply don't know how something like $2 + 2 = 4$ can be a deal maker, or a loving father, or vindictive, or play favorites, or tell us that we are ignorant pigs and shouldn't interrupt.

At a point like this, I start to get very frustrated. As far as I am concerned, Christianity is in deep, deep trouble, because it has contradictory pictures at its very heart. God as a person. God as a mathematical-like entity. If you are a person, you are in time and space. If you are a mathematical-like entity, you are not in time and space. Now I am fully aware that people like Brian Davies are only just getting going at this point. In Chapter 2, explicitly he argues that the eternal God can get involved, person-like, in his creation. God cannot suffer. (Remember Aquinas: "To sorrow, therefore, over the misery of others does not belong to God."[10]) Davies writes: "And it would be wrong to suppose that, when Aquinas says that God does not change or suffer as we do, he means that God is inert or static. What he means is that the 'maker of all things, visible and invisible,' cannot be thought of as being *acted on* by something external to him or as being *vulnerable* to any such thing. To think of God in those terms, Aquinas argues, would be to think of God as a creature, as something that owes its life history to things around

---

[7] Genesis 17:11.   [8] Matthew 3:17.

[9] St. Augustine, *Confessions*, trans. H. Chadwick (Oxford: Oxford University Press, [396] 1998), 396.

[10] St. Thomas Aquinas, *Summa theologiae*, I (London: Burns, Oates and Washbourne, 1952), 21:3.

it."[11] Yes, but then, what is God up to? My coauthor quotes his fellow Dominican Herbert McCabe:

> If the Creator is the reason for everything that is, there can be no actual being which does not have the Creator at its centre holding it in being. In our compassion, *we* in our feeble way, are seeking to be what God is all the time: united with and within the life of our friend. We can say in the psalm "The Lord is compassion" but a sign that this is metaphorical language is that we can also say that the Lord has no need of compassion; he has something more wonderful, he has his creative act in which he is "closer to the sufferer than she is to herself."[12]

I repeat: what then is God up to? Go back to the heart-rending end of the little boy who loved racing cars. "But the actual truth is the last few weeks of Harry's life were marked by terrible pain and suffering that no human, not least a 5-year-old boy, should endure."[13] If God is closer to Harry than Harry is to himself, I just don't know what that can mean if God is not in some sense encountering what Harry is encountering. We apparently can only empathize. God is right there in the trenches. And that means that God is spatiotemporal. Thus, $2 + 2 = 4$ is totally indifferent to Harry and his troubles.

I might add, without intending to be nasty, that in Chapter 3, I think Brian rather gives the game away. The Bible speaks of direct encounters with God. Jacob says: "I have seen God face to face." Brian will have none of it:

> Classical theists take God to be incorporeal, omniscient, omnipotent, and outside time and space. As I have noted, they also insist on the idea that God cannot be one of a kind, that God cannot be put in a list of things to be counted as we count the number of dogs and cats and so on. But if that is what God is (or is not), how is anybody able to know (in this life at any rate) that what they might take themselves to have directly encountered or seen or perceived *is* God? What could justify anyone appealing to direct experience to claim to know that what they have encountered or perceived or experienced is omniscient and omnipotent – let alone time-less? That, of course, is a rhetorical question to which I take the answer to be "Nothing."[14]

---

[11] This volume, p. 57.

[12] Herbert McCabe, *God Still Matters* (London: Continuum, 2002), 235–36.

[13] "Harry Shaw: Lewis Hamilton's 'Spirit Angel' Boy Dies," BBC News, June 4, 2019, www.bbc.com/news/uk-england-surrey-48506434.

[14] This volume, p. 77–78.

And again:

> Theistic personalists say that God is a person without a body who has lots
> of knowledge and power. But how could anyone by virtue of perception or
> direct experience be correctly able to identify something like this? Can one
> directly perceive what is incorporeal? Can one, just by perceiving some-
> thing, see that it has lots of knowledge? Can one by perceiving it see that it
> has power to the degree that theistic personalists take God to have power?
> These are more rhetorical questions to which I take the answer to be "No."[15]

Couldn't have said it better myself.

EVIL AGAIN

All of this aside, as you might expect, I don't have much to say about the
traditional arguments for the existence of God. Brian gives a good exposition
and I say little more. Thus far in this chapter you might feel justified in
concluding that I don't have much respect for Christians. Not at all! When
I read the great philosopher-theologians on their topics, my heart swells with
pride that I can presume to follow in their footsteps. These really are mega-
minds. Moreover, as one who approaches philosophical questions as a
historian of ideas, I am ever conscious of the fact that, as in the biological
world, the world of intellect and culture is evolutionary. Nothing just comes
into existence without a long and pertinent historical background. I am a
Darwinian and I believe that Darwin's theory of evolution through natural
selection is just about the most important empirical discovery ever – at least,
up in the Top Ten. It didn't come from nowhere. Darwin's genius was not
just to find a mechanism of change – natural selection or the survival of the
fittest – but to speak to the pressing question of design. Organisms are
design-like – they are as if someone had consciously planned how they
would work or function, such work or function being toward their well-
being and reproduction. The hand and the eye are not random bits of matter
stuck together. They are perfected toward ends – grasping and seeing – final
causes in the Aristotelian sense. Darwin came up with the solution, but it
was the theologian/philosophers who came up with the question. What is it
about organisms that is different and how do you explain it? Traditional
natural theology has contributed hugely to our present understanding –
secular or otherwise.[16]

---

[15] This volume, p. 78.

[16] I have made a cottage industry out of this claim: R. J. Richards and M. Ruse, *Debating Darwin*
(Chicago: University of Chicago Press, 2016); M. Ruse, *On Purpose* (Princeton: Princeton

Okay, time for being nice is over! As you have seen, I worry about issues like the existence of many religions or varieties of religions all making different faith claims. These are significant worries, but they fade beside the problem of evil. It is this why I totally and absolutely don't want anything to do with the Christian God. Even if you can make some sense of such a God as a Creator and so forth, anyone or anything that can let poor little Harry suffer in that way is simply not worthy of worship. Remember, I am working in the realm of reason. If I had faith, then, like the existence of different faith claims, the problem of evil as such would not arise because I would not then be in the business of reason and argument. I would be in the realm of adoration and worship and great thankfulness. Against critics I would say, simply, read 1 Corinthians 13: "For now we see in a mirror, dimly, but then we will see face to face. Now I know only in part; then I will know fully, even as I have been fully known." The problem of evil could not trouble me because faith trumps everything and arguments are simply irrelevant.

What does Brian Davies have to say about all of this? First, in some sense he wants to take God out of the moral realm, at least as is understood by us humans. "Biblical authors do not think of God as the best-behaved person around. They do not think of God as always acting in accord with moral obligations or as always displaying human virtues. Biblical texts never come even close to asserting that God is morally good in the sense in which we typically understand 'morally good.'"[17] Well, perhaps, but are you allowed to do this? We learn that God hands out good gifts, but "it does not speak of God being *morally obliged* to provide them, just as it does not say that God is morally *dubious* for sending weal and woe on some people. In biblical texts, God is not presented as a person subject to a moral code. If anything, such texts take God to be the ultimate source of moral codes."[18]

I agree that there are passages in the Bible that do lend themselves to such a reading. As we have seen, Job is always good for this sort of thing. But, with respect, a lot of the Bible does present God as a moral being – a human-like moral being. Take the parable of the Prodigal Son. For me, the important part comes at the end, when the father speaks to the older son.

"Listen! For all these years I have been working like a slave for you, and I have never disobeyed your command; yet you have never given me even a

University Press, 2017); M. Ruse, *The Darwinian Revolution* (Cambridge: Cambridge University Press, 2019). There is much, much more.

[17] This volume, p. 119.   [18] This volume, p. 119.

young goat so that I might celebrate with my friends. But when this son of yours came back, who has devoured your property with prostitutes, you killed the fatted calf for him!" Then the father said to him, "Son, you are always with me, and all that is mine is yours. But we had to celebrate and rejoice, because this brother of yours was dead and has come to life; he was lost and has been found."[19]

If this isn't a wise and loving father, I don't know what is. The older son is understandably hurt. The father doesn't brush him off, even if – as I rather suspect – his love is greater for that tearaway, the younger brat. Rather, he counsels his older boy with loving sensibility, helping to put things into perspective. So, just don't give me any guff about the Bible not proposing "to us the notion of God being a morally admirable person as we tend to think of morally admirable persons."[20] At times like this, I am all the way with C. S. Lewis and his eschewing of soft soap.

And then, finally, Brian tries to con us with the theological three-card trick of evil being a deprivation, a lack of goodness, so it could hardly be God's fault anyway: "evil or badness cannot be thought of as something created by God since its reality always consists in the absence of a due good."[21] One of my former graduate students has just sent me a picture of her two-year-old toddler sitting happily in a pumpkin patch (I am writing with Halloween just around the corner). The kid looks incredibly healthy and happy. The mother is obviously overjoyed. And her old prof feels that he has contributed to the development and thriving of a young person who is now truly showing her worth as a human being – as a scholar, as a wife, as a mother, as a loving member of society. Good, good, good. If anyone deserves credit for this, it is the Almighty. Thank you, God, thank you. And then there is poor little Harry, dying in agony. So happy when his hero, the racing driver Lewis Hamilton, dedicated a victory to him and arranged for one of his team's racing cars to be sent over to see and sit in. And, then, the end. I don't think Hamilton is God – I know people who do – but this time he was a good substitute. How you can then turn around and say that the illness and pain do not have the same ontological status simply escapes me. Giving joy to my student Elizabeth. Giving misery to Harry. Or, if you like, preventing happiness for Harry. If one exists, so does the other. That horrible disease causing such suffering is as real as the pumpkins surrounding Elizabeth's little boy.[22] And if you want to say that God would have

---

[19] Luke 15:24–32.   [20] This volume, p. 119.   [21] This volume, p. 122.
[22] I will not tell you his name, but I do note with surprise and regret that it is not Michael.

prevented Harry's misery if he could have done but, creating the best possible world as he did, meant that Harry had to suffer, then with Dostoevsky (who made a similar point in *The Brothers Karamazov*) I say he shouldn't have got into the creation business in the first place.[23]

SIMILARITIES AND DIFFERENCES

My suspicion is that, if you read the two parts of Chapter 5, on morality, side by side, you will be struck by the similarities as much as the differences. We both, for instance, have little time for those arguments supposedly proving the existence of God by the very existence of morality or moral codes. Brian roughs up John Henry Newman. I rough up C. S. Lewis. A fair division of labor, for Brian is a Catholic roughing up another Catholic, and I am my funny kind of Protestant roughing up a fellow Protestant. Again, you will note the absence of discussion about what many – every American evangelical – would think are the main topics of morality. Abortion, homosexuality, feminism, and so forth. This is not cowardice or a reluctance to get into quicksand that would swallow all other discussion. It is more from a shared sense that so many of these endless arguments, about a woman's right to choose and so forth, don't have a lot to do with morality as such, and are more about empirical or supposedly biblically derived prohibitions and so forth. We both agree that killing is wrong. The question is about what is a human being, and that is not directly a moral issue.

But let us not minimize our differences, especially when it comes to the claims of revealed theology. What of those Christian claims about the Trinity and so forth? I am back to where we were earlier. Christians are trying to square the circle, and it just cannot be done. If the two great leaders of the Protestant Reformation cannot agree on the Trinity, that surely tells us something. And we know what that something is: $1 + 1 + 1 \neq 1$. We have seen how and why Christianity gets backed into the Trinity. As soon as you have God down here on Earth as a man, you are trapped. Adding the Holy Spirit is just icing on the cake. Jews don't have this problem because they don't have a Messiah. Muslims don't have this problem because Jesus was a

[23] "'Tell me yourself, I challenge your answer. Imagine that you are creating a fabric of human destiny with the object of making men happy in the end, giving them peace and rest at last, but that it was essential and inevitable to torture to death only one tiny creature – that baby beating its breast with its fist, for instance – and to found that edifice on its unavenged tears, would you consent to be the architect on those conditions? Tell me, and tell the truth.' 'No, I wouldn't consent,' said Alyosha softly" (Fyodor Dostoevsky, *The Brothers Karamazov*, trans. Constance Garnett (London: Heineman, [1879] 1912), chapter 4).

prophet, not God. Of course, as Brian Davies shows, if you trawl through the Bible carefully enough, you can find supposed support for the Trinity.

> Jesus talks to his disciples by distinguishing between "my father" and "your father" while also seeming to claim to speak with divine authority (as in the Sermon on the Mount, with its refrain to the effect "You read such and such in the Old Testament, but I say to you ..."). Famously, of course, at the outset of John's gospel Jesus is identified as "the Word," which was "with" God and "is" God from "the beginning." At the end of that gospel one of Jesus' disciples addresses him as "My Lord and my God."[24]

Unfortunately, as I have pointed out, you can trawl through the Bible and find passages that do not support the Trinity. On the Cross. "Eli, Eli, lema sabachthani?" that is, "My God, my God, why have you forsaken me?"[25] That is just not one person, even if you use "hypostasis" or some other fancy language. This is the supreme moment of the drama. Jesus has been deserted. There is evidence to suggest that he didn't think it was going to come to this – all that stuff about some of us not tasting death and so forth – but it did. And that of course is what makes the final acceptance so tremendously important and powerful. "Father, into your hands I commend my spirit."[26] Say it again: $1 + 1 + 1 \neq 1$.

TWO FINAL QUESTIONS

Let me end this reflection – hardly a response because, as I have said, this is all more about me than about Brian Davies – by addressing a couple of mop-up points. First, if I am so down on Christianity, why am I not an atheist? Why do I speak of myself as an "agnostic"? The talk-show host and comedian Stephen Colbert – a deeply committed Catholic – characterizes folk like me as gelded atheists, except he puts his point in rather ruder language. A fair question that deserves a serious answer. Logically, because I am not A, it does not follow that I must be B, where B is not the contradictory of A. I might be, as I am, a C. Denial of Christianity is not assertion that there is nothing. I could be a Muslim. I am not. I am an agnostic. But I could be a Muslim. But why not an atheist? In the spirit of William James, I have accused Christians of being too scared of death to follow the facts. Am I not the same? In the end, am I also too scared of death to follow my arguments to their conclusion? Perhaps. But apart from the fact that I really, really am prepared for nothingness – and inclined to think that that is what we shall get, and that that is probably a lot better than many

---

[24] This volume, pp. 171–172.   [25] Matthew 27:46.   [26] Luke 23:46.

alternatives (although it would be fun to try my idea of bliss, an eternity of new Mozart/da Ponte operas) – two things stand in the way. First, there is so much that we do not know. What is the electron really? A particle or a wave or something else? Why quantum entanglement, with things happening on one side of the universe simultaneously being reflected on a far distant side? Why is there something rather than nothing? What is the real relationship between body and mind? I am right there with J. B. S. Haldane: the world is not only queerer than we do know, it is queerer than we can know.

My second mop-up point is simply to answer the question of why, if Christianity has the insoluble problems I suggest it has, has it had such a hold on people and continues to have such a hold? Answering the question, let me stress that, at one important level, I do not speak of Christianity as "wrong and inadequate." Intellectually, I don't think it is true. Overall, without making truth-value judgments, I am more inclined to view Christianity as a cultural phenomenon, which has grown and developed over 2,000 years. It started off as a variety of Judaism, and that in itself raised difficulties as the new did not always harmonize happily with the old – the need and nature of the Trinity, for instance. Then as the new religion attracted followers and spread and gained importance, other cultural phenomena and ideas like Greek philosophy bumped up against it and got absorbed. As with the internal issues, there was no reason to think that these new influences would harmonize perfectly with already existing beliefs, and in major respects they didn't. Were I a believer, then I would expect that, ultimately, they could be shown to harmonize – I take it that this is Brian Davies's position – but I am not a believer, and so, in a way, I would be more surprised if they did harmonize than that they do not.

This in no way implies that, as a sociological phenomenon, Christianity would be a dud. And obviously it is not. Hard though it may be to say, while technical issues of theology and philosophy absorb the attentions of professional theologians and philosophers, regular people have other concerns. Because something is wrong or intellectually inadequate doesn't mean that people will not believe it. Think supply-side economics. Take from the poor and give to the rich and we will all be a lot happier! Although this example does point the way to understanding the hold of Christianity. People are all too ready to believe things if it is in their interests so to believe. If I were a billionaire, I would be all in favor of supply-side economics! Without necessarily endorsing everything that E. O. Wilson says about religion, I suspect he has a point when he says we believe because we are happier and more efficient if we do believe, than otherwise. This is true of Christianity.

Take the Middle Ages.[27] Frankly, for most people in Europe, life was just dreadful. Even if you didn't die at birth, your chances of making it out of childhood were still not rosy. Your home was dirty, cold, and wet. Your job was tedious, harsh, and dangerous. If you were a woman, there was the constant risk of death in childbirth. No television! No video games! No iPhones! But there was Christianity to give life meaning – birth, marriage, children, old age, death. It all fit in and made sense.[28] Apparently, death was almost a social occasion and people went in fear of dying alone, without friends and family to cheer you on to the next world. And think of all those holidays, celebrating saints and so forth, when the lord of the manor was expected to provide a feast – pease pudding all around! Had I lived in the Middle Ages, I would have been a Christian! Who cares that it doesn't make sense and that most of it is made up? Think the cult of the Virgin Mary. What an honor to carry her effigy in the parade. Worth living for!

Let's not be too condescending about the distant past. The signatories on the Declaration of Independence were deists. Ben Franklin was eloquent on the subject. "Some books against Deism fell into my hands; they were said to be the substance of sermons preached at Boyle's Lectures. It happened that they wrought an effect on me quite contrary to what was intended by them; for the arguments of the Deists, which were quoted to be refuted, appeared to me much stronger than the refutations; in short, I soon became a thorough Deist."[29] Unfortunately, while this might have worked for a sophisticated, Enlightenment world-traveler at the end of the eighteenth century, by the third decade of the nineteenth century it was showing its inadequacies. Deism was simply not enough for a pioneer and family moving west, facing droughts and floods, unplowed land, wild animals, hostile indigenous people. *Little House on the Prairie* sort of stuff. One needed stronger theological fare.[30] The preachers, in the Second Great Awakening, provided it – an evangelical literalism, based on crude readings of the Bible, made that much easier by the ready availability of mass-printed copies of the Holy Book.[31] You need to know the proper relationship between man and wife? Turn to the Bible. "Wives, be subject to your

[27] I am elaborating here on examples introduced briefly in Chapter 1.
[28] E. Duffy, *The Stripping of the Altars: Traditional Religion in England 1400–1580* (New Haven: Yale University Press, 1992).
[29] Benjamin Franklin, *Autobiography* (Oxford: Oxford University Press, 2009).
[30] Amanda Porterfield, *Conceived in Doubt: Religion and Politics in the New American Nation (American Beginnings, 1500–1900)* (Chicago: University of Chicago Press, 2012).
[31] M. Noll, *America's God: From Jonathan Edwards to Abraham Lincoln* (New York: Oxford University Press, 2002).

husbands as you are to the Lord."[32] How to treat children? Turn to the Bible. "Those who spare the rod hate their children, but those who love them are diligent to discipline them."[33] Treatment of servants and slaves? Turn to the Bible. "Let all who are under the yoke of slavery regard their masters as worthy of all honor, so that the name of God and the teaching may not be blasphemed."[34] Religion gave a supportive ideology. Truth? Well, that's another matter. Remember this is all happening while, away in Europe, theologians are turning to Higher Criticism to show that the Bible is nothing but the fables of untutored peoples, long ago. I am not surprised that Christianity has the hold that it has.

Do I think that, with increasing intellectual sophistication, Christianity will fade away? If you look at the world's most advanced societies, Scandinavia, for example, you might indeed think so. But don't take my word for it. Philosophers are the world's worst forecasters. In 1790, the greatest philosopher of the modern era, Immanuel Kant, announced confidently that there will never be a Newton of the blade of grass. Sixty-nine years later, Charles Darwin published the *Origin of Species*. Enough said.

Brian Davies

INTRODUCTION

While Michael thinks that Christianity is all a matter of faith, considered as a life-transforming "experience," and while he holds that faith differs strongly from reason, I argue that a believing Christian might make use of both faith and reason while also noting that what we call "knowledge" frequently depends on faith – not considered as something dramatic but rather as a starting point for thought.

Again, while Michael thinks that natural theology is intrinsically irrelevant to Christianity, I argue that it gives us reason to think that God exists, as all Christians believe. And while Michael finds little philosophical value in the arguments of natural theologians, I hold that there are good philosophical grounds for saying that God exists.

Also, while Michael finds authors like Aquinas to be basically offering some version of Neoplatonism, I find things to learn from in them and am clear that they are thoroughly grounded in the biblical tradition. And while

---

[32] Ephesians 5:22.   [33] Proverbs 13:24.   [34] 1 Timothy 6:1.

Michael finds the traditional doctrines of the Trinity and Incarnation to be riddled with contradiction, I maintain that they can be defended as not being logically contradictory.

Yet I am glad to say that Michael and I agree on some very important matters. Drawing on his Quaker background, and on the writings of John Hick, Michael endorses the view that God is seriously incomprehensible. For Michael, God is not a *scientific* explanation of anything. And he thinks that religion and science need not be thought of as *necessarily* opposed to each other since there are questions taken seriously by religious people with which science is not concerned. I endorse these conclusions. That is why I have tried to speak in favor of classical theism as found in the Catechism of the Catholic Church and in theologians such as Thomas Aquinas. I am not suggesting that Michael is a "closet Catholic," let alone a secret Thomist. But I am struck by the fact that he frequently talks about the mystery of God in a way that orthodox Catholics should find congenial.

I also appreciate Michael's impatience with new atheists such as Richard Dawkins and Christopher Hitchens. Michael thinks that these thinkers often attack theists by wrongly assuming that all theists subscribe to a crudely anthropomorphic understanding of divinity. And I think that Michael is right about this.

Of course, there have always been theists whose writings about God seem to be anthropomorphic, just as there have been theists who think that empirical investigation might lead to a knowledge of God's existence. Yet, as I have indicated, I lack sympathy with people such as these. In some of his contributions to previous chapters, Michael appears to revert to an anthropomorphic approach to God. He seems, for example, not to worry about talking of God as possibly failing to *think through* (emphasis mine) creating the universe.[35] Again, Michael seems erroneously to construe the orthodox doctrine of the Incarnation as if it involved Jesus moving from heaven to reside on earth as I might move from New York to Paris. But this anthropomorphic talk about God is less common in what Michael has to say in this book than is his emphasis on God's distinction from creatures. And I am pleased about that.

Yet I have some serious worries when it comes to what Michael argues in some of his chapter sections. So, in the space now allowed me, I shall briefly explain what a few of these worries are.

---

[35] This book, p. XXX.

FAITH AND REASON

I think that Michael includes too much under the noun "faith." He seems to suppose that both belief in God's existence and belief in doctrines such as those of the Trinity and the Incarnation must equally count as faith. Yet many Christians have made distinctions concerning faith that Michael appears to ignore. They have said, for example, that while some Christians might, as a matter of fact, hold all their religious beliefs on faith, knowledge of God's existence is something that can, in principle, be had apart from faith. They have also said that while some truths about God *can* be *known*, some *must* be grounded in divine *revelation*. Michael's use of "faith" therefore seems to me to be undiscriminating since it does not reflect what has been said about faith in the history of Christian theology. To a high degree it strikes me as merely stipulating that faith is what Michael takes it to be. And while such stipulation tells us something interesting about Michael, it does not much address the theology of faith in many of its influential forms. St. Anselm of Canterbury, very much the student of St. Augustine of Hippo, famously spoke about faith as something that should positively *seek* understanding; yet Michael does little to reflect on this view directly and in detail. Nor does he note how and why people such as Aquinas feel the need to strongly distinguish between knowledge of God (e.g., that God exists) and faith in divine revelation (the "articles of faith" as Aquinas and the Catholic Church call them).

In his part of Chapter 2 Michael expresses sympathy for the notion of faith as running against reason. He says: "If faith is to mean anything, it must be a leap of trust, into or toward the Unknowable."[36] And I can make sense of this sentence because I take all orthodox Christian faith to be acceptance of God's revelation and because I take God to be seriously unknowable to us in this life. But Michael's next sentence, offered as a gloss on its predecessor, asserts: "As Kierkegaard saw, reason giving you a comfortable backup destroys the whole thing." Here Michael seems to take "faith" to include any claim about God, including the claim that God exists. But he ought not to be doing that while proposing to discuss what "faith" has meant to Christians over the centuries. And I do not see that Michael's references to Kierkegaard should automatically be taken as relevant even to what Christians have said about divine revelation.

For the most part, Christians have agreed that divine revelation cannot be strictly proved to be true. But many of them have also noted that reason is

[36] This book, p. XXX.

relevant when it comes to what revelation teaches. Some have stressed that the articles of faith admit of rational *defense*, even though no such defense can amount to *proof*. Again, it has been argued that the articles of faith cannot be shown to be self-contradictory. And orthodox Christians seem in principle open to giving a hearing to those who say that key elements in Christian belief are empirically refutable. Here I am thinking of theologians who, because they believe in the *literal* resurrection of Jesus, are willing to say that belief in the resurrection *would* be refuted if one could establish beyond reasonable doubt that the bones of Jesus are still somewhere near Jerusalem. Orthodox Christians who say such things do not believe that they can *demonstrate* the consistency of doctrines such as those of the Trinity and the Incarnation. But they are not thinking of faith as having *nothing* to do with reason. And, in keeping with these views, I would add that I cannot make much sense of the view that Christian faith should be thought to be a good and valiant jousting against reason.

My main reason for saying so is that orthodox Christians believe that certain propositions are *true*. I do not mean that faith, whether religious or nonreligious, is a "merely" intellectual matter. My point is that any belief is belief that such and such is true, and that Christian faith is in this sense irreducibly propositional. So, I take it that if people hold a doctrine on faith and are indifferent to evidence for or against it, we should think that they did not hold it on faith as true. That is why I find it hard to understand the notion of faith that, as *genuine faith*, must think of reason as an *opponent* of some kind, which seems to be Michael's position.

What leads him to this conclusion? I suspect it is his supposition that faith is best thought of as an *experience*. Faith, he explains, is a "sense of being embraced by love, an experience over which one has no control."[37] But I am worried about this definition of "faith." As I argued in my part of Chapter 1, we all rely on faith for a whole lot of things that we believe. But we are not here relying on some experience over which we have no control. As I have argued, faith can be thought of as mundane and as being the rule rather than the exception. While having faith in the truth of what my teachers or doctors have to say, I am just believing them, just as I take God to be telling me about God (and me) in the revelation that Christians refer to as the Bible (a revelation that Catholic Christians take to be ongoing as the Church goes through the messy and complicated business of trying to interpret what

[37] This book, p. XXX.

God is revealing in sacred texts). In this sense, faith is *assent*, which is not the same as *experience*.

I am experienced in the ways of cats since I have lived with many cats. But when I tell you *what* cats are, I am not just reporting my experience of living with cats. I am not reporting any experience at all. Similarly, orthodox Christian talk about the reality and nature of God and the articles of faith is not a report of an experience. It is a profession of belief. That is why it can be communicated or preached to others as being true, as experiences can never be. In saying this, I am taking experiences (sensations, surges of emotion, and so on) to be private while taking thoughts (as expressed in propositions) to be things that all of us can equally share. Michael invites us to sympathize with David Copperfield's falling in love with Dora in Dickens's *David Copperfield*.[38] He does so when trying to do something to rescue the notion of Christian faith. But I do not think that the Copperfield comparison does that. It asks us to consider how we might have felt as Copperfield might have felt had he been a nonfictional character. And I do not see how doing that is much help when trying to understand what actual Christian faith amounts to.

Michael might say that those with Christian faith are continually over-whelmed by a sense of God's presence, a sense that he lacks. But he would then be ignoring what many faithful Christians have said while feeling no such sense. For a recent example, consider Mother Teresa of Calcutta (1910–1997), who in 2016 was proclaimed by the Catholic Church to be a saint. From diaries of hers published since her death it seems clear that she felt little consolation or joy or lively sense of God's presence in her life of faith.[39] I take this to indicate that even a saint can lack what Michael calls the "experience" of faith.

PROBLEMS WITH CHRISTIANITY

Michael has several problems with Christianity. One is what he calls the "problem of pluralism."[40] Then there are the doctrines of the Trinity and the Incarnation, both of which Michael takes to be exercises in "squaring

---

[38] This book, p. XXX.

[39] Mother Teresa, *Come Be My Light: The Private Writings of the "Saint of Calcutta,"* ed. Brian Kolodiejchuk (New York: Doubleday Religion, 2007). I should note that many other well-known Christians have spoken of their sense of darkness and lostness before God. St. John of the Cross (1542–1591) is one example. Another is St. Thérèse of Lisieux (1873–1897). Hence the phrase "the dark night of the soul," which is common in discussions of Christian spirituality.

[40] This book, p. XXX.

the circle."[41] Finally, Michael is opposed to the notion of original sin, to accounts of Christ's death that regard it as a "blood sacrifice," and to the miracles of Jesus when considered as lending credence to orthodox Christian teachings concerning him. So, at this point I want to briefly offer some comments on ways in which Michael develops his position on these matters.

(A) The Problem of Pluralism

When it comes to Michael's "problem of pluralism," I deny that there is a problem. Michael presents it by first noting the enormous differences to be flagged when it comes to religious beliefs. Then he says that he does not know "how you could possibly hope to reconcile all these faith-derived positions." I am far from convinced that all the positions he refers to are best characterized as "faith-derived." More important, however, is the question "Why should a Christian want to reconcile them?"

John Hick wanted to do that. Yet Michael doubts that Hick said enough to "get out of the pluralism mess."[42] But why should any religious believer think that there is a pluralism mess? Michael himself says things that indicate why such a person should not. For example, he writes: "Either the Catholics are right, or the Mormons are right. They cannot both be right. Either the Pope is the representative of Peter and what he says goes, at least when he is speaking ex cathedra. Or this is an illusion. Either Joseph Smith found and translated those golden plates, or the Mormon religion is the biggest con game of the nineteenth century."[43] Michael's language here is somewhat inflated. But his basic point is correct. Truth cannot contradict truth. In that case, though, why should religious believers who think that they are in possession of religious truth worry about different religious believers who disagree with them? To say, "There may be many religions, but we all worship the same God" makes little sense. If someone's beliefs about God are sufficiently out of sync with what the true God is, then that person is not believing in the one true God.[44] But why should that fact embarrass any group of theists sharing the same view of God? They might regret that there so much disagreement on what God is. They might modestly pause when it comes to what they think true about God given that others have rejected what they hold. In the end, though, diversity of belief is not a problem when it comes to one who asserts such and such a belief,

---

[41] This book, p. XXX.   [42] This book, p. XXX.   [43] This book, p. XXX.
[44] Cf. Peter Geach, "On Worshiping the Right God," which is chapter 8 of P. T. Geach, *God and the Soul* (London: Routledge & Kegan Paul, 1969).

especially if that person presents reasons for asserting as they do. To be sure, if all faith is, in a serious way, impervious to reason, then religious pluralism leaves believers with a bunch of competing claims and no way to adjudicate between them. But I have been arguing that all faith is not seriously impervious to reason.

(B) Trinity and Incarnation

Michael is confident that the orthodox doctrines of the Trinity and the Incarnation are both logically self-contradictory. When talking about these doctrines, I defended the claim that such is not the case. In his rejection of the doctrines, Michael does nothing to refute what I say on this matter. He seems to think that the doctrines of the Trinity and the Incarnation can be dismissed without paying attention to matters that are extremely important when thinking about them – matters to do with relations and substance, what subjects and predicates are, and so on. Instead, he provides what I can only describe as a caricature when it comes to the orthodox doctrines of the Trinity and the Incarnation and the theological history lying behind them as formulated by Church Councils and as discussed by orthodox theologians (both Eastern and Western) since they were formulated.

Michael seems clear that the doctrine of the Incarnation holds that "Jesus came down to earth to help us."[45] But the doctrine does not assert that some nameable human being in heaven came "down" to help us. The orthodox doctrine of the Incarnation asserts that Jesus began to exist only when he was born. It says that the second person of the Trinity assumed a human nature with the birth of Jesus. Nothing here about a preexisting *Jesus*. I might also note that Michael is wrong to say that the orthodox doctrine of the Trinity holds that Jesus "stays" on after his death "in the form of" the Holy Spirit.[46] Indeed, he does little to accurately explain what the doctrines of the Trinity and the Incarnation actually amount to. He even manages to misrepresent some famous objections to them.

One of these he calls "Docetism," which he thinks Martin Luther favored. But what does Michael mean by "Docetism"? He describes it as the claim that God is *one*, though there are problems with seeing "how God, Son, and Spirit function apart." Yet this is not what historians of theology think of as Docetism (from the Greek *dokeow*, meaning "I seem"). That was an early Christian heresy according to which Jesus' humanity and suffering were

[45] This book, p. XXX.   [46] This book, p. XXX.

illusory. And Luther certainly had no time for it. Michael's "Docetist" quote from Luther is actually an endorsement of the orthodox view that Jesus is one person with two unconfused natures (the unity of divinity and humanity lying in the *person*, not the *nature*).

Again, Michael refers to "Ebionitism," to which, he says, Calvin inclined "a bit."[47] And, for Michael, Ebionitism is the view that "you keep God, Son, and Spirit separate but then have trouble with the One." Yet Ebionites (of whom we know little historically) seem to have been a group of early Jewish converts to a form of Christianity that rejected the teachings of St. Paul and held that Jesus was nothing but human – a conclusion to which Calvin was most certainly never even remotely inclined. Michael suggests that he was so because he wrote, "'The Son of God descended miraculously from heaven, without abandoning heaven.'" But here Calvin is saying that the Word (the second person of the Trinity) assumed a human nature without ceasing to be divine. What I have just been noting in criticism of Michael is *commonplace* among historians of theology.[48] And if pressed to say what I take to be the most serious problem with his discussion of the orthodox doctrine of the Incarnation, I would say that it pays no serious attention to its claim that Jesus is *one* subject with two *distinct* natures.

(C) Miracles

I am glad that Michael offered a discussion of miracles in his discussion of Christianity. For reasons of space, I have so far avoided discussion of that topic. But now I can feel free to say something about it while commenting on what Michael has to say about it. And I begin by saying that I do not take miracles to "prove" that God exists.

You will, of course, now wonder what I take the word "miracle" to mean. Michael says that he is "a bit of a Humean" when it comes to miracles.[49] I assume that he is, therefore, agreeing with Hume when he says that a miracle is "a violation of the laws of nature."[50] And perhaps we can make sense of that understanding if we take miracles to be what could never happen if, so to speak, the world were left to itself while proceeding in the

---

[47] This book, p. XXX.
[48] Cf. F. L. Cross and E. A. Livingstone, eds., *The Oxford Dictionary of the Christian Church*, 3rd ed. (Oxford: Oxford University Press, 1997).
[49] This book, p. XXX.
[50] This is Hume's definition of miracle in section 10 of his *An Enquiry Concerning Human Understanding*.

law-bound way in which it seems to operate. People regularly die and stay
dead. And so on. Things in nature operate in predictable ways, and their
doing so is what allows us to talk about what is possible for this or that thing
in the world given the thing's nature. It is what allows us to say, for example,
that when cats mate they produce cats and not mice. In this sense we can
understand and value talk about "laws of nature" and might agree that a
miracle, if it occurred, would be a "violation" of some natural law. But why
suppose that a miracle constitutes proof of God's existence?

Suppose that I have no belief in the existence of God and that I come
across, or am told about, a miracle in the above sense of "miracle." Why
should I conclude that God *must* therefore exist? Why might I not say that
here we have something that is just scientifically inexplicable? And why
might I not add that "scientifically inexplicable" is not equivalent to "produced by God"? Scientists might not be able to explain scientifically why
such and such has happened, but knowing *that* is knowing something about
them, not about *why* the such and such has happened. Of course, if we *knew*
that God exists, and if we *knew* that God is omnipotent, we might say that
God is the most likely candidate to invoke as the cause of a miracle. But we
would not then be taking a miracle as proof of God's existence.

To be fair to him, Michael is not criticizing the view that *any* miracle is
proof of God's existence. In his discussion of miracles, he chiefly asks us to
discount the claim that the reported miracles of Jesus should be given
credence and taken as proof of God's existence. Yet now I must ask, "Who
has ever said that the miracles of Jesus are proof of God's existence?" Many
miracles of Jesus are reported in the gospels, but none of them is presented
as proof of God's existence. The gospels do not argue "Jesus did miracles X,
Y, and Z; therefore, God exists." The existence of God is *taken for granted* by
the gospel writers. Their line seems to be that the miracles of *Jesus* testify to
what *he* truly is.

Christians since New Testament times have tended to say that the gospel
writers are onto something here. Michael's view, though, is that the gospel
accounts of Jesus performing miracles can be quickly dismissed if read as
purportedly historical accounts of miracles in Hume's sense of "miracle." He
says, "It is more likely that the stories are made up than that they are true."[51]
But what is Michael's basis for this confident and sweeping conclusion?

Hume's argument against believing in miracles seems to amount to the
claim that *reports* of miracles should always be deemed to be false since

[51] This book, p. XXX.

common experience tells against them. But that is not a good argument. To be sure, what Hume takes to be a miracle is not what we would expect to occur as we expect it to be the case that eggs we put into hot oil will shortly become fried. But the gospel writers would have been as aware of that as we are. Their point was that certain miracles were *observed* to occur. And saying that what they reported as having occurred is to be disregarded just because such things hardly ever occur is, by itself, no refutation of them having occurred.

As Michael notes, Hume says: "'No testimony is sufficient to establish a miracle, unless the testimony be of such a kind, that its falsehood would be more miraculous, than the fact, which it endeavors to establish.'" The idea here, as Michael understands and agrees with it, is that background knowledge should always trump accounts of what does not square with it. So, for example, testimony to the effect that billions of dead people have not been raised from the dead as, say, Jesus is said to have been. But this conclusion invites at least two questions.

First, if we "know" that dead people do not rise from the dead, are we not claiming to know based on testimony just as much as do people who now believe that Jesus was raised from the dead? Or is it that we have personally observed the rotting and non-resurrection of all who have died? Second, why should New Testament accounts of the miracles of Jesus be disregarded as serious testimony that is worthy of belief as *evidence* in their favor?

Belief in the universal and necessary corruption of the dead is clearly based on testimony. It is based on many reports. But these reports do not seem to me to establish what always *must* happen when someone dies. They give us reason to be skeptical should it be said that someone has been raised from the dead, but that does not mean that we have to be left without *reason* when believing on someone's say-so that someone has been raised from the dead. If we *knew* that miracles are *flatly impossible*, things would be different. Hence, for example, we can be confident that reports of there being a square circle should be disregarded from the outset. But Michael distances himself from the claim that miracles are impossible. He allows for their possibility. Yet if miracles are not impossible, why should we suppose that *all* reports of them, including those to be found in the gospels, should be taken to be likely "made up"?

In his discussion of miracles, Hume says that we should believe because of *evidence*. But he does not consider anything that might be taken as evidence for the miracles associated with Jesus. Nor does Michael. Both offer an abstract argument based on what usually happens. Neither of them considers why we might take certain New Testament texts as evidence for the miracles of Jesus, and especially for that of his resurrection. Michael says nothing about reasons why some New Testament scholars have concluded that the gospel accounts of Jesus and his resurrection do not amount to indubitable historical evidence. But speaking as someone who has looked into what such scholars have said, and while being impressed by some of their arguments, I am also impressed by what other New Testament scholars have argued in favor of the view that we have many reasons to suppose that what the gospels report is basically true.[52] Of course, "having good reasons to believe such and such" is not the same as having *proof* that such and such is the case. But reasons that fall short of proof should not be quickly dismissed. Fred might lack proof that his wife is faithful to him. But he might have good reasons for thinking that she has never cheated on him. In contexts such as these, the devil is in the details. And I think that Michael has not sufficiently explored the details when describing the gospel miracle stories as "made up." He likes some of these stories considered nonhistorically and as parables to read while thinking about ways in which good people might behave. Hence his preferred (non-"magical") reading of the changing of water into wine in John's gospel.[53] But this is not how these accounts are presented by New Testament authors.

(D) The Death of Jesus and Original Sin

The name "Jesus" derives from a name originating in a Hebrew verb meaning "to save" or "to deliver." That explains Matthew 1:21, in which Jesus' mother is told to call him "Jesus" since "he will save his people from their sins." And, for Christians, the name is appropriate since from New Testament times onward Christian theologians have emphasized that Jesus is the savior of humanity. But in what sense?

Michael notes that some Christians have taken Jesus to save people from their sins because his crucifixion was "a blood sacrifice that wiped out or made null our sins";[54] and he does not like this idea. He expresses revulsion "at the idea that blood sacrifice, of the most barbaric kind, is necessary for the cleansing of our sins."[55] What Michael does not note is that this "blood sacrifice" notion of Jesus' death is also strongly rejected by many

---

[52] For a biblical scholar who is radically skeptical concerning the story of Jesus in the gospels, see Bart Ehrman, *How Jesus Became God: The Exaltation of a Jewish Preacher from Galilee* (New York: Harper Collins, 2014). For a biblical scholar with a very different perspective, see Peter J. Williams, *Can We Trust the Gospels?* (Wheaton: Crossway, 2018).
[53] This book, p. XXX.   [54] This book, p. XXX.   [55] This book, p. XXX.

contemporary Christian theologians. Hence, for example, Herbert McCabe can write, "If God will not forgive us until his son has been tortured to death for us then God is a lot less forgiving than even we are sometimes. If a society feels itself somehow compensated for its loss by the satisfaction of watching the sufferings of a criminal, then society is being vengeful in a pretty infantile way. And if God is satisfied and compensated for sin by the suffering of mankind in Christ, he must be even more infantile."[56] Comments like this are now common among professional theologians (of different Christian denominations), and I wish that Michael had noted this fact. At one point he refers to St. Irenaeus (c. 130–c. 202) as holding that the real meaning of the Cross was that Jesus was showing unbounded love toward us all. But Michael does little to explain how prevalent this Irenaean approach to Jesus, even in qualified forms, has been among Christians. Indeed, he does hardly anything to give his readers a sense of the history of Christian soteriology (reflections on how Jesus saves us).

Christians have said *much* more about the death of Jesus than Michael notes. Consider, for example, what Aquinas has to say on this, having first made clear why he thinks that "simply and absolutely speaking, God could have freed people other than by Christ's passion, for nothing is impossible with God" (*Summa theologiae*, 3a, 46, 2). Aquinas is aware that Christians have used a range of words when reflecting on Jesus's saving work – words such as "redemption," "satisfaction," "sacrifice," and "atonement." And he patiently tries to tease out the merits and demerits of talking about Jesus using these terms. But his own account does not lay special emphasis on any of them. It also comes with the conviction that God can simply forgive sins by fiat. As Aquinas tries to develop his soteriology, therefore, he reflects on the *whole* of Jesus' life and teachings, including what seems to have been going on *as* he freely went to his death *following* opposition to him on the part of various Jews and Romans. The resulting discussions of Aquinas are complex, nuanced, and not easily summarized. But readers of Michael on the death of Jesus should realize that they, and discussions comparable to them, exist and are respected in many theological circles. "Christian" teaching on the death of Christ is not as simple as you might think when reading what Michael has to say about it.

The same, I think, goes when it comes to Michael's references to the doctrine of original sin. Michael presents this doctrine as standing or falling with belief in Adam and Eve as historical individuals. And for some

---

[56] Herbert McCabe, *God Matters* (London: Continuum, 1987), 92.

Christians it *does*. But for many it does *not*. Hence, for example, Pope John Paul II (1920–2005) acknowledged the truth of the basic tenets of Darwinian evolutionary theory in a text addressed to the Pontifical Academy of Sciences dated October 22, 1996. He said:

> New knowledge has led to the recognition of the theory of evolution as more than a hypothesis. It is indeed remarkable that this theory has been progressively accepted by researchers, following a series of discoveries in various fields of knowledge. The convergence, neither sought nor fabricated, of the results of work that was conducted independently is in itself a significant argument in favor of the theory.

I take this to be an indication that Roman Catholics, at least, are not obliged to think about original sin while assuming the historical accuracy of the accounts of Adam and Eve in the early Genesis narratives. I might add that many Catholic theologians have tried to theologize about original sin while not taking Adam and Eve to have been historical figures.[57]

Finally, I should also note that Michael is wrong to say that Roman Catholic teaching asserts that people such as he and Richard Dawkins are "smeared with original sin," *unlike* Cardinal Theodore McCarrick, who was convicted on charges of sexual assault in 2018. Michael writes: "I simply do not know what to say to someone who says that Dawkins and I, through no fault of our own, are tainted in a way that McCarrick, through no merit of his own, is not."[58] In response to this comment, all I can say is that Roman Catholic teaching on original sin is very clear that it affects *everyone*, both the virtuous and the vicious.

---

[57] Cf. Timothy McDermott, "Original Sin (I)," *New Blackfriars* 49 (January 1968), and Timothy McDermott, "Original Sin (II)," *New Blackfriars* 49 (February 1968). Again, cf. McCabe, *God Still Matters*, chapter 15, "Original Sin." The list could go on at length.

[58] This book, p. XXX.

Select Bibliography

Alston, W. 1991. *Perceiving God.* Ithaca: Cornell University Press.

Anscombe, G. E. M. 1974. "'Whatever has a beginning of existence must have a cause': Hume's Argument Exposed." *Analysis* 34: 145–151.

1981. *Collected Philosophical Papers, vol. 3: Ethics, Religion and Politics.* Oxford: Blackwell.

2000. *Intention.* Cambridge, MA: Harvard University Press.

2008. "What Is It to Believe Someone?" In *Faith in a Hard Ground: Essays on Religion, Philosophy and Ethics.* Ed. M. Geach and L. Gormally. Exeter: Imprint Academic.

2015. "Grounds of Belief." In *Logic, Truth and Meaning: Writings by G. E. M. Anscombe.* Ed. M. Geach and L. Gormally. Exeter: Imprint Academic.

Anselm, St. 1903. *Anselm: Proslogium, Monologium, an Appendix on Behalf of the Fool by Gaunilon; and Cur Deus Homo.* Trans. S. N. Deane. Chicago: Open Court.

Aquinas, St. T. [1259–65] 1963. *Summa theologiae.* London: Eyre and Spottiswoode.

1975. *Summa contra Gentiles.* Trans. V. J. Bourke. Notre Dame: University of Notre Dame Press.

Augustine, St. [396] 1982. *The Literal Meaning of Genesis.* Trans. J. H. Taylor. New York: Newman.

1998. *Confessions.* Trans. H. Chadwick. Oxford: Oxford University Press.

Ayer, A. J. 1946. *Language, Truth and Logic,* 2nd ed. London: Gollancz.

1976. *The Central Questions of Philosophy.* London: Pelican Books.

Barnes, J., ed. 1984. *The Complete Works of Aristotle.* Princeton: Princeton University Press.

Barrow, J. D., and F. J. Tipler. 1986. *The Anthropic Cosmological Principle.* Oxford: Clarendon Press.

Beanblossom, R. E., and K. Lehrer, eds. 1975. *Thomas Reid's Inquiry and Essays.* Indianapolis: Bobbs-Merrill.

Boyle, R. [1688] 1966. "A Disquisition about the Final Causes of Natural Things." In *The Works of Robert Boyle.* Ed. T. Birch, 5: 392–444. Hildesheim: Georg Olms.

Braine, D. 1988. *The Reality of Time and the Existence of God.* Oxford: Clarendon Press.

Browne, J. 1995. *Charles Darwin: Voyaging, Volume 1 of a Biography.* London: Jonathan Cape.

Brunner, E., and K. Barth. 2002. *Natural Theology.* Eugene: Wipf and Stock.

Calvin, J. 1536. *Institutes of the Christian Religion.* Grand Rapids: Eerdmans.

Clifford, W. K. 1879. *Lectures and Essays.* Ed. L. Stephen and F. Pollack. London: Macmillan.

Cooper, J. M., ed. 1997. *Plato: Complete Works.* Indianapolis: Hackett.

Coyne, J. A. 2015. *Faith vs. Fact: Why Science and Religion Are Incompatible.* New York: Viking.

Craig, W. L. 1979. *The Kalām Cosmological Argument.* London: Macmillan.

Crane, T. 2017. *The Meaning of Belief: Religion from an Atheist's Point of View.* Cambridge, MA: Harvard University Press.

Cross, F. L., and E. A. Livingstone, eds. 1997. *The Oxford Dictionary of the Christian Church*, 3rd ed. Oxford: Oxford University Press.

Darwin, C. 1859. *On the Origin of Species by Means of Natural Selection, or the Preservation of Favoured Races in the Struggle for Life.* London: John Murray.

⸻ 1871. *The Descent of Man, and Selection in Relation to Sex.* London: John Murray.

⸻ 1985. *The Correspondence of Charles Darwin.* Cambridge: Cambridge University Press.

Davidson, D. 1963. "Actions, Reasons and Causes." *Journal of Philosophy* 60: 685–700.

Davies, B. 2004. *An Introduction to the Philosophy of Religion*, 3rd ed. Oxford: Oxford University Press.

Davies, B., and P. Kucharski, eds. 2016. *The McCabe Reader.* London: Bloomsbury T&T Clark.

Davies, B., and B. Leftow, eds. 2006. *Aquinas: Summa theologiae, Questions on God.* Cambridge: Cambridge University Press.

Dawkins, R. 1983. "Universal Darwinism." In *Evolution from Molecules to Men.* Ed. D. S. Bendall, 403–25. Cambridge: Cambridge University Press.

⸻ 1986. *The Blind Watchmaker.* New York: Norton.

⸻ 2003. *A Devil's Chaplain: Reflections on Hope, Lies, Science and Love.* Boston: Houghton Mifflin.

⸻ 2006. *The God Delusion.* New York: Houghton, Mifflin, Harcourt.

Dawkins, R., and J. R. Krebs. 1979. "Arms Races between and within Species." *Proceedings of the Royal Society of London, B* 205: 489–511.

Dennett, D. C. 1984. *Elbow Room: The Varieties of Free Will Worth Wanting.* Cambridge, MA: MIT Press.

⸻ 2006. *Breaking the Spell: Religion as a Natural Phenomenon.* New York: Viking.

Descartes, R. 1964. *Meditations.* In *Philosophical Essays*, 59–143. Indianapolis: Bobbs-Merrill.

Desmond, A. 1998. *Huxley: From Devil's Disciple to Evolution's High Priest.* London: Penguin.

Dickinson, E. 2003. *The Collected Poems of Emily Dickinson.* New York: Barnes and Noble.

Duffy, E. 1992. *The Stripping of the Altars: Traditional Religion in England 1400–1580.* New Haven: Yale University Press.

Feser, E. 2009. *Aquinas: A Beginner's Guide.* London: Oneworld.

⸻ 2017. *Five Proofs of the Existence of God.* San Francisco: Ignatius Press.

Foot, P. 2001. *Natural Goodness.* Oxford: Clarendon Press.

Franke, W. 2007. *On What Cannot Be Said: Apophatic Discourses in Philosophy, Religion, Literature, and the Arts, vol. 1: Classic Formulations*. South Bend, IN: University of Notre Dame Press.

Geach, P. T. 1956. "Good and Evil." *Analysis* 17: 33–42.

1969. *God and the Soul*. London: Routledge and Kegan Paul.

1973. "An Irrelevance of Omnipotence." *Philosophy* 46: 7–20.

1976. *Reason and Argument*. Oxford: Basil Blackwell.

Grisez, G. 1975. *Beyond the New Theism*. Notre Dame: University of Notre Dame Press.

Gunton, C. 2002. *Act and Being*. Grand Rapids: William B. Eerdmans.

Haldane, J. B. S. 1927. *Possible Worlds and Other Essays*. London: Chatto and Windus.

Hanfling, O. 1981. *Logical Positivism*. Oxford: Blackwell.

Harris, S. 2004. *The End of Faith: Religion, Terror, and the Future of Reason*. New York: Free Press.

Hauerwas, S. [1988] 2001. "On Being a Church Capable of Addressing a World at War: A Pacifist Response to the United Methodist Bishops' Pastoral in Defense of Creation." In *The Hauerwas Reader*, 426–58. Durham, NC: Duke University Press.

Hause, J., ed. 2018. *Aquinas's "Summa theologiae": A Critical Guide*. Cambridge: Cambridge University Press.

Heidegger, M. 1959. *An Introduction to Metaphysics*. New Haven: Yale University Press.

Hick, J. 1973. *God and the Universe of Faiths: Essays in the Philosophy of Religion*. New York: St. Martin's Press.

2005. *An Autobiography*. London: Oneworld Publications.

Hume, D. [1757] 1963. *A Natural History of Religion*. In *Hume on Religion*. Ed. R. Wollheim. London: Fontana.

[1779] 1963. *Dialogues Concerning Natural Religion*. In *Hume on Religion*. Ed. R. Wollheim, 93–204. London: Fontana.

2000. *A Treatise of Human Nature*. Ed. D. F. Norton and M. J. Norton. Oxford: Oxford University Press.

2007. *An Enquiry Concerning Human Understanding*. Oxford: Oxford University Press.

Huxley, J. S. 1942. *Evolution: The Modern Synthesis*. London: Allen and Unwin.

Huxley, T. H. 2009. *Evolution and Ethics with a New Introduction*. Ed. M. Ruse. Princeton: Princeton University Press.

James, W. 1902. *Varieties of Religious Experience: A Study in Human Nature*. New York: Longman.

John Paul II. 1998. *Fides et Ratio: Encyclical Letter of John Paul II to the Catholic Bishops of the World*. Vatican City: L'Osservatore Romano.

Kant, I. 1949. *Critique of Practical Reason*. Chicago: University of Chicago Press.

1959. *Foundations of the Metaphysics of Morals*. Indianapolis: Bobbs-Merrill.

[1787] 2017. *Critique of Pure Reason*, 2nd ed. Trans. and ed. J. Bennett.

Kenny, A. 1969. *The Five Ways*. London: Routledge and Kegan Paul.

Kierkegaard, S. 1992. *Concluding Unscientific Postscript to Philosophical Fragments, Volume 1 (Kierkegaard's Writings, Vol. 12.1)*. Trans. H. V. Hong and E. H. Hong. Princeton: Princeton University Press.

Kuhn, T. 1962. *The Structure of Scientific Revolutions*. Chicago: University of Chicago Press.

1993. "Metaphor in Science." In *Metaphor and Thought*, 2nd ed. Ed. Andrew Ortony, 533–42. Cambridge: Cambridge University Press.

Lakoff, G., and Johnson M. 1980. *Metaphors We Live By*. Chicago: University of Chicago Press.

Leibniz, G. F. W. 1714. *Monadology and Other Philosophical Essays*. New York: Bobbs-Merrill.

Lewis, C. S. [1952] 2015. *Mere Christianity*. New York: Harper Collins.

1955. *Surprised by Joy: The Shape of My Early Life*. London: Geoffrey Bles.

Mackie, J. L. 1955. "Evil and Omnipotence." *Mind* 64: 200–212.

1977. *Ethics*. Harmondsworth: Penguin.

1982. *The Miracle of Theism*. Oxford: Clarendon Press.

Malcolm, N. 1977. "The Groundlessness of Belief in God." In *Reason and Religion*. Ed. S. C. Brown. Ithaca: Cornell University Press.

Marmion, D., and R. V. Nieuwenhove. 2011. *An Introduction to the Trinity*. Cambridge: Cambridge University Press.

McCabe, H. 2002. *God Still Matters*. London: Continuum.

2005. *The Good Life*. London: Continuum.

McCall, T., and M. Rea, eds. 2009. *Philosophical and Theological Essays on the Trinity*. Oxford: Oxford University Press.

McDermott, T. 1968a. "Original Sin (I)." *New Blackfriars* 49: 180–89.

1968b. "Original Sin (II)." *New Blackfriars* 49: 237–43.

McGrath, A. E. 1997. *Christian Theology: An Introduction*, 2nd ed. Oxford: Blackwell.

Metzger, B. 1987. *The Canon of the New Testament: Its Origins, Development, and Significance*. Oxford: Clarendon Press.

Miller, B. 1992. *From Existence to God: A Contemporary Philosophical Argument*. London: Routledge.

Moore, G. 1983. "Incarnation and Image of God." *New Blackfriars* 64: 452–68.

Moore, G. E. 1903. *Principia Ethica*. Cambridge: Cambridge University Press.

1925. "A Defence of Common Sense." In *Contemporary British Philosophy*. Ed. J. H. Muirhead, 2: 193–223. London: Allen and Unwin.

1939. "Proof of an External World." *Proceedings of the British Academy* 25.

Newman, J. H. 1870. *A Grammar of Assent*. New York: Catholic Publishing Society.

Noll, M. 2002. *America's God: From Jonathan Edwards to Abraham Lincoln*. New York: Oxford University Press.

O'Connell, J., and M. Ruse. 2020. *Social Darwinism* (Cambridge Elements on the Philosophy of Biology). Cambridge: Cambridge University Press.

Owen, H. P. 1965. *The Moral Argument for Christian Theism*. London: George Allen & Unwin.

Paley, W. [1802] 1819. *Collected Works, vol. 4: Natural Theology*. London: Rivington.

Pinker, S. 2011. *The Better Angels of Our Nature: Why Violence Has Declined*. New York: Viking.

Plantinga, A. 1974. *The Nature of Necessity*. Oxford: Oxford University Press.

1980. *Does God Have a Nature?* Milwaukee: Marquette University Press.

Porterfield, A. 2012. *Conceived in Doubt: Religion and Politics in the New American Nation*. Chicago: University of Chicago Press.

Rahner, K. 1998. *The Trinity*. New York: Crossroad.

Re Manning, R., ed. 2013. *The Oxford Handbook of Natural Theology*. Oxford: Oxford University Press.

Richards, R. J., and M. Ruse. 2016. *Debating Darwin*. Chicago: University of Chicago Press.

Rowe, W. 1979. "The Problem of Evil and Some Varieties of Atheism." *American Philosophical Quarterly* 16: 335–41.

Ruse, M. 1986. *Taking Darwin Seriously: A Naturalistic Approach to Philosophy*. Oxford: Blackwell.

1996. *Monad to Man: The Concept of Progress in Evolutionary Biology*. Cambridge, MA: Harvard University Press.

2001. *Can a Darwinian Be a Christian? The Relationship between Science and Religion*. Cambridge: Cambridge University Press.

2003. *Darwin and Design: Does Evolution Have a Purpose?* Cambridge, MA: Harvard University Press.

2010. *Science and Spirituality: Making Room for Faith in the Age of Science*. Cambridge: Cambridge University Press.

2012. *The Philosophy of Human Evolution*. Cambridge: Cambridge University Press.

2013. *The Gaia Hypothesis: Science on a Pagan Planet*. Chicago: University of Chicago Press.

2017. *Darwinism as Religion: What Literature Tells Us about Evolution*. Oxford: Oxford University Press.

2017. *On Purpose*. Princeton: Princeton University Press.

2019. *The Darwinian Revolution*. Cambridge: Cambridge University Press.

2019. *A Meaning to Life*. Oxford: Oxford University Press.

Russell, B. 1959. *My Philosophical Development*. London: Allen and Unwin.

Sartre, J. P. 1948. *Existentialism and Humanism*. Brooklyn, NY: Haskell House Publishers Ltd.

Schleiermacher, F. 1928. *The Christian Faith*. Edinburgh: T. and T. Clark.

Spencer, H. 1857. "Progress: Its Law and Cause." *Westminster Review* 67: 244–67.

Stevenson, C. L. 1944. *Ethics and Language*. New Haven: Yale University Press.

Stump, E. 2016. *The God of the Bible and the God of the Philosophers*. Marquette: Marquette University Press.

Swinburne, R. 1977. *The Coherence of Theism*. Oxford: Clarendon Press.

1993. *The Coherence of Theism*, revised ed. Oxford: Clarendon Press.

2004. *The Existence of God*, 2nd ed. Oxford: Clarendon Press.

2010. *Is There a God?*, revised ed. Oxford: Clarendon Press.

Weinberg, S. 1977. *The First Three Minutes: A Modern View of the Origin of the Universe*. New York: Basic Books.

1999. "A Designer Universe?" *New York Review of Books* 46, no. 16: 46–48.

Whewell, W. [1853] 2001. *Of the Plurality of Worlds. A Facsimile of the First Edition of 1853: Plus Previously Unpublished Material Excised by the Author Just before the Book Went to Press; and Whewell's Dialogue Rebutting His Critics, Reprinted from the Second Edition*. Ed. M. Ruse. Chicago: University of Chicago Press.

Williams, C. J. F. 1994. "Neither Confounding the Persons nor Dividing the Substance." In *Reason and the Christian Religion: Essays in Honour of Richard Swinburne*. Ed. A. G. Padgett. Oxford: Clarendon Press.

Williams, P. J. 2018. *Can We Trust the Gospels?* Wheaton: Crossway.

Wilson, E. O. 1978. *On Human Nature*. Cambridge, MA: Harvard University Press.

    1992. *The Diversity of Life*. Cambridge, MA: Harvard University Press.

Wittgenstein, L. 1922. *Tractatus Logico-Philosophicus*. London: Routledge & Kegan Paul.

    1974. *On Certainty*. Ed. G. E. M. Anscombe and G. H. von Wright; trans. D. Paul and G. E. M. Anscombe. Oxford: Blackwell.

Zell-Ravenheart, O. 2009. *Green Egg Omelet: An Anthology of Art and Articles from the Legendary Pagan Journal*. Franklin Lakes, NJ: New Page Books.

Index

CPSIA information can be obtained
at www.ICGtesting.com
Printed in the USA
BVHW030629100221
599714BV00019B/92

9 781108 792196